AF560801

RURAL ECONOMY OF INDIA

• Globalization • High Growth Trajectory
• Strategy for Inclusive and Holistic Development

RURAL ECONOMY OF INDIA

• Globalization • High Growth Trajectory
• Strategy for Inclusive and Holistic Development

Edited by :
DR. NIRAJ KUMAR VERMA

Foreword by :
PROF. PULIN B. NAYAK
Department of Economics
Delhi School of Economics
University of Delhi
Delhi - 110 007

DEEP & DEEP PUBLICATIONS PVT. LTD.
F-159, Rajouri Garden, New Delhi - 110 027

RURAL ECONOMY OF INDIA

ISBN 978-81-8450-406-4

Typeset by RAHUL COMPOSERS
358, Pocket-B, Phase-2, Sector-16B, Dwarka, New Delhi - 110 075

Printed in India at MAYUR ENTERPRISES
WZ Plot No. 3, Gujjar Market, Tihar Village, New Delhi - 110 018

Published by DEEP & DEEP PUBLICATIONS PVT. LTD.
F-159, Rajouri Garden, New Delhi - 110 027 • Phone : 25435369, 25440916
E-mail : ddpubs@gmail.com • ddpubs@yahoo.com
Showroom :
2/13, Ansari Road, Daryaganj, New Delhi - 110 002 • Telefax : 23245122

Contents

SECTION C

INCLUSIVE GROWTH STRATEGY AND HOLISTIC DEVELOPMENT

DEPARTMENT OF ECONOMICS
DELHI SCHOOL OF ECONOMICS
UNIVERSITY OF DELHI

Foreword

The Indian economy has been moving at an unprecedented pace during the past decade. Even though the international financial turmoil of 2007-08 did contribute to some slowing down of the GDP growth after we had consistently achieved a 9 per cent plus growth rate in the four preceding years, the economy has again substantially recovered its momentum and grown at a rate of over 8 percentage points in the past year. This is therefore, at one level, extremely satisfying and also a pointer to the possibility that we may step up the growth rate even further.

Yet there is good reason to ask whether there is any reason for complacency. At a cut off level of an expenditure of Rs 20 per person per day, around 77 per cent of the population of the country is below the poverty line, as assessed by the National Commission for Enterprises in the Unorganised Sector (NCEUS), which was chaired by the late Dr Arjun Sengupta. India is among the worst performers in terms of some of the most standard health and education indicators. The comparison is particularly glaring when set against the performance of China. The infant mortality rate is 50 per thousand in India compared with 17 in China. The maternal mortality rate is 230 per 100,000 live births in India against 38 in China. About 48 per cent of children in India in the age group 0-5 are severely malnourished. India's sex ratio is among the worst in the world. It is in fact worse than some of the poorest sub-Saharan countries.

If articulation and formulation of sophisticated planning and development models could have been the panacea for all of India's ills, then India today would not have been home to the largest numbers of the poor and destitute people in the world. Indian policy makers have tried to grapple with the age old problems of poverty and ill health over more than six decades after Independence, but apparently without any major tangible results for the bottom third of the population. This has been a collective failure of our political economic system.

The time has perhaps now come to have a relook at the core issues of diminishing land resources, factor productivity decline, loss of bio diversity, natural resource degradation, and widening income inequality, among others. We perhaps need to seriously work towards a paradigmatic shift in the conceptualization of our developmental problems from a holistic economic, sociological and political perspective.

I believe that the book put together by Dr. Niraj Kumar Verma would go a considerable way towards a reappraisal of the key problems that the country is confronted with at present.

Delhi - 110 007

PROF. PULIN B. NAYAK
Department of Economics
Delhi School of Economics
University of Delhi

Preface

Rural Development has come out as a distinctive field of policy and practice, and of research. In rural economics, there are typical characteristics like continuing population pressure, and ever declining land-man ratio, small and fragmented agricultural holdings, highly iniquitous distribution, low productivity, etc. which are putting road blocks in its development. Rural development has regained its importance when the concept of poverty reduction has come into force. Notwithstanding increased availability of milk, fruits, vegetables, fish and other produce, the agriculture sector is facing the new challenges of diminishing land resources, factor productivity decline, threatened loss of bio-diversity, natural resource degradation, widening economic inequality, etc. India's achieving double-digit economic growth is largely contingent on the country's farming sector expanding by four percent per annum. We cannot afford to exclude the rural population. It was the rural sector that helped India sustain through the economic meltdown. Route to substantial economic growth in India is through the development of the country's farming and agriculture sector. Growth in agriculture is on an average two or three times more effective in raising incomes of the poor. Promotion of non-farm jobs, self-employment, entrepreneurship amongst youth and women are very important. Diversification of the rural economy hinges on changes in agriculture as well as on emerging opportunities in non-farm sector. A vibrant rural economy generates demand for manufactured goods and services. The need is to transform the rural economy of the country, making agriculture a vibrant and remunerative enterprise, removing the 'technological fatigue' and ushering in Second Green Revolution. Diversification adds to value-chain. Agro-business, agro-industries, food-processing help raise the income levels of farmers and increase the export basket of the country.

Indian planners and policy-makers do realize how critically important it is to have more than four percent growth in agriculture to give any meaning to "Inclusive Growth". Major investments are needed both in public and private sectors, to realize it. Falling or constant rates of growth in agriculture is puzzling. Now, the concern is about the distributional aspects of growth. Constraints on efficiency and productivity in agriculture must be revisited.

The 11th Plan has put the concept of 'Inclusive Growth' to the centre stage. The challenges of Inclusive Growth are myriad. Incidentally, the agriculture sector in India is lagging behind. According to 11th Plan, higher level of infrastructure development is envisaged "especially in rural areas".

After several years of high growth, India of 21st century has the distinction of being only second to US in terms of combined wealth of its Corporate billionaires co-existing with the largest number of homeless, ill-fed and illiterates of the world. Appropriate strategy would be, of-course, a mid-course making growth more inclusive, broad-based and participatory. Provision of public services to the poor needs to be addressed effectively.

My thanks go to Mr. G.S. Bhatia, Managing Director, M/s Deep & Deep Publications Pvt. Ltd., New Delhi, for his invariably excellent work. I owe him special thanks for completing the work in record time.

Lastly, I sincerely hope that this book meets the expectations of the readers.

DR. NIRAJ KUMAR VERMA

Acknowledgements

First and foremost, the editor expresses his sincere gratitude to Eastern Regional Office (ERO) of University Grants Commission (UGC) for granting National Seminar to the Post-Graduate Department of Economics, H.D. Jain College, Ara under Veer Kunwar Singh University, Ara, which, in the first place, made this seminar possible to be held in the Department of Economics of H.D. Jain College, Ara successfully and secondly, towards the publication of this edited book. The then Vice-Chancellor of Veer Kunwar Singh University, Ara, Prof. Sachindra Kumar Singh and Officers of the University deserve special thanks for patronage in this effort. The editor takes this opportunity to express sense of gratitude to Prof. Qamar Ahsan, Vice-Chancellor, M.M.H. Arabic Persian University, Patna, Late Prof. K.K. Sinha, Emeritus Professor, UGC and Former Head (Economics), College of Commerce, Patna. Dr. T.N. Jha, Former General Manager, NABARD, Patna and Faculty, Central University, Bihar and Dr. Rakesh Raman, Associate Professor (Economics), BHU, Varanasi for their August presence and scholarly address during the Seminar. Special mention goes to Dr. Monazir Hassan, Member Parliament (Lok Sabha) who was of immense help and was chief guest on the occasion.

Chairman of the organizing committee and Principal of H.D. Jain College, Ara, Dr. Janeshwar Singh was a major pillar of this seminar and subsequent efforts. Coordinator of the Seminar and Head of the Department of Economics, Prof. Dineshwar Kumar Singh deserves special mention, since he was a major source of inspiration and encouragement all the way and supported the move through his positive will, gestures and efforts. The editor is thankful to Prof. Vinod Kumar Singh, the then H.O.D. (Economics) of Veer Kunwar Singh University for his co-operation. Special mention goes to Prof. Raghawendra Prasad Singh, Professor of Economics, VKSU, Ara, who took great pains and made great effort in organizing this seminar. He and Dr. Satya Narayan Singh of the Department of Economics, VKSU, Ara had always time for the task of organizing this seminar. Prof. Pratap Narayan Singh, Professor of Economics of the University was of great help.

The editor is thankful to all his Departmental colleagues Dr. Narendra Kumar Singh, Dr. Naresh Prasad Singh, Dr. Baij Nath Singh, Dr. D.K. Bhattacharya and Dr. (Mrs.) Shabnam Perwin and Dr. Himanshu Shekhar of the Department of Chemistry of the University. They contributed enormously towards the success of this Seminar. Prof. Arun Kumar Sinha, Professor of Chemistry of the College deserves special mention since he guided the seminar from day one and was a constant source of inspiration.

The editor takes this opportunity to thank all advertisers and all those who helped in organizing the National Seminar directly or indirectly. Next, all the learned contributors deserve special mention and editor thanks them for contributing their papers in the book.

Last but not the least, the editor is highly indebted to M/s. Deep & Deep Publications Pvt. Ltd., New Delhi and its Managing Director, Mr. G.S. Bhatia for kind co-operation and help in publishing this book.

DR. NIRAJ KUMAR VERMA

List of Contributors

Aviral Pandey, Research Scholar, Department of Economics, Banaras Hindu University, Varanasi (U.P.).

Bakshi Amit Kumar Sinha, Research Scholar, Department of Economics, Veer Kunwar Singh University, Ara (Bihar).

Dr. Anil Kumar Singh, Reader in P.G. Department of Political Science, H.D. Jain College, Ara (Bihar).

Dr. Baij Nath Singh, Reader in Economics, H.D. Jain College, Ara (Bihar).

Dr. Chandrika Prasad, Lecturer, Deptt. of Economics, Nalanda College, Biharsharif, Nalanda (Bihar).

Dr. Dhirendra Kumar Singh, Reader in Economics, D.K. College, Dumraon (Buxar).

Dr. Jawahar Lal, Principal, D.K. College, Dumraon (Buxar).

Dr. Kawita Kumari, Lecturer, Department of Education, Veer Kunwar Singh University, Ara (Bihar).

Dr. Kumkum Jha, Lecturer, Deptt. of Economics, B.S. College, Danapur (Bihar).

Dr. Kumkum Narain, Reader and H.O.D. Economics, B.S. College, Danapur (Bihar).

Dr. Mira Mridubhashini, Head of Department of Economics, A.N. College, Patna (Bihar).

Dr. Mridula Kumari, Lecturer in Economics, College of Commerce, Patna, Magadh University (Bihar).

Dr. Naresh Prasad Singh, Lecturer in Economics, H.D. Jain College, Ara (Bihar).

Dr. Niraj Kumar Verma, Reader in Economics, H.D. Jain College, Veer Kunwar Singh University, Ara (Bihar).

Dr. Rajesh Kumar, Head, Deptt. of Economics, M.V. College, Buxar (VKS University, Ara) (Bihar).

Dr. Rashmi Akhoury, Department of Economics, College of Commerce, Patna (Bihar).

Dr. Reeta Kumari Bhagat, P.G. Deptt. of Economics, J.D. Women's College, Patna (M.U.).

Dr. Reeta Kumari, Senior Lecturer, Department of Economics, B.S. College, Danapur (Bihar).

Dr. Rekha Jha, Lecturer, Deptt. of Economics, Jamshedpur Women's College, Jamshedpur (Jharkhand).

Dr. Sandhya Rani, Deptt. of Economics, Maharaja College, Ara (Bihar).

Dr. Shabnam Perwin, Lecturer, Deptt. of Economics, H.D. Jain College, VKS University, Ara (Bihar).

Dr. Shabnam Verma, Principal In-charge, Deptt. of Education, Veer Kunwar Singh University, Ara and Academic Councilor, IGNOU, Patna College, Patna (Bihar).

Dr. Shashi Prabha, Women's Training College, Patna University, Patna (Bihar).

Dr. Shiwani Singh, Patna (Bihar).

Jagadish Deka, Lecturer, Faculty of Commerce, Rangia College, Rangia, Distt. Kamrup (Assam).

Navlata, M.A. (Eco.), NET, Research Scholar, Ranchi University, Ranchi (Jharkhand).

Pravin Kumar, Research Scholar, Department of Economics, Banaras Hindu University, Varanasi (U.P.).

Prof. Dineshwar Kumar Singh, Head, Department of Economics, H.D. Jain College (Veer Kunwar Singh University), Ara (Bihar).

Rajesh Kumar Pandey, Research Scholar, P.G. Department of Political Science, V.K.S. University, Ara (Bhojpur) (Bihar).

Reena Kumari, JRF, Department of Economics, Banaras Hindu University, Varanasi (U.P.).

Ritesh Kumar, Research Scholar, Deptt. of History, B.R.A. Bihar University, Muzaffarpur (Bihar).

Sindhu, Research Scholar, J.P. University, Chapra (Bihar).

Introduction

Rural India is inextricably bound up with the challenge of meeting the first Millennium Development Goal of reducing by half the proportion of people living on less than a dollar a-day and the proportion of people who suffer from hunger. Despite decades of planned development and poverty eradication programmes, poverty continues to exist in India. Rural India is the backwater of development, bereft of modern advancement and laggard in getting economic benefits. Development of rural area is of utmost importance. For us, with the population of more than one billion, food security is an issue of concern. Majority of our workforce lives in rural areas. Creating work opportunity for rural folk is of added significance. A healthy rural sector provides an economic and employment buffer in times of crisis. Now, the government is sensitive to change the economic complexion of rural areas. Programmes like Bharat Nirman and MGNREGS are pointer of Government's sensitivity to the issue of rural development.

Dr. Jawahar Lal, Sindhu and Dr. Dhirendra Kumar Singh are of the view that globalization has provided free and deregulated environment for the business in India. It has made significant impact on human resource management and industrial relations in India.

Prof. Dineshwar Kumar Singh and Bakshi Amit Kumar Sinha, in their paper have discussed the importance of human development approach towards achieving the Millennium Development Goals especially for the state of Bihar.

Dr. Naresh Prasad Singh has outlined the trends in rural employment in India and suggested measures for achieving sustainable high growth rate in agriculture.

Dr. Niraj Kumar Verma has tracked some of the problems besetting Indian agriculture and suggested measures to improve and rejuvenate Indian agriculture.

Dr. Baij Nath Singh has outlined the importance of rural development in India and analysed the effectiveness of various anti-poverty and employment generation programmes undertaken in India from time-to-time.

Dr. (Mrs.) Shabnam Perwin has outlined India's trade relations and its prospects with outside world and suggested measures to improve it further.

Miss Navlata and Dr. Rekha Jha have addressed some of the burning issues confronting Indian agriculture. They, in their paper have suggested that subsidies are hampering productivity enhancing investment.

Dr. Rajesh Kumar has suggested to usher in Second Green Revolution in India. He has opined to introduce genetically to modified seeds and diversification of agriculture to improve Indian agriculture.

Dr. Sandhya Rani has outlined the status of agriculture marketing in India and problems besetting it. She has traced agriculture marketing in post-reform era.

Dr. Chandrika Prasad has outlined problems besetting agriculture in Bihar and suggested measures to improve it.

Dr. Shabnam Verma and Mr. Ritesh Kumar have detailed the development of self-help groups and its impact on rural finance in India.

Dr. Anil Kumar Singh has discussed rural development programmes in pre-independence India in a detailed fashion.

Dr. Mira Mridubhashini and Dr. Kumkum Narain have discussed state of agriculture in Bihar and have outlined the importance of agriculture diversification in the state.

Dr. Jagadish Deka has analysed the problems besetting agrarian and rural economy of Assam and suggested measures to remove poverty from rural areas of Assam.

Dr. Shiwani Singh has traced reforms in the banking sector in India and its impact on agriculture sector.

Mr. Rajesh Kumar Pandey has outlined the importance of social audit in Bhilwara district of Rajasthan and its role model for the other areas under NREGA.

Prof. Dineshwar Kumar Singh and Bakshi Amit Kumar Sinha have outlined the importance of micro-finance and self-help groups in the state of Bihar and its role in ushering inclusive growth.

Dr. Mridula Kumari has suggested various measures to achieve the target of inclusive growth and to bridge rural-urban, gender and other divides plaguing India.

Dr. Rashmi Akhoury has tried to establish link between globalization, employment and inclusive growth in the context of India and suggested measures to incorporate human face to inclusive growth.

Dr. Reeta Kumari has focused on the emergence of 'two Indias', of late, and suggested measures to improve languishing and neglected sector of Indian economy so that goal of inclusive growth can be realized.

Mr. Aviral Kumar Pandey, Mr. Pravin Kumar and Ms. Reena Kumari have outlined the importance of Rural Non-Farm Sector to achieve inclusive growth in India and states within it.

Dr. Reeta Kumari Bhagat has discussed in detail, problems and prospects of rural India and challenges in achieving inclusive growth in India.

Dr. Shashi Prabha has discussed importance of education in economic development and suggested measures to remove anomalies and chasm within education in India.

Dr. Kumkum Jha in her paper has suggested measures to realize inclusive growth in true spirit. She has outlined various anomalies prevailing in India.

Dr. Kawita Kumari has outlined deprivation and neglect of education in certain social groups of India which is resulting in stunted human development in these groups. As a result of it, all sections of the society are not benefiting equally on account of education.

DR. NIRAJ KUMAR VERMA

SECTION A

Globalization and Sectoral Chasm

Globalization : A Paradigm Shift in Human Resource Management

JAWAHAR LAL, SINDHU AND
DHIRENDRA KUMAR SINGH

Globalization has resulted into competitive corporate culture and made transformation in HRM practices in both public and private sectors on individualistic lines. HRM and Industrial Relations saw declining role of trade union movements in post-globalization era. FDI, technology transfers, MNCs, etc. led to reduction in gap between national and international business culture and practices.

INTRODUCTION

The post-World War II period witnessed an unexpected expansion of national companies of mostly capitalist countries into international or multinational companies. The Post-1990s period has given great help to international business due to globalization of world economies along with the strides in information technology. Most of the countries initially adopted capitalist economic systems and later shifted to communist, socialist or mixed economic systems/socialistic pattern of societies as a result of revolutions or demands of the masses. These types of economic systems necessitated the Governments to play the role of businessmen also as a part of discharging their responsibilities of being the custodian of the nation. This role made the Governments to use the public sector mainly as a means to achieve their objectives and control the private sector towards its ends.

Government in capitalistic economic system provides free and deregulated environment to the business to operate and formulate competitive corporate as well as human resource management strategies (Human Resource Management Journal, 1997:50). Further, globalization provides free and deregulated environment for the business in all those countries who have opened their doors and windows for the rest of the globe. As such business in such economies centres its strategies on customer, but not on human resource. Globalization along with the capitalistic economic system resulted in insignificant role for business regulating devices including industrial relations institutions (Sundeep Khanna, 1996).

Globalization tends to result in exchange of the cultures across the countries. It led to internationalization of capital, human resources markets, material, management and manufacturing posing severe competition to the companies of developing countries like India. The sole objective of business during the early days was profit maximization through cost minimization of all inputs including labour. Owners of business of those days exploited labour by following individual approach to human resource management. Thus, individualistic approach to HRM in those days resulted in individual-based industrial relations. The cumulative effect of such exploitation led to the formation of trade unions with their militant tendency and revolutionary approaches. These developments changed the individualistic approach to collective approach of HRM.

India followed the mid-way of economic system, i.e. mixed economy in 1991. The huge fiscal deficit and crisis in balance of payment forced the Government to globalize its economy and create a favourable climate for restoration of capitalist tendency or market-based economic system.

OBJECTIVES

The main objectives of this paper are:

- To study the impact of globalization on human resource management structure in public and private sector organizations in India.
- To examine the impact of structural changes in human resource management on the industrial relations on institutions and patterns in India.
- To identify the cause and effect relationship among globalization, human resource management and industrial relations in India.

METHODOLOGY

The effect of globalization on significant areas of human resource management and industrial relations in India has been studied from the view points of organization structure, job design, human resource planning, employment, performance appraisal, human resource development, career planning, salary and benefits. Further, the impact of paradigm shifts in the structure and practice of HRM on industrial relations has been analyzed.

ORGANIZATION STRUCTURE

Generally, companies design and structure their organizations based on functional or departmental and matrix structure. So far organizational structure is concerned, it is a managerial tool in the process of achievement of organizational objectives by implementation of strategies. Thus, companies modified their organizational structure based on the strategy to establish the link between strategy and the structure.

Companies with multiple portfolios started adopting different structures for different portfolios rather than one structure for the entire company. As such, the human resource management implications vary from one portfolio to another portfolio of the same company. Further, human resource management policies and practices also vary from one strategic situation to another strategic situation. Thus, globalization led to structural shifts in varying degrees in different types of business firms. These new structures created an opportunity to the managements to deal with the employees individually in employment, development and compensation. HRM policies and practices took paradigm shift from the individual contribution to team contribution and from collectivistic HRM approach to the individualistic HRM approach in case of employing, developing and compensating the employees which is in contrast with HRM principle and practices followed before globalizations.

JOB DESIGN

The next design function in human resource management is job characteristic approach. Further, some companies found that team design, rather job design is more appropriate in the post globalization business strategies, resulting in de-jobbing (Vikram Chhachi, 1996:7-21).

Team design and de-jobbing consequent upon employee's multi-skills lead to surplus of workforce and thereby resulted in retrenchment, flexible work and work sharing barring the traditional formal communication channels and lines of command (Team Power, 2003:34). Employees learnt how to adopt themselves to these shifts in job design due to fear of loss of job or cut in compensation package. In addition, organizations also provided training programme and enabled the employees in acquiring multi-skills to cope with the new demands of competitive and challenging strategies. Thus, globalization resulted in significant shifts in job design to de-jobbing, multi-skilling, teams and employee empowerment.

HUMAN RESOURCE PLANNING

Globalization along with information technology enabled

the production technology transferable from country to country easily and at a fast rate. This development, in turn led to facility of outsource. In addition, the shifts in organization structure and from job design to team design brought vital changes in human resource planning and practices. After globalization, the Government stopped influencing the human resource planning of public and private sector industries, as part of its strategy of attracting foreign investment. Similarly, trade unions influence of human resource planning for internal candidates also disappeared during the post-globalization era.

Thus, globalization has been contributing to the shifts in human resource planning for skill-mobility outsourcing plans and plan for candidates purely based on suitability to the job. In addition, globalization either minimized or eliminated the influence of trade unions and Government on human resource planning.

EMPLOYMENT PRACTICES

National business environment has become more volatile due to the foreign direct investment, technology transfers, fast expansion of the operations of multinational companies and traditional companies, mobility of human resource, dispersion of manufacturing facilities with the help of information technology and soft political and economic policies of the governments towards foreign companies owing to globalization. These developments reduced the gap between national business environment and international business environment. Multinational and domestic companies started appropriate techniques in empowering right human resource at a fast rate rather than relying heavily on traditional techniques. The recent techniques of recruitment followed by many sun-rising companies were 'Employees Referrals' in which the present employees recommend prospective employees and motivate them to apply in the organization. Such shifts in the recruitment practice reduce the importance of trade unions and political influences.

Other shifts in the recruitment practices include walk-in, consult-in, e-recruitment and outsourcing. All these new practices of recruitment help the companies to formulate and implement strategies efficiently in the dynamic environment. The complex strategies let the organization select the candidates and employ them with multiple skills rather than expert skills in one area. As such, these companies started selecting the candidates with basic multi-skills and developing them as well as empowering them. These employees are fully committed towards achievements of organizational strategies. In addition, the other shifts in selection function like on-line selection tests and on-line interviews enable the companies to reduce the cost of recruitment and time duration in recruitment procedure.

PERFORMANCE APPRAISAL

The most important area in human resource management is performance appraisal. Punishment to the employees was one of the techniques in performance appraisal but later on organization started performance appraisal by identifying the employees weaknesses and initiate training and development programmes in order to develop employees. After globalization most of the companies followed such type of performance appraisal techniques which eliminate the influence of trade unions and tend to follow individualistic approach to HRM.

HUMAN RESOURCE DEVELOPMENT

Initially, industrial relations institutions were less concerned with training and development aspects of human resource development. The managements during the post-globalization era took interest in career planning and developing those employees whose skills were in demand. Thus, globalization resulted in dependence of the companies on contractual staff rather than regular staff that reduces the budget on human resource development. Contract staff to some extent takes their training and development by themselves and they never become the members of companies' trade unions. Thus, globalization in this respect contributes for the decline in membership of trade unions and thereby their finances and activities.

SALARIES AND BENEFITS

Before globalization, government of India favoured socialistic pattern of society and consequently believed in minimization of inequalities in distribution of income and salaries.

After globalization the higher salary and benefits are given to those employees whose skills are in great demand. Globalization also sets trends for adjustment of salaries based on performance. As such different employees working on the same job get different salaries based on their performance levels and demand and supply factors in most of the private sector companies. Consequently individual bargaining based on demand and supply factors displaced the collective bargaining in this regard paving the way for individualistic HRM.

COLLECTIVE BARGAINING

Collective bargaining is process of negotiations about the terms and conditions of employment between employer and a group of employees or one or more trade unions with a view to reaching an agreement (I.L.O., 1957:3). The post-globalization scenario tends to drive collective bargaining in a reverse direction as terms and conditions of employment vary from employee to employee. The decaying trend of trade unions and/or emergence of non-union organizations during the last 1980s contributed to the shift from collective bargaining to individual bargaining in private sector. Collective bargaining institutions in public sectors have become inactive regarding the monetary issues that could not be individualized due to public nature of organizations. The fundamental charges in trade unions and collective bargaining invariably bring the shifts in nature and degree of industrial disputes.

INDUSTRIAL DISPUTES

Though several measures are taken to manage human resource, satisfy the demands of employers and employees, disputes between employees and employer take place due to conflict of interest between capital and labour. The collective forms of industrial dispute like work-to-rule, strikes by all or a group of employees, lay-offs and lockouts were common before globalization. It is not exaggeration to state that there was no issue of newspaper and magazine without a report on strikes/ lock-out before 1990s, but not later. It is quite abnormal to listen to strikes and lockouts in India after globalization. This is mostly due the individualistic approach adopted by the business in managing their human resources.

PARTICIPATION IN MANAGEMENT

The next important issue of industrial relations in institutions is workers' participation in management following the concept of industrial democracy. Before globalization this concept was not successful due to non-cooperation of the managements. After globalization and economic liberalizations the direction towards market economics in India changed. Globalization led to optimum utilization of human resources through participative management idea and contributed to the attainment of the goals of workers' participation in management which was hitherto non-existent before globalization. Thus, globalization sustains the drive of workers' participation in management.

CONCLUSION

The analysis of Paradigm Shift in Human Resource Management indicates that globalization brought paradigm shift in human resource management structure and pattern in India in terms of de-layering, team and virtual structures, downsizing, multi-skilling, de-jobbing and other soft skills in employee selection, outsourcing of human resource, on-line training and employees' own initiatives for self-development, use of performance appraisal for employee development, compensation based on demand and others. These paradigm shifts change the traditional collective approach of human resource management to individual approach of human resource management in case of employment, development and compensation and team-based structure. The paradigm shifts in human resource management structure brought fundamental change in industrial relations in institution and structure. Globalization provided free and de-regulated environment to business to operate, which in turn resulted in severe compensation and formulation of competitive strategies. This competitive situation forced the companies to develop competency building-*cum*-low cost centered human resource strategies. Thus, globalization tends to bring significant shifts in human resource management, i.e. from collective to individual human resource management and thereby a fundamental change in industrial relations, i.e. collective relations to individual relations.

SECTION B

High Growth Trajectory for Rural and Agrarian Economy

Millennium Development Goals and Bihar : Through the Lens of Human Development

Dineshwar Kumar Singh and
Bakshi Amit Kumar Sinha

The focus is on Human Development Approach to strengthen the economy for steady and sustainable growth. Analysis has been done regarding Bihar's position on Human Development Index with regard to Millennium Development Goal of the United Nations. Various measures like achieving universal primary education, promoting gender equity and empowering women, reducing child mortality, combating serious health hazards like HIV, Malaria, ensuring environmental sustainability and developing a global partnership for development are measures to achieve the millennium goals for the poverty stricken state like Bihar vis-a-vis India. Boost to the social sector as well as facilitating physical infrastructure, etc. will go a long way in changing the face of Bihar.

INTRODUCTION

This paper looks on the Millennium Development Goals (MDGs) through the human development in Bihar. Bihar is most backward state in the country which always found its position at bottom in context of the Human Development Index (Planning Commission's reports). Only 5 years are left to complete all goals of millennium development, the deadline drawn by National Assembly for the MDGs. The period of MDGs is from 1990 to 2015. I would like to checkout the stand of Bihar in achieving progress especially in the two era of government exactly. Is there any significant change in Bihar or not, measuring through the yardstick of MDGs?

This is high time to think about the other way, which is advancing the richness of human life, rather than the richness of the economy in which human beings live, which is only a part of it. A bunch of the people are still outside the circle of the growth or partly. If the rest people who are like rural or poor or backward people contribute in the economy, one can see increase with a sustainable growth as a whole. About 90 percent people reside in the rural areas in Bihar. Therefore, this paper is representative of the position of rural economy.

APPROACH OF THE PAPER

So, this paper presents the human development approach to strengthen the economy for steady and sustainable growth. This analyzes information from key reports on the importance of access to Human Development in achieving the Millennium Development Goals (MDGs) introduced by United National Assembly. The MDGs are globally adopted by National Assembly (NA) as Human Development adopted by United Nation Development Programme (UNDP). The MDGs are taken on targets for reducing extreme poverty by 2015. They address income, poverty, hunger, disease, lack of education, gender exclusion, environmental degradation and exclusion from global participation whereas the human development fully think about longevity, knowledge (skills), standard of living, gender equality, poverty, etc.

I go through the Millennium Development Goals (MDGs) to locate the Bihar's position with the help of Human Development Indicators (Index) (HDIs).

Millennium Development Goals are:

1. Eradicate extreme poverty and hunger,
2. Achieve universal primary education,
3. Promote gender equality and empower women,
4. Reduce child mortality,
5. Improve maternal health,
6. Combat HIV/AIDS, malaria and other diseases,
7. Ensure environmental sustainability, and
8. Develop a global partnership for development.

MDG[1] Eradicate extreme poverty and hunger: 1st goal of the millennium development has two targets to achieve this goal. 1st target is to reduce by half, between 1990 and 2015, the proportion of the people whose income is less than $1 a day whereas the other target is to uplift at least half of the people who suffer from hunger. The data available compares goal achieved with respect to target in poverty ratio.

TARGET 1

Poverty Ratio in Bihar and India

State	*Bihar*			*India*		
	Rural	*Urban*	*Total*	*Rural*	*Urban*	*Total*
1983-84	64.4	47.3	62.2	45.7	40.8	44.5
1987-88	52.6	48.7	52.1	39.1	38.2	38.9
1993-94	58.2	34.5	55.0	37.3	32.4	36.0
1990-00	44.3	32.9	42.6	27.1	23.6	26.1
2004-05	42.1	34.6	41.4	28.3	25.7	27.5

Source : Planning Commission, Government of India.

The poverty ratio in Bihar is very high among all the states. It is very high even compared to national poverty share. Bihar has to reduce poverty ratio from 55% to 27.5% till 2015

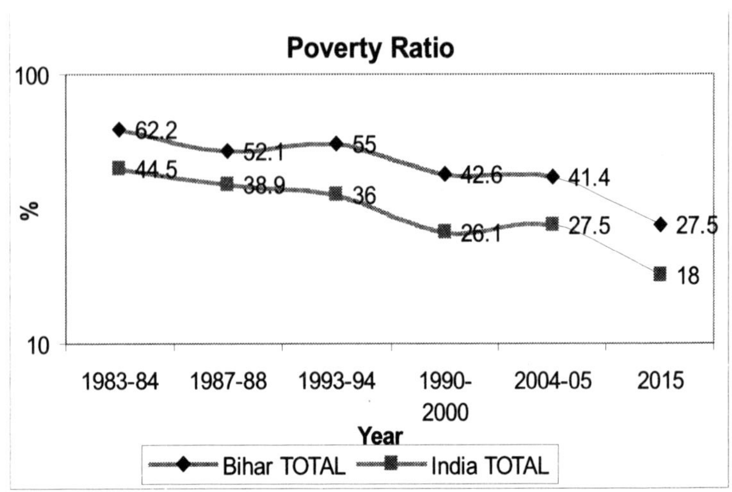

where as national target is 18% from 36.0%. There has been poverty reduction of only 51% in 15 years in Bihar. By looking at the graph, it is observed that overall poverty ratio of Bihar was 55.0% in 1993-94 whereas in 2004-05 it was 41.4%. This reduction has come about because the decrease in rural poverty.

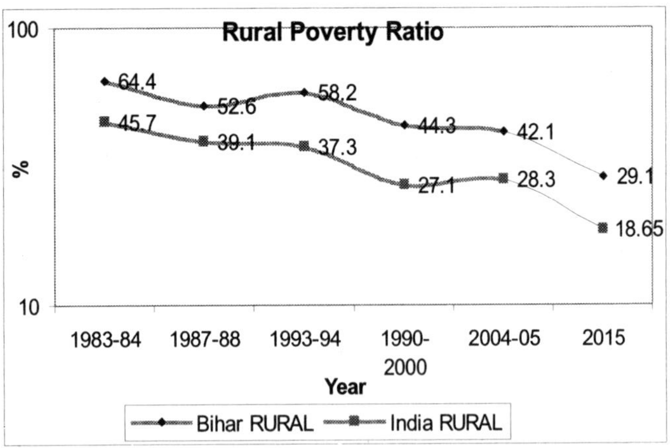

There is no achievement during the period of 1993-94 to 2004-05 in urban poverty reduction in Bihar. So the Bihar's

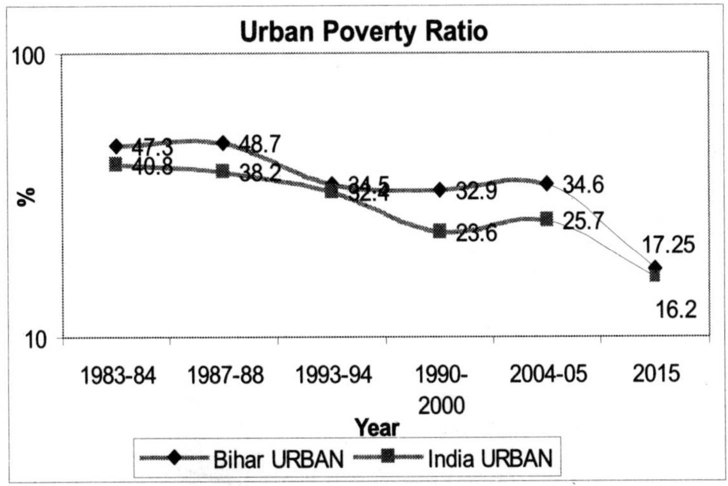

target is still lagging in reducing the number of urban poor. Instead of decreasing, it increased 0.1 percentage point, whereas, national poverty is reduced by 6.7 percentage point. In the context of rural poverty, it declined from 58.2% to 42.1% whereas national poverty reduced from 37.3% to 28.1%.

MDG² Achieve universal primary education: Education, in the present day context, is perhaps the single most important means for individuals to improve personal endowments, build capability levels, overcome constraints and, in the process, enlarge their available set of opportunities and choices for a sustained improvement in well-being. It is not only a means to enhance human capital, productivity and, hence, the compensation to labour, but it is equally important for enabling the process of acquisition, assimilation and communication of information and knowledge, all of which augment a person's quality of life. Education is important not merely as means to other ends, but it is an attribute that is valued in itself, by most individuals. More importantly, it is a critical invasive instrument for bringing about social, economic and political inclusion and a durable integration of people, particularly those 'excluded', from the mainstream of any society.

The MDGs 2nd goal is to ensure that, by 2015, children everywhere, boys and girls alike, will be able to complete a full course of primary schooling.

Target 2
Primary Enrolment Ratio

State		*1997-98*	*2000-01*	*2006-07*
Bihar	Male	90.9	98.24	106.34
	Female	59.5	60.49	82.32
India	Male	98.5	104.91	114.42
	Female	81.5	85.92	107.84

Source : Ministry of Human Resource Development, Government of India.

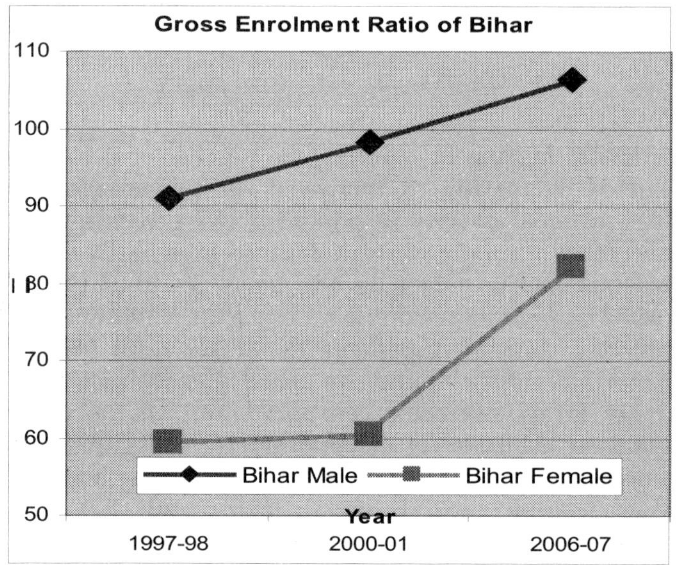

MDG[3] *Promote gender equality and empower women:* To eliminate gender disparity in primary and secondary education, preferably by 2005, and to all levels of education, not later than 2015. This target is for empowering the women.

Only 36% women take household decisions at the national level whereas only 32% women participate in taking household decisions in Bihar in 2005-06. The gender literacy gap was very wide around 30 percentage points in 1991 and just 26 percentage points in 2001 in Bihar whereas, in India it was 25

TARGET 3
Drop-out Rates during 1997-98 and 2004-05

State	*Classes I-V*		
	Boys	*Girls*	*Total*
Bihar (1997-98)	54.6	59.6	56.5
Bihar (2004-05)	53.4	48.6	51.6
India (1997-98)	37.5	41.5	39.2
India (2004-05)	31.8	25.4	29.0

Source : Ministry of Human Resource Development (2003), Education in India: School Education (Numerical Data), 1997-98", Government of India; Ministry of Human Resource Development, Selected Educational Statistics: 2004-05, Government of India.

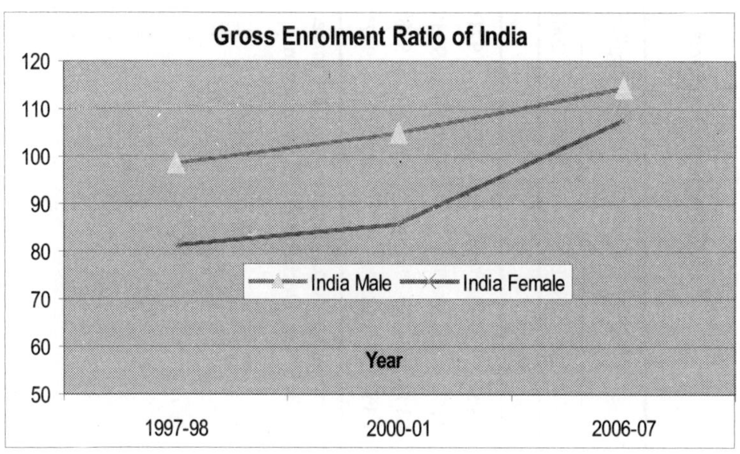

percentage point in 1991 and 21 percentage point in 2001. The position of women in rural work participation ratio in Bihar is only 9.5% in 1991, but it has increased in 2001 to 20.2%, where India rural women work participation ratio has decreased from 27% to 17% between 1991 and 2001. So, the women empowerment has still to go a long way.

MDG[4] *Reduce child mortality*: For most individuals, the choice to live a healthy life free from illness and ailments—and a reasonable life span, are crucial attributes in the notion of

Target 4
Gender Disparity

		Literacy		*Sex Ratio*@		*Work Participation Ratio*		*Decision Taken by Women*
		1991	*2001*	*1991*	*2001*	*1991*	*2001*	*2005-06*
(1)	*(2)*	*(3)*	*(4)*	*(5)*	*(6)*	*(7)*	*(8)*	*(9)*
Bihar	Male	51.4%	60.3%	907*	921*	48.2%	48.0%	32.7%
	Female	22.0%	33.6%	953**	938**	9.5%	20.2%	
India	Male	64.1%	75.3%	927*	933*	52.5%	44.3%	36.7%
	Female	39.3%	53.7%	945**	927**	26.7%	16.6%	

Note : * All age groups, ** 0-6 yrs. age group, @-female per 1000 male.
Source : Census 1991 and 2001, NFHS 3 for Decision taken by women.

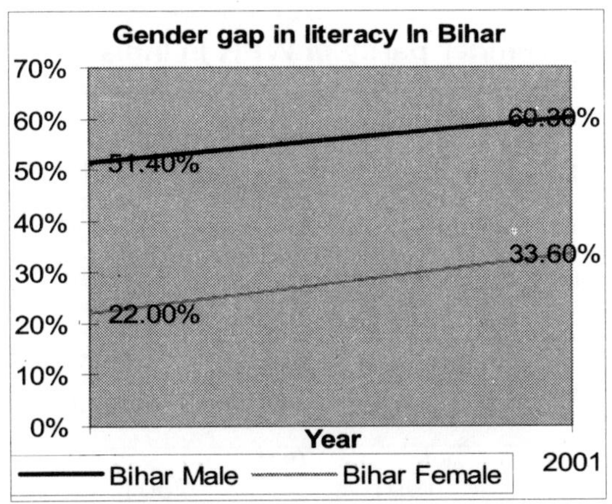
Gender gap in literacy In Bihar
70%
60%
50%
40%
30%
20%
10%
0%
60.30%
51.40%
33.60%
22.00%
Year
2001
Bihar Male
Bihar Female

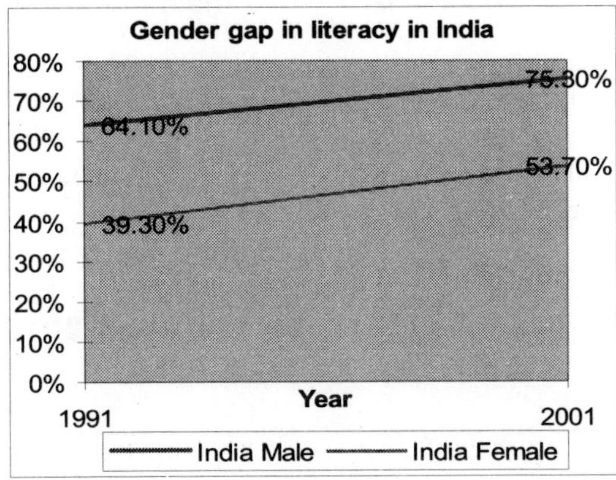
Gender gap in literacy in India
80%
70%
60%
50%
40%
30%
20%
10%
0%
75.30%
64.10%
53.70%
39.30%
Year
1991
2001
India Male
India Female

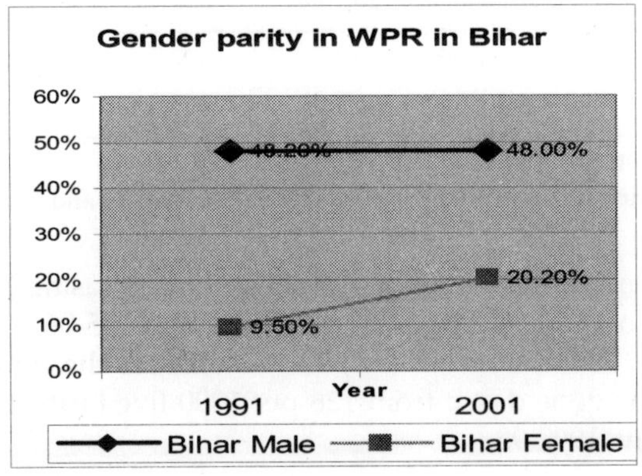
Gender parity in WPR in Bihar
60%
50%
40%
30%
20%
10%
0%
48.00%
20.20%
9.50%
Year
1991
2001
Bihar Male
Bihar Female

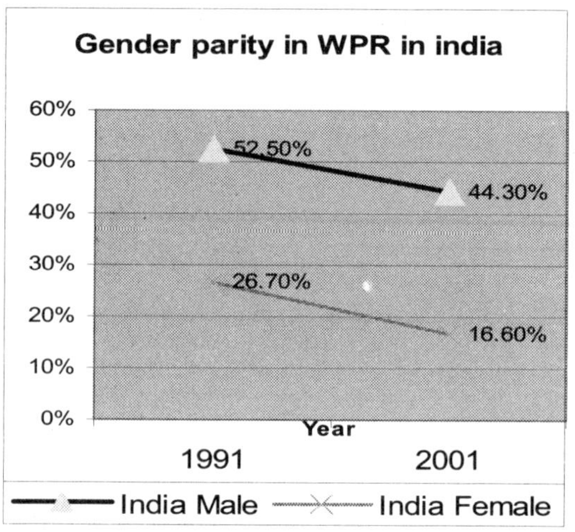

personal well-being. Similarly, for a society, a transition from high incidence of morbidity and mortality to a state where people generally enjoy long and disease-free lives is considered a desirable and valued social change.

TARGET 5

Reduce by Two-third, between 1990 and 2015, the Under-five Mortality Rate

	Infant Mortality@			*Under-five Mortality*@		
	1992-93	*1998-99*	*2005-06*	*1992-93*	*1998-99*	*2005-06*
Bihar	89.2	72.9	61.7	127.5	105.1	84.8
India	78.5	67.6	57.0	109.3	94.9	74.3

Note : @ mortality per 1000 live Birth.

Source : National Family Health Survey, 1992-93, 1998-99 and 2005-06.

Infant mortality rates are significantly decreasing in Bihar as well as in India. It has been achieved by 2005-06 at 62 per 1000 of live births from 89 in 1992-93, whereas the under five mortality has gone down from 126 per 1000 live births to 85 by 2005-06 from 1992-93.

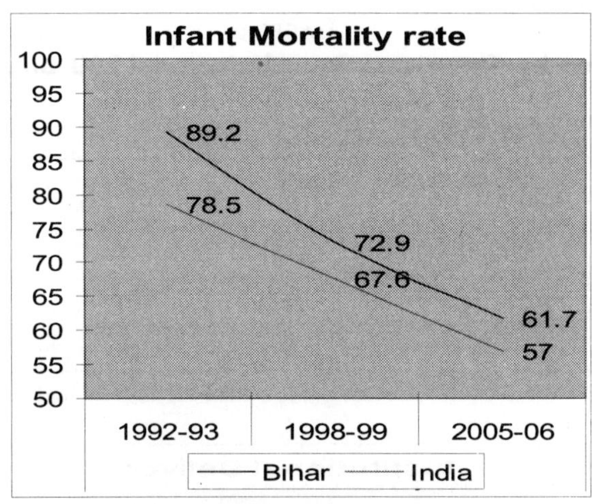

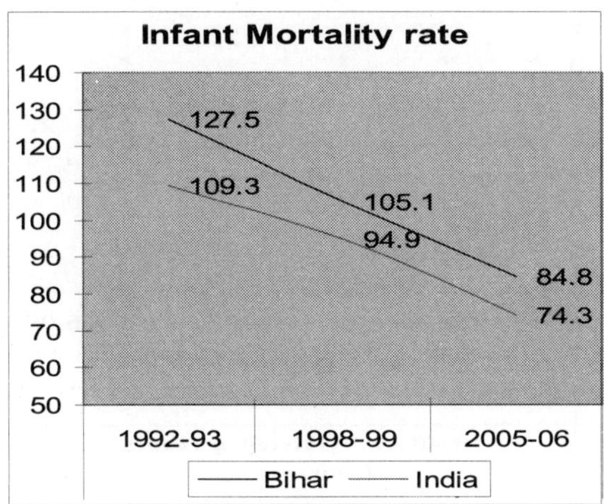

MDG[5] To Improve maternal health: Maternal deaths due to complications in pregnancy and childbirth are among the leading causes of death among women in a number of States in India. It depends on caring about mother during the pregnancy.

Not only women health but child health is also affected by maternal health. Bihar is lagging behind in the context of maternal health. Delivery assisted by health professional was only 32.6% in 2005-06 whereas national delivery less than half was assisted by health professionals. Only 22% childbirth has

Target 6
Reduce by Three-quarters, between 1990 and 2015, the Maternal Mortality Ratio

	Institutional Delivery			*Delivery Assisted by Health Professionals*		
	1992-93	*1998-99*	*2005-06*	*1992-93*	*1998-99*	*2005-06*
Bihar	12.2	14.3	22.0	19.0	24.8	32.6
India	25.5	33.6	40.8	34.2	42.3	48.8

Source : National Family Health Survey, 1992-93, 1998-99 and 2005-06.

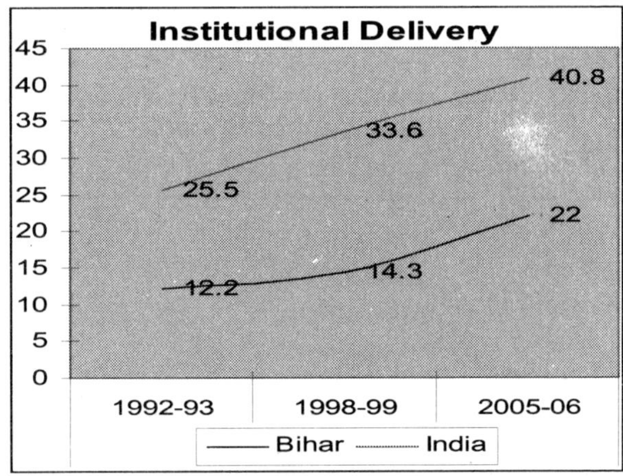

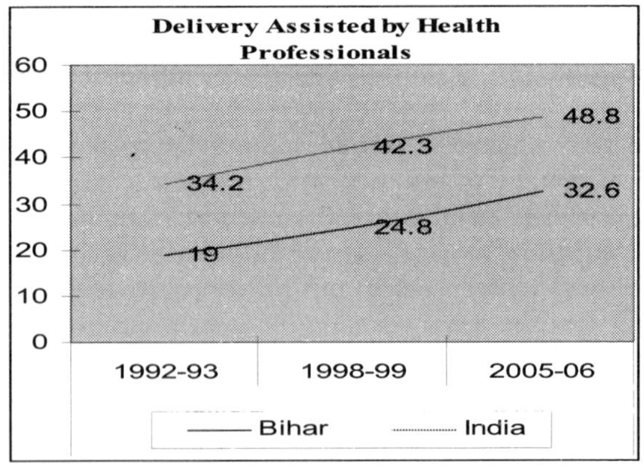

been delivered in health institutions in Bihar upto 2005-06 which is 10 percentage point increase from 1992-93. National childbirth in health institution was 25% in 1992-93 but increased significantly upto 40% in 2005-06.

MDG[6] Combat HIV/AIDS, Malaria and Other Diseases: Good health is most important for human development, because one cannot develop its skill or productivity without well-being. Health is most dependent on awareness. HIV/AIDS awareness, mass immunization and malnutrition are to be tackled on priority basis.

Poverty is directly related to health and health is related with awareness of the people. Only 11.5% female had heard about AIDS in 1998-99 and 35% female were aware of AIDS in 2005-06 in Bihar 70% men were aware of AIDS in 2005-06, in India, 80% male and 57% female were aware of AIDS. Most of the critical diseases can be controlled by vaccination. The vaccination coverage in Bihar has increased to 32.8% from 10.7% between 1992-93 and 2005-06. The national immunization coverage was 43% in 2005-06. 55% children were under-weight in Bihar in 2005-06 whereas the national child malnutrition in 2005-06 was 42%. So, we will have to spread the awareness about AIDS/HIV, universal immunization and nutritious food among the people especially in women.

MDG[7] Ensure environmental sustainability: Integrate the principles of sustainable development into country policies and programmes and reverse the loss of environmental resources.

After bifurcation of Bihar, the most forested area is in Jharkhand. Forest covered area is only 6.9% in Bihar whereas the national average of forested area is 23.4%. So, Bihar has to determine its environmental sustainability.

The basic household facilities are safe drinking water, electricity, toilet, latrine facilities, etc. In this context, 27% households with electricity facility in 2005-06 increased from 16.6% coverage in 1992-93, whereas the national electrified households was 67% in 2005-06. The toilet/latrine facility available for the households in Bihar was 16.5% only in 1992-93, and it increased to 25.2% in 2005-06. The safe drinking water facility is also not available for all. It is indicating the backwardness of the basic household infrastructure in Bihar as

TARGET 7
Have Halted by 2015 and Begun to Reverse the Spread of HIV/AIDS, Malaria and other Major Diseases

	Who have heard of HIV/AIDS			*Fully immunized*			*3 yr. Children Under Weight*		
	1998-99F	*2005-06F*	*2005-06M*	*1992-93*	*1998-99*	*2005-06*	*1992-93*	*1998-99*	*2005-06*
(1)	*(2)*	*(3)*	*(4)*	*(5)*	*(6)*	*(7)*	*(8)*	*(9)*	*(10)*
Bihar	11.5	35.2	70.0	10.7	11.0	32.8	62.6	54.4	55.9
India	40.3	57.0	80.0	35.4	42.0	43.5	53.4	47.0	42.5

Note : F—Female, M—Male.

Source : National Family Health Survey, 1992-93, 1998-99 and 2005-06.

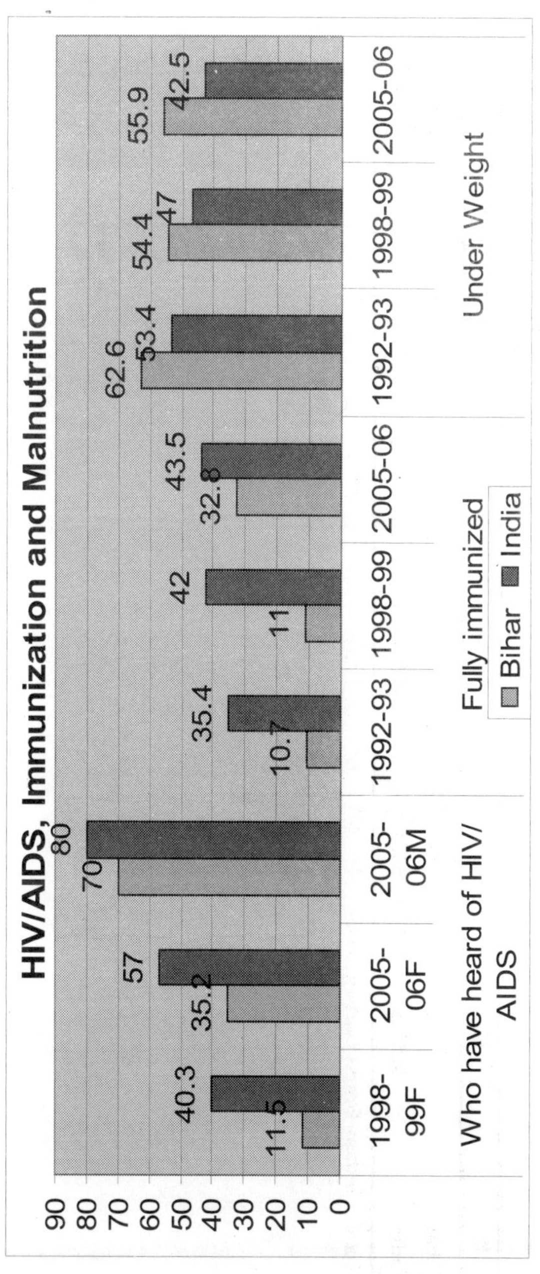
HIV/AIDS, Immunization and Malnutrition
90
80
70
60
50
40
30
20
10
0
11.5
40.3
35.2
57
70
80
10.7
35.4
11
42
32.8
43.5
62.6
53.4
54.4
47
55.9
42.5
1998-99F
2005-06F
2005-06M
1992-93
1998-99
2005-06
1992-93
1998-99
2005-06
Who have heard of HIV/AIDS
Fully immunized
Under Weight
Bihar
India

TARGET 8

Ensure Environmental Sustainability

(Area in km²)

State	*Geographical Area*	*Forested Area*	*Forest Covered*	*Outside forest Area covered with tree*	*No. of tree/ hectare culturable area*	*Forest covered + Tree Area*
(1)	*(2)*	*(3)*	*(4)*	*(5)*	*(6)*	*(7)*
Bihar	94163	6473 (6.87%)	5579 (5.92%)	2522 (2.68%)	10.80	8101 (8.60%)
India	3257263	769626 (23.4%)	677088 (20.6%)	91663 (2.79%)	12.14	861289 (23.4%)

Source : Indian Forest Survey, 2005.

Target 9
Halve by 2015 the Proportion of People without Sustainable Access to Safe Drinking Water and Basic Sanitation

	Households with safe Drinking Water Facility			*Households with Toilet/ Latrine Facility*			*Households with Electricity Facility*		
	1992-93	*1998-99*	*2005-06*	*1992-93*	*1998-99*	*2005-06*	*1992-93*	*1998-99*	*2005-06*
(1)	*(2)*	*(3)*	*(4)*	*(5)*	*(6)*	*(7)*	*(8)*	*(9)*	*(10)*
Bihar	63.6	75.4	96.1	16.5	16.8	25.2	16.6	18.2	27.7
India	68.2	77.9	87.9	30.3	36.0	44.6	50.9	60.1	67.9

Source : National Family Health Survey, 1992-93, 1998-99 and 2005-06.

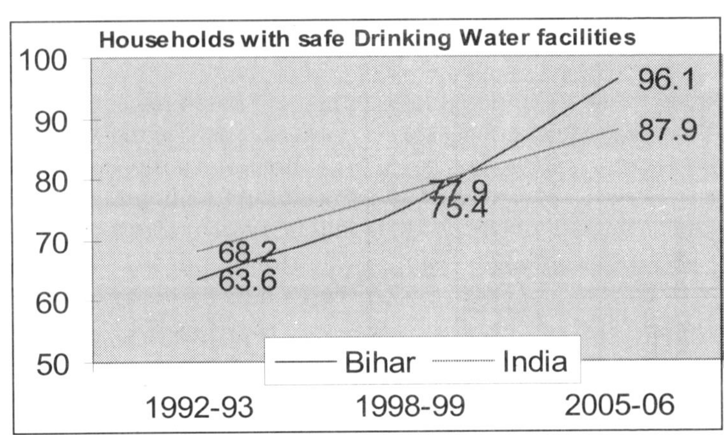
Households with safe Drinking Water facilities
100
90
80
70
60
50
96.1
87.9
77.9
75.4
68.2
63.6
Bihar
India
1992-93
1998-99
2005-06

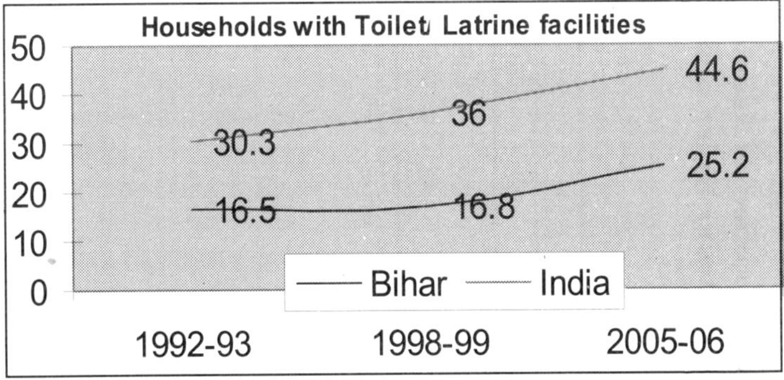
Households with Toilet/ Latrine facilities
50
40
30
20
10
0
44.6
36
30.3
25.2
16.5
16.8
Bihar
India
1992-93
1998-99
2005-06

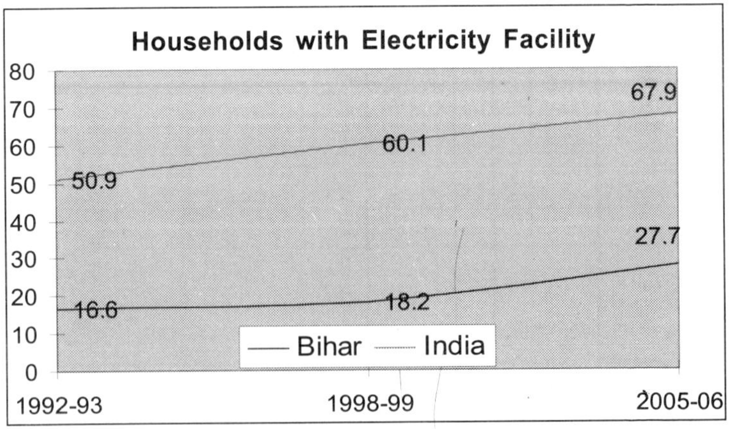
Households with Electricity Facility
80
70
60
50
40
30
20
10
0
67.9
60.1
50.9
27.7
16.6
18.2
Bihar
India
1992-93
1998-99
2005-06

	Telephone Lines per 100 Population			*Cellular Subscribers per 100 Population*			*Internet Users per 100 Population*		
	1991-92	*1999-00*	*2004-05*	*1992-93*	*2004-05*	*2006-07*	*2001*	*2004*	*2006*
(1)	*(2)*	*(3)*	*(4)*	*(5)*	*(6)*	*(7)*	*(8)*	*(9)*	*(10)*
Bihar	0.15	0.60	1.80	—	1.67	7.52	—	—	—
India	0.67	2.82	8.95	—	7.02	18.31	1.41	1.93	3.5

Source : Department of Telecommunication, Government of India.

well as the nation. One can easily locate the disparity between Bihar and the National households' basic facilities.

MDG[8] Develop a global partnership for development: The economic reforms in India took the form of globalization, privatization and liberalization in 1991. The National Assembly set the target. In cooperation with the private sector; it made available the benefits of new technologies, especially information and communication technologies.

The development system depends on use of the new technology, information and communication participation. The baseline density in Bihar was only 0.2 telephones per 100 people in 1991-92 against 0.7 telephones per 100 people in India. It is increasing significantly upto 2 telephones per 100 head and 9 telephones per 100 head at the Bihar and national level respectively in 2004-05. The cellular service in Bihar is very speedily growing everywhere in India as well. The internet users are also increasing with a steady rate in both Bihar and India.

SUMMING UP

The development scenario in Bihar is characterized not only by its economic backwardness, but by its social backwardness as well. This social backwardness is reflected in the low literacy rates, poor health standards, low status of women and children, and many other indicators of social development. This low level of social development leads to low levels of human development, in the absence of which it is very difficult for the state to embark on a process of steady economic development. It is observed there that Bihar lies at the bottom of all the states in terms of its human development in all these three decades. One can observe from Appendix II that Bihar is the most backward state in India. We can see the position of Bihar in achieving its goals of millennium development. It is far below the target. The disparity among the states of India and Bihar development is increasing over the time. It is because of the very poor physical infrastructure (Road, Electricity, Transport, etc.), unorganized market structure, lack of industrialization, low literacy, poor health infrastructure, low level of living standard, low credit-deposit ratio, traditional agriculture system, etc. So, state should strike at the grass-root level to rectify these problems. If the society or the people develop, the economy will be automatically developed. One can observe the Millennium Development Goals as well as Human Development from Appendix I.

Notes and References

1. 'Planning Commission Government of India', New Delhi, National Human Development Report, 2001: UNDP, Oxford.
2. Different Round of National Sample Survey, Government of India.
3. Eleventh Five-Year Plan (2007-12): Government of India, Planning Commission (54th NDC Meeting), 'Rural Drinking Water and Sanitation in the Eleventh Plan Period—Excerpts'.
4. Census of India and Bihar, 1991 and 2001.
5. Ministry of Health and Family Welfare, National Family Health Survey, 1992-93, 1998-99 and 2005-06'.
6. Ministry of Human Resource Development, 'Selected Educational Statistics of Several Years'.
7. Indian Forest Research Institute, Dehradun, Indian Forest Survey, 2005'.
8. Telecom Regulatory Authority of India, 'Several Telecom Reports'.
9. http://www.un.org/millenniumgoals/
10. http://www.undp.org.in/
11. Different reports of MDGs submitted by Government of India.

APPENDIX I
Mapping MDG with HDI

Human Development Index	*Millennium Development Goals*
Human Poverty Index	Eradicate extreme poverty and hunger.
Educational Index	Achieve universal primary education,
Gender Parity Index	Promote gender equality and empower women,
Health Index	Reduce child mortality, Improve maternal health, Combat HIV/AIDS, malaria and other diseases,
Physical Environment	Ensure Environmental Sustainability and Develop a global partnership for development.

APPENDIX II

Human Development Index of 15 Major States of India

State	*1981*		*1991*		*2001*	
	Value	*Rank*	*Value*	*Rank*	*Value*	*Rank*
Andhra Pradesh	0.298	09	0.377	09	0.416	10
Assam	0.272	10	0.348	10	0.386	14
Bihar	*0.237*	*15*	*0.308*	*15*	*0.367*	*15*
Gujarat	0.36	04	0.431	06	0.479	06
Haryana	0.36	05	0.443	05	0.509	05
Karnataka	0.346	06	0.412	07	0.478	07
Kerala	0.500	01	0.591	01	0.638	01
Madhya Pradesh	0.245	14	0.328	13	0.394	12
Maharashtra	0.363	03	0.452	04	0.523	04
Orissa	0.267	11	0.345	12	0.404	11
Punjab	0.411	02	0.475	02	0.537	02
Rajasthan	0.256	12	0.347	11	0.424	09
Tamil Nadu	0.343	07	0.466	03	0.531	03
Uttar Pradesh	0.255	13	0.314	14	0.388	13
West Bengal	0.305	08	0.404	08	0.472	08
All India	0.302	—	0.381	—	0.472	—

Source : 2001, Planning Commission, Government of India, 'National Human Development Report'.

High Growth Trajectory and Rural Development in India

NARESH PRASAD SINGH

Tracing trends of rural employment in India, both labour force participation rate (LFPR) and work participation rates (WPR) picked up during the period 1999-2000 to 2004-05 after the period of jobless growth. RNFS employment among males increased from 23 per cent in 1983 to 34 percent in 2008-09. It is suggested that development efforts targeting rural areas should be done in decentralized manner, land reforms be enforced, greater access to credit be ensured and other basic inputs should be provided. Unorganized sector should not be left behind while making efforts towards betterment of socio-economic conditions of rural people.

INTRODUCTION

The year 2009 has been one of the toughest and most challenging year for the Indian Economy. Despite severity of the global downturn and doomsday forecasts, Indian economy has shown marked resilience and has emerged as a respectable and matured economy, which can wither any storm unaided. World has come to respect India as never before.

Indian economy showing the signs of recovery, grew by 7.9 percent during the second quarter of 2009-10 (July-September 2009). This is the highest GDP growth which Indian economy obtained since the beginning of global financial recession in September 2008. This growth rate makes India the second fastest growing economy among major countries after China which recorded 7.9 percent growth in April-June 2009 period. As per World Bank's projections India could return to 8-9 percent growth rate by 2011.

This paper attempts to examine the high growth rate in the Indian economy in the context of different sectors of rural development. In section-1, I have discussed the impact of high growth rate on rural employment in India. In section-2, discussed the sustainable high growth in agriculture. In section-3, examined the impact of high growth on Socio-Economic conditions of informal workers, and lastly in section-4, analyzed the problems of urbanization and migration in India.

1. Employment Growth in Rural India

The agricultural sector is passing through a complex crisis of low productivity, poor competitiveness and adverse climatic conditions. The compound annual growth rate of agriculture and the allied sector from 2000-01 to 2004-05 was 2.02 percent, the lowest annual growth recorded in the sector since 1980-81. They have also shown the widespread decline in the sector, covering all sub-sectors.

How does employment growth pick up when output growth is stagnant ? Under normal circumstances, this trend should have further reduced the employment in the rural economy. However, further probing reveals that the acceleration in rural employment growth is probably a response to the crisis that is gripping the sector. Under conditions of distress, when income levels fall below sustenance, then the part of the normally non-working population is forced to enter the labour market to supplement household income. It is argued that it is probably the distress in the agrarian sector that has led to the growth of employment in rural India. In other words, it can be argued that the recent growth in rural employment is "distress-driven employment" or "earnings capacity poor" driven employment.

The neo classical framework of analyzing labour supply starts with the premise that labour supply decisions are entirely done by individual decision makers. The neoclassical theory presume that individual decision-makers maximize their satisfaction based on a division of time between leisure and work, which generate the typical backward bending labour supply curve (Robbins, 1930). However, there it little truth in such an analytical structure, when it comes to traditional agriculture-based families living at subsistence levels. A choice between leisure and work based on one's earnings becomes pertinent only when an individual is trying to maximize his marginal utility, and he is well above the subsistence level. When, at subsistence level, the earnings level declines then the individual may need to work more hours per day and more days per week to keep his income levels constant.

However, some argue that individual decision-making at subsistence income levels does not attempt to optimize the individual utility levels under conditions of poverty. Rather, members in households at subsistence level try to acquire the basic subsistence income for all members in the family. Thus the labour supply of a house-hold is a joint utility function of the household. When the earnings of the working members of the poor household do not meet the subsistence level of the family, the workers may increase their total time of work, cutting down on leisure.

TRENDS IN RURAL EMPLOYMENT

After the decline in labour force participation and work participation rates (WPR) during 1993-94 to 1999-2000, both the indicators recovered during the period 1999-2000 to 2004-05 marking the resurgence of employment growth after the period of jobless growth. This was true in the case of both males and females. The male labour force participation rates (LFPR) in the rural sector increased from 533 per thousand to 546 per thousand while for females it increased from 235 to 249. Similarly, the male WPR increased from 522 to 535, and for females it increased from 231 to 242 per thousand. Prima facie it looks encouraging that both male and female participation rates have increased. Yet, the sudden spurt of females LFPR and WPR casts doubts on these encouraging trends. Since 1983, the highest recorded female LFPR was in the period 1987-88 at 254 per thousand. It is common knowledge that 1987-88 was a year of severe drought in the economy, when the female LFPR peaked. Since the peak the female LFPR had continuously declined to reach the lowest in 1999-2000 at 235, thereafter, it suddenly shot up to 249 per thousand in 2004-05, the highest since 1987-88 peak of female LFPR. Similarly, the female WPR, which had a secular decline from 1983 to 1999-2000, the lowest 231, increased in 2004-05 to 242.

One cannot argue that this rise in female participation rates is due to cracking up of the traditional patriarchal system in India. Institutional changes in traditional social system do not occur in a short period, but they involve over a long period of time. A more plausible reason seems to be the distress-related feminization of work. It is the submission of this paper that the new peak in female LFPR in 2004-05 is a phenomenon similar to the 1987-88 surge in female LFPR that occurred due to the drought. Women previously engaged in domestic work joined the primary income earner, mainly as unpaid family

TABLE 1

LFPR and WPR in Rural India

Year	*Labour Force Participation Rate*		*Work Participation Rate*	
	Male	*Female*	*Male*	*Female*
1983	540	252	528	248
1987-88	532	254	517	245
1993-94	594	237	538	234
1999-2000	533	235	522	231
2004-05	546	249	535	242

Source : NSS Reports on Employment and Unemployment situation in India.

workers in the agricultural farms, replacing hired labour, as the farm output declined to subsistence level.

However, the male LFPR and WPR had also increased during the latest period, unlike the period 1983 to 1987-88 when it declined. This rise in male participation rates also, as argued later, is a sign of the distress-related employment. The stagnation in rural agricultural wages and low productivity has forced the male workers to search for employment in non-farm sector, while otherwise non-working males such as aged dependents have joined the workforce for subsistence.

RURAL NON-FARM EMPLOYMENT

The total share of employment in the agriculture sector had declined from 77 percent of the workforce in 1983 to 66 percent in 2004-05. The largest decline was in the period 1999-2000 to 2004-05, where a reduction of 5 percent point was recorded. Correspondingly, the rural non-farm sector (RNFS) employment share among males increased from 23 percent in 1983 to 34 percent in 2008-09. This increase in RNFS employment was spread within the manufacturing sector, construction sector, trade, hotel and restaurant, transport, storage and communication. Such a rise in RNFS employment is to be suspected for its quality. The sudden spurt in RNFS employment in the period 1999-2000 to 2004-05 is probably a distress driven strategy of households to seek employment in other sectors. Such a shift in industrial composition, owing to agrarian distress would make the RNFS a residual low value adding, low productivity sector. The trends broadly suggest that the agrarian distress has driven male workers out of agricultural sector in search of employment in the RNFS sector, while women substitute men in their previous agricultural employment.

1. Achieving Sustainable High Growth in Agriculture

Indian agriculture is the back-bone of our economy. About 65 percent of India population is dependent for employment and income on agriculture and it continues to play a vital role in the country's economy. The Indian agriculture, since independence, has achieved tremendous progress. The food-grain production has increased from a mere 15 million tones during 1950's to more than 230 million tones now.

After all in India the situation is worse because our average productivity also lies below the optimum level, and compares poorly with that of many countries. During the post green revolution period, agricultural production has increased rapidly. But since the last 10 years, India has witnessed a fatigue in the green revolution with the growth rate in food production falling below the population growth. The growth rate of food-grain production decelerated to 1.2 percent during 1990-2007, lower than annual population growth rate averaging 1.9 percent. Vanguard states like Punjab and Haryana are among the first to be hit by this stagnation.

How to raise the agricultural productivity is, therefore, a major concern with agricultural policy planners today. The Government set-up a National Commission on farmers in 2005 under the Chairmanship of Prof. M.S. Swaminathan. Many of the recommendations made by the Commission have already been implemented and others are in various stages of implementation.

One key strategy to raise farm production was to identify districts in which there was scope of significantly improving productivity of major foodgrain crops by focused intervention from the government. The Rs. 5000 Crore National Food Security Mission (NFSM) was started with this assumption. This mission focuses on making available quality seeds and fertilizers, credit and extension support in about 300 identified districts. The resultant increase in productivity of rice, wheat and pulses would result in additional production of additional 10 million tones of rice, 8 million tones of wheat and 2 million tones of pulses per year by 2012. NFSM has yielded satisfactory results in the first year of its implementation.

Another major scheme, the Rashtriya Krishi Vikas Yojana (RKVY), was launched to encourage states to invest more on agriculture and allied activities. The Centre is providing funds to the tune of Rs. 25,000 crores to states during the 11th Plan to invest in agriculture, with additional funds coming from states, this will lead to substantial investment in agriculture. This will result not only in higher production of foodgrains, other crops and animal products, but will also lead to generation of assets and contributes to long terms growth of the sector.

The government has waived the debt of Indian farmer in 2008-09. In one stroke, over Rs. 71,000 crore has gone in to loan accounts of about four crore indebted farmers. While debt relief was a one-time intervention, the government has been encouraging banks to lend more and more to the farming sector. Kisan Credit Card have also been introduced to make borrowing easy and more transparent. Loans up to Rs. 3,00,000 lakh are given at a low rate of interest of 7 percent a year.

Raising of the minimum support prices (MSP) for major crops successively in the last four years has had a very favourable impact on farming, it has insured remunerative prices to farmers. It has also led to record procurement of foodgrains which has in turn made ample availability and stable prices of food commodities. Recently, the government has modified the formula for fixing MSP so as to include the cost of crop insurance also in the MSP and thus compensate farmers better for their produce. The investments being made now will lead to better technology adaptation, higher use of inputs and establishment of marketing facilities. Along with rural development and employment schemes, these will result in sustainable growth in agriculture in the 11th Plan and beyond.

Seeing the emerging economic opportunities in the farm sector, private companies and individual entrepreneurs have also been entering with investments and services. Some areas in which they have shown interest include marketing, storage and logistic facilities, weather information, insurance, credit, food processing, fish farming, dairying, poultry, floriculture, herbal medicines and exports.

It cannot be denied that there are problems that need to be addressed quickly and firmly to harness the full potential of agriculture and allied sectors. Some, such as dependence of a large number of farmers on rains and small farm holdings, make it difficult to bring about fast transformation of agriculture. The only way to tackle them is to adopt focused strategies, and the government is doing just that. These strategies have been rigorously tested in the last three-four years and they have succeeded in achieving a fast growth, better prices to farmers, adequate availability of foodgrains and reasonable stable food prices.

2. Socio-Economic Conditions of Informal Workers

The term informal sector was first initiated by Keith Hart (1970) in a study of urban Ghana. He describes the informal sector as that part of the urban labour force, which falls outside the organized labour market. The concept has been further refined by a mission of International Labour Organization in 1972, which studied the employment situation in Kenya within the framework of the World Employment Programme. The study reveals that informal sector has the characteristics like easy entry for the new enterprises, reliance on indigenous resources, family ownership, small operations, unregulated and competitive markets, labour-intensive technology and informally acquired skills of workers.

Most of India's workforce is unorganized in nature. While almost the entire farm sector can be characterized as informal, roughly 80 percent of the workforce in the non-farm sector is informal. Over half of India's national output from the unorganized sector, while employment in the formal sector has been stagnant in the last decade, employment creation in the informal segment is tremendous. Out of 399 million workers in 1999-2000, it is estimated that 371.2 million workers are employed in the unorganized segment of the economy, whereas only 27.8 million workers are engaged in the organized sector.

The informal sector plays a major role in Indian economy. It is providing gainful employment opportunity to millions of people and is also contributing significant share to the nation's output. It is estimated that about two-fifths of India's Gross Domestic Product generate from the informal sector and about 90 percent of the families are depending on this sector directly and indirectly for their survival. Despite this, a large number of workers engaged in this sector in both rural and urban areas are illiterate, poor and vulnerable. They live and work in unhygienic conditions and are susceptible to many infectious and chronic diseases. These workers have neither fixed employer-employee relationship nor do they obtain statutory social security benefits. They do not have the bargaining power to fight discrimination and victimization for protecting their rights to a desired standard of living. In the last few years, socio-economic conditions of workers have became more deplorable.

The emergence of informal sector is a major source of employment and income generating sector in developing countries in the recent years. It is primarily a manifestation of increasing pressure of burgeoning population, immaturity of employment market and insufficient alternative income generating sources for rural labour. The rising inflation rate and growing poverty further aggravated the situation and force of labourers to enter into the informal sector for their living.

CONCLUDING OBSERVATIONS

The Indian economy is passing through a phase of socio-economic and political changes. Due to rapid urbanization, growing industrialization, unprecedented rural-urban migration and tremendous population explosion, the entire gamut of human life has changed drastically. In the recent years, there has been tremendous increase in prices, and increases in the pay structure and service conditions of the workers, belonging to the organized sectors. But it is surprising and a pity to learn that no such corresponding improvement has taken place in the wages and working conditions of the workers in the unorganized sectors; the workers who are working under the umbrella of unorganized nature, they do not have strength to fight for their survival due to illiteracy, inadequate alternative sources. The welfare authorities should take necessary policy steps to enhance their livelihood status.

3. Urbanization and Migration in India

India is undergoing radical changes in demographic patterns as streams of people migrate to regions which offer better opportunities than their homes. Migration from rural to urban areas is of different types. One is to settle down permanently in the urban areas of one's choice. This is called translocatory migration. Other is one in which migrants hang on to the rural base and migrate repeatedly and for varying durations, either to the same urban area or to different ones. This is termed circulatory migration.

Migration is a positive phenomenon and if regulated and managed properly can reap benefits for both the sending and receiving regions. Employment is one of the main reasons for migration. Migration from rural to urban areas also follows a certain patterns. One, it depends upon the "pull" factors at the urban and "push" factors at the rural end. Thus, migration of agricultural labourers from Bihar to Punjab during the harvest season is of this type. Then there is migration which is caused by rural poverty and urban opportunity of getting work.

The rural to urban migration and the urbanization are associated with a vertical shift in the labour force from the agricultural sector to the urbanized-industrial sector. In India migration is from rural agricultural sectors to urban informal sectors as well. The total urban population of India has grown from 62.44 million in 1951 to 286.12 million in 2001. Thus, the urban population has increased very fast. Although the realization is bitter, their arrival causes undue stress to the urban system which has to deal with pavement dwelling, slums, disease, crime and ultimate degeneration. The urban system breaks down often due to this stress. Water shortage, electricity, transportation, education, housing security and other services fail.

SUGGESTIONS

Government should take measures to enhance the basic facilities to the rural population. Rural development and poverty alleviation programmes should implement on a decentralized basis throughout the country. Rural development implies both the economic betterment of rural people as well as greater social transformation. In order to provide the rural people with better prospects for economic development, increased participation of them in the rural development programmes, decentralization of planning, better enforcement of land reforms and greater access to credit are envisaged. Connectivity of villages providing economic opportunities to all the segments of people is an urgent need. Finally, the Governments should take effective steps to provide health facilities, power supply and water supply to reduce the rural-urban migrants.

REFERENCES

The Economic Times, July 2009 to December 2009.

Government of India (2007), Report of Expert Group on Agricultural Indebtedness.

Sundaram, K. (2007), Employment and Poverty in India, 2000-05, *E & P Weekly*, 28 July.

Abraham, V. (2009), Employment Growth in Rural India, *E & P Weekly*, 18 April.

Kurukshetra, Ministry of Rural Development, April 2009 to December, 2009.

Southern Economist, January 2009 to November 2009.

Sakthivel, S. and Joddar, P. (2006), Unorganized Sector Workforce in India, *E & P Weekly*, May 27.

Abraham, V. (2007), Growth and Inequality of Wages in India, *Indian Journal of Labour Economics*, Vol. 50, No. 4.

Economic Advisory Council to the Prime Minister (2009), *Review of the Economy*, 2008-09, January.

Rejuvenating Indian Agriculture

NIRAJ KUMAR VERMA

Agriculture plays an important though declining role in the Indian economy. The divergence between the growth rate of overall GDP and that from agriculture has been increasing. Agriculture suffering from consistently low rates of growth demands attention. The development of agriculture requires credit, access to quality seeds and proper irrigation facilities. Corporate sector can be partner in the development of agriculture. Agriculture subsidies are fiscally unsustainable. Need is for process-based farm activities. Agricultural diversification will lead to commercialization of agriculture.

" .... *I have believed and repeated several times that India is to be found not in its few cities but in its villages."*

—Mahatma Gandhi

India is one of the fastest growing economies of the world

and is currently the focus of a great deal of international attention. It is the seventh largest country in the world in terms of its geographical size. Today it has a population of nearly 1.1 billion which makes it the second most populous in the world. The leading forecasting institutions expect that India will play a bigger role in world markets in future. It is likely to consolidate its position as worlds leading exporter of rice. India is third largest economy in Asia after Japan and China, as measured in terms of its Gross Domestic Product and it is continuing to grow rapidly. The Indian economy has seen high growth rates of more than 8% since 2003. In 2005 and 2006, GDP grew at a rate of over 9%. High growth rates have significantly reduced poverty in India.

Cereals are the staple food in India, providing over half of the calories consumed, while the pulses are the main protein supplement in the diet. Rising incomes and the influence of globalization have contributed to changes in diet with a slight decrease in cereals consumption and increase in pulses, edible oils, fruits and vegetables, milk and meat, which is growing from a low base. However, although diets are diversifying, India still lags behind Brazil and China in terms of daily calorie intake per capita.

TABLE 1
Food Consumption—Daily Calories Per Capita

	1990-92	*1998-2000*	*2003-05*
Brazil	2860	3001	3223
China	2696	2917	2957
India	2396	2463	2512

Source : FAOSTAT.

Agriculture plays an important, though declining role in the economy. Its share in overall GDP fell from 30% in the early nineties to below 17.5% in 2006. This is high compared to China and Brazil, at 12% and 5% respectively. Over this period the share of industry has stayed relatively constant, reaching nearly 28% in 2006. Meanwhile, the service sector has grown rapidly (accounting for about 65% of total GDP growth from 2000-05) to almost 55% of GDP in 2006.

Despite India's economic development, over 70% of population still live in rural areas. Agriculture is the key employer with around 60% of the labour force, down from 70% in the early nineties. This compares with 44% in China (2002) and 21% in Brazil (2004). Overall agricultural gross domestic product (GDP) growth in the country has been below population growth for nearly a decade. Investment in agriculture is only about 1.3 percent of GDP.

It is a nation with over 300 million poor people, a number hat has barely declined over the last three decades of development. Rapid growth will be essential to reduce the number of the poor. India has successfully reduced the share of the poor in the population by 27.4 percentage points from 54.9 in 1973 to 27.5 in 2004. There is growing consensus that poverty line (Rs. 356 monthly per capita consumption expenditure for rural areas and Rs. 539 for urban areas in 2004-05) is too low. The composition of the poor has been changing and rural poverty is getting concentrated in agricultural labour and artisanal households. Agricultural labour households accounted for 41% of rural poor in 1992-93 as well as in 2004-05. The share of self-employed in agriculture among the rural poor had fallen from 32% to 21.6% during the period (*Source* : 11th Five Year Plan document).

The occupational composition of rural poor varied across states. In general, in developed States, poverty was highly concentrated among the agricultural labour households and in contrast, in backward states poverty extended to other occupational groups including self-employed in agriculture. The poor are geographically concentrated in India. They also happened to be in states were a significant proportion of agriculture is irrigated, and not rain fed.

The farmers constitute the largest consumer group in the country and no growth can be sustainable unless the problems of this sector are addressed. Farming is also the largest private sector enterprise in the country. The National Commission on Farmers (NCF) under the Ministry of Agriculture, Govt. of India has defined "Farmers" to include landless agricultural labourers, sharecroppers, tenants, small, marginal and sub-marginal cultivators, farmers with larger holdings, fish, dairy, sheep, poultry and other farmers involved in animal husbandry, pastoralists, plantation workers as well as those rural and tribal families engaged in a wide variety of farming-related occupations such as sericulture. The canvas is vast and there are myriad issues, both supply side and demand side, to be addressed.

AGRICULTURE STRUCTURE

India's agricultural areas is vast with total arable and permanent cropland of 170 million hectares in 2003-04. It has the second largest arable area in the world after the United States. OECD in its 2007 agricultural monitoring report stated that Indian agriculture is dominated by a large number of small scale holdings that are predominantly owner occupied. The average size of the holding in the late nineties was about 1.4 hectares and continues to decline. Out of India's 116 million farmers, around 60% have less than one hectare. The share of medium to large farms (about 4 hectares) is very small at just over 7% of all holdings, but these farms account for around 40% of the land.

In India, agricultural value added per worker has grown by only 15% in real terms from 1990 to 2004. By comparison, productivity in China rose by over 60%, it more than doubled in Brazil. India is among the world's leading producer of paddy rice, wheat, buffalo milk, cow milk and sugarcane. India is now the largest milk producer in the world and the second largest producer of paddy rice, sugarcane, wheat, cow milk, groundnuts and certain fresh vegetables. But it is also a leading consumer.

India is the world leader in products like banana and mangoes. India is the fifth largest cultivator of biotech crops in the world, ahead of China. In 2006, about 3.8 million hectares of land were cultivated with genetically modified crops, by about 2.3 million farmers. The main GM crop is Bt cotton, which was introduced in 2002. Agricultural exports represent 9% of the value of total exports while the share of agriculture in total imports is just 5%. India is a next exporter of agricultural food products with a small surplus of just under

TABLE 2
Top 10 Sectors of India and World Rank

Commodity	*Rank India*	*World Rank 2005*	*Production Avg. 2003-05*	
			Billion $	*Million T*
Paddy rice	1	2	27.5	129.2
Buffalo milk	2	1	25.2	50.5
Wheat	3	2	10.9	69.7
Cow milk	4	2	10.0	37.5
Fresh vegetables	5	2	6.6	34.9
Sugarcane	6	2	5.2	250.0
Potatoes	7	3	3.6	25.0
Groundnuts	8	2	3.4	7.1
Spices	9	1	3.3	1.1
Buffalo meat	10	9	3.1	1.5

$ 4 billion. The single biggest export is milled rice, accounting for 16% of the value of agricultural exports in 2003-04.

THE DIVERGENCE

The divergence between the growth rate of overall GDP and that from agriculture has been increasing. This means, on the one hand, rising demand for food, specially for milk, meat, vegetables and fruits, and, on the other, slow growth in the supplies of food grains. Agricultural strategy in India has to be robust enough to face adverse food scenario. Apart from stepping up public investment in irrigation on which some progress has been made in the last few years, other major challenges in agriculture are rejuvenating dry land areas through soil and water conservation, revamping agricultural research and extension, developing the marketing infrastructure including transport and cold storage to meet the growing needs of diversified and high value agriculture by linking the group of farmers to processes and reviving and strengthening of various public support system for small and marginal farmers.

More investments to revitalize the rural economy and increase the spending power of more than half of the population dependent of agricultural will have cascading effects on other sectors of the economy. For inclusive growth, key sectors of agriculture and rural development are interlinked. Agriculture suffering from consistently low rates of growth demands attention. As land is fixed, only productivity increase and diversification can raise incomes of the rural population. One measure may be extension of irrigation to most of 60% of cultivable land still without access to it.

Agricultural growth requires due access to credit, emphasis on seeds, irrigation, etc. Water management for restoring water bodies and ground water recharge as well as revitalizing the extension system can aid productivity. Critical gaps in linking the farm sector to downstream manufacturing remain. The rural economy goes beyond agriculture and, as revealed by NSSO data, the self-employment category in rural India is the fastest growing occupation. This is corroborated by the findings of Fifth Economic Census, showing rapid increase in enterprises in rural areas. There is need to remove constraints to rural enterprise.

Stagnation in crop yields, providing protection against risks and boosting farmers' income require series of measures. Rainwater harvesting, weather-based crop insurance, technology transfers, infrastructure development, credit, etc. are some of the measures for improving agrarian scenario. Technology up-gradation and R & D, vital for improving productivity of agriculture require consideration. Agriculture today is practiced in traditional manner for centuries. Enhancing productivity involves newer ways of farming and dissemination of new inputs and techniques with linkages. R&D need focused attention to infuse technology into agriculture. R&D and innovation are central to the sustainability of growth in the current global scenario.

India's efforts in achieving food security for all remain unimpressive. According to FAO of the United Nation, 200 million people, ¼th of the world undernourished population, live in India. India is the second largest producer of foodgrains in the world, yet over 300 million people go without two square meals a day. We still compare very poorly with the world's highest productivity—just about 15-20%. India currently ranks 126 among 177 countries in the UNDP's human development index. The country at present finds itself in the midst of a paradoxical situation: endemic mass hunger co-existing with the mounting food grains stocks. The food grains stocks available with the FCI stand at an all time high for last many years. Ironically, food worth Rs. 58,000 crore by government's own admission is wasted every year. Reason, the country processes just 2% of the produce from its $ 182 billion food industry. But a large part of perishables are wasted as the government has failed to create a farm-to-fork supply chain.

There is vast untapped production reservoir available in Bihar, Orissa, Eastern U.P., West Bengal and Assam even with the technologies available on the shelf. These states are well endowed with water resources; the major problem is water management, not availability. Productivity of rice in Punjab is 36 quintals per hectare, while it is 22 quintals in U.P, M.P and Bihar. There is urgent need to improve yields of wheat, rice, pulses and oilseeds in the Indo-Gangetic plains and Eastern India.

There are possibilities of demand driven agriculture. The interest shown by the corporate sector and the new focus on agriculture as a part of public policy can transform this sector a bit. Growth was higher in areas of flower exports, organic food production, food processing and dairy, where there was surge in the new opportunities due to rising urban demand and globalization. The National Horticulture Mission and the National Fisheries Development Board are likely to generate additional income to farmers and diversify their activities. Agriculture becomes an attractive and important component of rural livelihoods. Fisheries and Aquaculture have potential to provide the poor with more food, better nutrition and increased incomes.

The 11th Plan strategy for soil and moisture conservation rests on watershed development in the rain fed areas under the aegis of the National Rain-fed Area Authority. Green Revolution of the sixties was triggered by yield improving technologies. There is no comparable break-through in technology in recent years, except in case of Bt cotton. R&D in public domain is suffering on account of paucity of funds-about 0.7 percent of agricultural GDP, compared to 1.2% in China. State Agricultural Universities need more resources and motivation to introduce newer technologies. High priority should be accorded to introduction of bio-technology and genetic research. Agriculture extension, which has been in disarray for quite some time has to be revived for making knowledge available to small farmers—mostly women—who now predominate farming in India. Participation of private sector in agricultural research, extension and marketing should be given a push for faster agricultural growth. It should be supplemented by public sector research for problems of resource—poor farmers in less endowed regions and less remunerative farming activities. Biotechnology can harbinger a new horizon of agricultural growth and rural prosperity.

Declining farm size resulting from sub division and fragmentation of land continues to put down pressures on the productivity of land. We need a different kind of agriculture—an efficient and modernized agriculture in which education and awareness are extensive, infrastructure and technologies are widening and deepening, yields and efficiency are high.

Land degradation in the form of depletion of soil fertility, erosion and water logging has increased. There has been decline in surface irrigation expansion rate and reduction in ground water table. Public and private investment in agriculture has declined. High value agriculture should be diversified, growth should be shared and equity realized by focusing on small and marginal farmers.

Procurement policy is limited to few crops and few states. The cost of cultivation has risen due to increase in input prices. Agricultural wages have increased due to MGNREGA. Farmers have to undergo distress sales due to lack of procurement in states like Bihar, part of U.P., M.P. and Orissa. Production of rice needs to be shifted to eastern region. For that, rural infrastructure of these reasons needs radical transformation. Procurement, buffer stocking and PDS require a more prudent and efficient management. Private sector should be encouraged in activities related to storage.

Agricultural subsidies are fiscally unsustainable. Instead productive investment in agriculture will make it remunerative. Public investment declined from 3.4% of agricultural GDP in the early eighties to 1.9% in 2001-03. During the same period, subsidies rose from 2.9% to 7.4% of agricultural GDP (GOI, 2007). Small size of farm is not a constraint for farm productivity, as the experience of China and east Asian countries show.

MGNREGA is a programme with a major focus on water conservation, drought-proofing, minor irrigation works, renovation of traditional water bodies, distilling of tanks, flood control land protection and drainage in water-logged areas. In states like Andhra Pradesh and Karnataka, works undertaken under this scheme have resulted in increasing water table with significant increase in agricultural productivity. With inclusion of small land marginal farmers under this scheme, irrigation potential in the rain-fed areas and drought-proof small holder agriculture can be enhanced. Real investment in irrigation has come down. There is urgent need to increase the investment in irrigation.

There is need to unleash large scale process-based farm activities. If agriculture could be diversified and the agro-business industry developed, there will be boost to rural economy. Agriculture diversification can play a vital role in diversifying and commercializing agriculture, adding value to the agriculture produce, and create surplus for export of processed food.

Crop diversification will give wider choice in the production of a variety of crops in a given area and it will also expand production related activity on various crops. Diversification from less remunerative to more remunerative crops will enhance the income levels of our farmers. Diversification towards more competitive and high value crops will be particularly remunerative. Crop sub-sector is the principal source of generating income in India followed by livestock, fisheries and forestry.

With more than 60% of gross cropped area under the cereals and pulses, their share in the value of total agriculture output is now less than 25%. Given rising incomes and higher income elasticity for high value commodities like horticulture, livestock and marine products, future growth is likely from high value sector. Post-harvest processing and value edition of crop produce can be achieved by food processing which will help raise the incomes of the farmers. Existing aged tea gardens require re-plantation and rejuvenation. Other financial support for other plantations like coffee, rubber and coconut may improve the prospects of other plantations. Horticulture, Floriculture and plantations require big push to diversify the agriculture.

Disparities in productivity across regions and crops persist to great extent. Shrinking of farm size is also responsible for slow progress of agriculture. More than $2/3^{rd}$ of the population lives in states that are food deficient. That requires transport of lacks of tons to foodgrains involving higher cost and pilferage.

The rain-fed agriculture is facing some problems like organizational and technological constraints resulting in lower level of productivity. Most of the irrigation canals are chocked with silt, garbage, and sewage. Soil should be enriched with balanced infusion of nutrients.

Every second Indian farmer is indebted. In 2003, out of 89.33 million farmer households in the country 43.42 million households were indebted.

According to Arvind Panagariya the key problem of Indian Agriculture is lack of rural infrastructure like rural roads and electricity. The subsidies to farmers are also disproportional since they are cornered by comparatively rich farmers. Indian agriculture requires a shift in public expenditure from subsides towards productivity enhancing investment. Our agriculture requires effective public-private partnership which can change the face of our rural areas. In the light of diverse conditions prevailing in India, requirement is to incorporate differentiated strategies. 'Technological Fatigue' is on account of paucity of research and outreach of extension in the agriculture.

Rural non-farm sector is another area which requires urgent attention since it is going to a major source of secondary livelihood and income generation in the countryside. There is need like the one in Kuttanad in Kerala where experiment was done with rotational cropping when prawns was cultivated with rice cultivation. Another simultaneous farming was that of rice, fish, poultry and livestock. These instances show the need to diversify so that farming can be sustainable. Development of forward linkages is also necessary in the form of processing and packaging. After the excessive use of chemical fertilizers under green revolution, organic farming can be a more healthier and sustainable option. We could make use of mud waste, farm-yard manure, waste cakes, municipal wastes and green wastes. These organic supplements provide 40 to 45 percent micro nutrient for increasing phosphorous, nitrogen and micro-nutrients in the soil.

What is most distressing about Indian agriculture is that it accounts for 25% of GDP. But, 12 percent of the GDP is spent on providing subsidies to agriculture rather than on transfer of technology.

Agriculture, floriculture, fresh fruits, mushrooms, spices, sugar, molasses, rice, tropical fruit juices, pulp concentrates, and agro-chemicals, account for 18.45 percent of export. Infrastructure, international bio-safe packaging, phyto-sanitation and quarantine measures are required to boost agriculture export. There is urgent need to develop food processing industries in India since only 2 percent of fruits and vegetables are processed as against 70-80 percent in developed countries. It requires better infrastructure and logistic support.

CONCLUSION

The time for 'pilots' has gone and now we need a movement like one that triggered the green revolution. The poor have to be enabled to increase their incomes by diversifying away from agriculture, to increase their income levels and rely on non-farm sources for at least a subsidiary income. In certain parts of India, (e.g. Kerela, Andhra Pradesh, Gujarat) the success of social mobilization schemes especially among women, like SHGs have borne fruit in reducing poverty, and it is essential to make sure that this programme goes to scale in the country in regions which need it most, the eastern and northern parts where it has hardly taken roots.

The milk revolution has many lessions for extrapolation to pulses, oilseeds and millets. Indian agriculture needs a new vision to make rapid progress in the new millennium.

Agriculture production and its relationship to resources, technologies, markets, services, policies, and institutions in their local cultural context need careful assessment. Crop rotation, diversification, R&D and extension, management of natural resources, etc. can be tools to improve agricultural outlook. Indian agriculture must be revamped, rejuvenated and revitalized in a befitting manner, only then the lot of rural populace will change for the better and the concept of inclusive growth and holistic development realized in true spirit, as envisaged in the 11th Plan. It is worth to end with the famous statement of Pandit Jawahar Lal Nehru made in 1947- "Everything else can wait but not agriculture".

References

Bajaj, Khushagra, (2008), 'Improving Agricultural Productivity is Crucial', *The Economic Times*, 21 July, p. 15.

Gulati, Ashok and Kavery, Ganguly (2008), Beyond Grain Security : Agriculture Tomorrow, *The Business Standard*, New Delhi.

Mishra, P.K. (2008), 'Rejuvenating Agriculture with a Focus on Farmers', *Kurukshetra*, March, pp. 41-43.

Rajalakshmy, G. (2009), 'Sustained Growth in Agriculture : Innovation and Diversification', *Southern Economist*, Vol. 47, No. 20, Feb. 15, pp. 19-23.

Razi, Shahin (2009), 'Food Security : The Next Big Challenge', *Kurukshetra*, Sept., pp. 3-7.

Seshasayee, R. (2007), 'Agriculture Rejuvenation will Push Demand', *Yojana*, March, pp. 7-9.

Sud, Surinder (2007), 'Budget and Agriculture', *Yojana*, March, pp. 24-26.

Swaminathan, M.S. (2007), 'No Recipe For Agricultural Renewal', *Yojana*, March, pp. 27-28.

Wani, G.M., (2008), 'Capacity Building and E-extension for Enhancing Agriculture Productivity in India', http://www. arti-clesbase.com.

Need to Reform the Plan Strategy of Indian Rural Development for High Growth Rate

Baij Nath Singh

Backwardness of rural economy, widespread unemployment and massive poverty and other ills plague our rural economy. Per capita and per acre productivity is quite low. To change the rural scenario, various rural development programmes like MNP, IRDP, TRYSEM, DWCRA and others were undertaken by Government of India from time to time. But the achievements were limited. Leakages in the implementation existed. There is need to continue rural development programme with greater thrust and higher budgetary allocations. Besides, irrigation facilities should be augmented, credit made available to develop the agriculture scenario in India.

INTRODUCTION

Rural development has become an established objective for formulating plans and programmes for economic development of any country. In a predominantly agriculture based economy like India, where approximately 68 percent total population lives in rural areas and nearly 18 percent of the total national income is generated in the agriculture sector, rural development is a must for high growth rate of the Indian economy. But unfortunately majority of the population lives in rural areas under the problems of poverty, unemployment and low standard of living. Therefore, after independence, the ultimate objective of all planned development efforts are for the well beings of the masses and since the very beginning of the economic planning (1950), rural development has been the main concern of our country. Development is no longer identified with a mere increase in national income or even per capita national income. The increased income should be so distributed as to result in a significant diminution of inequalities of income and wealth. The abolition of absolute poverty with minimum level of employment or remuneration to all, who seek employment, should be arranged. Public distribution of goods and services at lower rates for the poor, is also a step for development, as it increases welfare. Development is also expected to include the areas of health, education, roads, water, electricity, cultural values and welfare. By all these aspects, the standards of living improve. Thus, the purpose of development becomes the enrichment of the total quality of life. It is now recognized that development is not only the provision of opportunities for development, but also their actual utilization by the people for whom they are intended and involves the creation of the facilities necessary for such utilization. Development could be described as Sarvodaya or promoting the welfare of each individual. In our country, still 32% of the population is living below the poverty line, of which more than 80% are estimated to be living in rural areas. Backwardness of the rural economy, unemployment and mass poverty can be mitigated by emphasizing and successfully implementing rural development programmes. A special favour towards rural development in our future economic plans is essential.

HISTORICAL OUTLINE OF RURAL DEVELOPMENT BEFORE INDEPENDENCE

Before India came under the British Rule, Indian villages were having self-sufficient economy. According to the industrial commission of 1918, "when Europe, the birth place of Industrial Revolution, was inhabited by uncivilized tribes, India was famous for the wealth and high artistic skills of her craftsmen. However, with the starting of the British Rule, this rural self-sufficiency and expertise were broken. They had no programme for rural development. With a view to transform the Indian Economy into a raw material generator and a market for British manufactured goods, industrialization was thwarted in India and only its stunted growth was permitted by the Britishers having supremacy on their colonies. Indian cotton was bought at very cheap rate. Manufactured cloth at Manchester and Liverpool textile mills and that foreign manufactured cloth was sold in India at a very high rate. The British made every effort to give a setback to traditional industries of India. The story of the manner in which the world-famous Dhaka Muslin Industry was destroyed by Britishers by chopping-off hands of the weavers is tragic. Thus, the well known rural industries and handicrafts rapidly declined, and it hampered the rural development programme. The Indian village people became victims of stagnation and poverty, under the British rule.

Rabindra Nath Tagore was the pioneer of rural development of India, starting activities at Shantiniketan. However, the real efforts regarding rural upliftment were done by Mahatma Gandhi. He made so many efforts to revive village and cottage industries as a part of rural development. He discovered "Charkha" and made it popular as a part of the earning of the masses, which in turn became a part of the struggle for independence. Gandhiji wanted to create Indian villages as self-sufficient and for that; he made so many efforts to remove unemployment and poverty.

RURAL DEVELOPMENT PROGRAMMES DURING POST-INDEPENDENCE PERIOD

People living in the rural areas are facing three major problems. These are utter backwardness of the rural economy, widespread unemployment and massive poverty. Therefore, rural development programmes were put at the centre in our economic planning. There are some special characteristics of rural society, which give rise to the problem of rural development as distinguished from other kinds of development:

(i) Dominance of agricultural land with uneven distribution of land and other relevant assets,
(ii) Dominance in work of agriculture and allied activities,
(iii) Dominance of self-employment and family labour among the landowning working force,
(iv) Dependence of rural income on seasonal factors, with uncertainty and big fluctuations in income, and
(v) Lower level of development factors in rural areas as compared to urban areas such as education, training, research, communication and information, banking services, electricity, transport facilities, etc.

NEED FOR RURAL DEVELOPMENT PROGRAMMES

Agriculture, the all-pervasive sector of the rural economy, has in the last sixty-four years of economic planning, grown at a meagre rate of 2.7%. Being just about a little above the population growth, it has not given rise to any significant additions to the living levels of the rural people. The large rain-fed area, constituting 67% of the total cultivated area, is yet without irrigation facilities. The few green revolution areas are beset with some serious problems as degradation of soil, water logging and salinity. With traditional inputs and old farming practices prevalent in the most of the regions, the productivity per hectare and per worker is very low in comparison with the advanced countries. The traditional industries in the rural areas are far from developed technologies. There is very little of diversification of industrial products. Like the farm activities confined to few crops, the non-farm activities are also confined to a few products. The service sector in rural area is very small with a little variety of services.

Indian rural areas are marked by unemployed masses, with increase at a speedy rate because of large annual addition to population. Most of the unemployed persons are in agricultural sector. The number of workers is larger than their requirement. In rural areas we see the disguised and seasonal unemployment. As per the latest estimates of the Planning Commission for 1993-94, at least 37% of the rural population lives below the poverty line. These people are not able to meet fully their requirements for existence. Due to above mentioned serious economic problems in rural areas, it was essential to implement rural development programmes since the inception of Indian Economic Planning.

INTRODUCTION OF SOME RURAL DEVELOPMENT PROGRAMMES

To increase welfare in rural areas, several rural development programmes were undertaken from time to time. They are known as employment programmes, area development programmes, minimum needs programmes and programme of land reforms.

(I) Employment Programmes

Such type of programmed focuses on the creation of employment. The unemployed are helped through financial assistance to purchase productive assets. There is also a provision for the acquisition of skills and training in selected jobs, so as to enable the unemployed to undertake work of various kinds on their own. The programmes, which provide these facilities, are the Integrated Rural Development Programme, the Training of Rural Youth for Self-Employment Programme and the Development of Women and Children in Rural Areas. Some programmes aim at the creation of wage-employment opportunities. The projects undertaken are those with high labour-absorption capacity. The projects chosen are such as roads, buildings, irrigation and flood control devices.

Provision also exists for the creation of assets like social forestry, soil conservation and works benefiting the people belonging to the scheduled castes and scheduled tribes. Such programmes are known as the National Rural Employment Programmes and the Rural Landless Employment Guarantee Programmes. Another programme offering wage-employment is Employment Assurance Scheme. The scheme provides 100 days of employment to a maximum of two adults per family during lean agricultural season.

(2) Area Development Programmes

Such types of programmes aim at reducing poverty caused by unfavourable agro climatic conditions like those associated with droughts, deserts, etc. The various programmes are Drought Prone Area Programme, Desert Development Programme, Hill Area Development Programme and Integrated Tribal Development Programme.

(3) Minimum Needs Programme

This programme, launched in 1974, aims at providing access to people to certain basic services and facilities of social consumption in all areas up to nationally accepted norms. One set of elements includes measures for the improvement of health services, housing, water supply, nutrition, sanitation and education. The public distribution system is also a part of this set. All these increase the living standards. Another set includes provision of roads and electrification of villages. These increase energy of various types. In short, the Minimum Needs Programme aims at raising the standard of living as also the productivity of the rural people.

(4) Programmes of Land Reforms

This programme envisages changes in the agrarian relations between the land and tiller of soil on the one hand and the tiller and the owner of land on the other.

(5) People's Participation

Provisions have been made to secure people's involvement in the various programmes of rural development. The Panchayati Raj Institutions as also the non-government organizations are the two important agencies through which people have been empowered to make decisions regarding rural development.

Indian Economic Planning is working for the overall economic development of the country. Rural Development Programme is a significant part of that. During these so many years, there are limited achievements and unlimited shortcomings in this context.

Limited Achievements

In their primary objective of eradicating poverty, rural development programmes are successful to a reasonable extent. The number of persons living below poverty line has decreased. As a proportion of rural population, the decline is from 56.4% in 1973-74 to 37.3% in 1993-94. There is also an improvement in the lives of the poor in terms of more drinking water, sanitation facilities, housing facilities, literacy, health facilities, etc. There is also an increase in the work-opportunities of various types in both the farm activities and the non-farm activities. The total employment generated is considerable. There has been an increase in the physical assets like all-weather roads, minor irrigation projects, social forestry, schools, health centres, electricity projects, etc. These provide a useful support for agricultural and industrial sector.

Shortcomings

However, the achievements regarding rural development are important, yet these are very limited. These are far short of resolving the problems of rural India. The eradication of poverty, the primary objective of special programmes, is still a far cry, with about 35% of rural population below the poverty line. Most of the rural people still live a life of low standard. The incidence of poverty continues to be very high in the poor states like Bihar, Madhya Pradesh, Rajasthan, Uttar Pradesh and Orissa. The rural people live in a backward economy with a high birth rate.

The implementation and the success of rural development programmes are also deficient in some respects. While the financial expenditure on these programmes is quite large, the results in physical terms have not been commensurate with the spending. Another aspect of the unsatisfactory performance of these programmes is the big leakages in their implementation. An evaluation of the Ministry of Rural Development (For January-December 1992), shows that as many as 57% of the workers working under Jawahar Rojgar Yojana were non-poor. There is also wastage of expenditure. A part of the expenditure never reaches the identified poor because of institutional laxity, political intervention and bureaucratic lapses.

There is little improvement even *in the scope of the* Minimum Needs Programmes. Take for example, the primary education. As many as 90% of the children have been enrolled. However, there have been heavy dropouts. The net result is very low literacy rate among the rural children. Rural Water Supply, Rural Health Services, Rural Electricity, Rural road, etc. services are not achieved for the most of the rural people. The so-called "Feel Good Factor" is not seen in the rural India.

SUGGESTIONS AND RECOMMENDATIONS

(1) Rural Development Programmes must continue with greater thrust. Preferential treatment in terms of higher budgetary allocations may be provided to the states, where the numbers of Below Poverty Line household per district currently are more than one lakh.

(2) It is necessary to provide technical skills to the rural youth, so that they can get jobs. To develop technical skills among the potential rural youth, the increase in establishment of technical institutes will prove to be of great help.

(3) For effective implementation of rural development programmes, it is imperative for the panchayats to have requisite strength of the trained staff. So, efforts must be made for the requisition of sufficient professionalized staff either from other departments or through new recruitment.

(4) For monitoring the performance of rural development programmes, it is essential to activate the role-play of monitoring and vigilance committees.

(5) While planning and implementing programmes of wage-employment, it is felt necessary that availability of skills among the local people and natural resources should be the guiding principle. This will be a step forward in the sustainable development of human skills and available natural resources.

(6) Approximately 66% of the cultivated land is non-irrigated, major portion of the cultivated land is depended on rain and the rain is quite irregular in our country. Therefore, there is a need for increase in irrigation facilities. It will help to increase the employment opportunities and due to this, there will be welfare of the rural population.

(7) The cent percent electrification all over the country is essential to support production activities at rural level.

(8) The farmers and other entrepreneurs should be provided adequate credit in time. It will enhance production activities and the opportunities of employment.

(9) People's participation in rural development programmes is essential. If the rural population possesses awareness for the development activities, the programmes regarding development and welfare would become successful. To increase awareness in the rural people, primary education should be given to all in actual terms.

(10) Health services at the rural level must be improved. Most of the Indian villages do not have full time doctors or active primary health centres. By improving health services, we can increase efficiency and productivity of the people. Use of some local medicinal plants and ayurvedic medicines should also be done.

(11) For the last 30 years, some environmental problems like pollution of air and water have taken place. To protect our environment, useful tree-plantation is necessary. In this nationwide programme, we should take the help of rural unemployed people, so that they may get some work and earning.

CONCLUSION

Personally, I feel that above-mentioned steps will be useful in rural development programmes. Whole-hearted efforts by the government and the people can create heaven on Indian earth "Feel Good Factor" should be seen in every village of India. The recent parliamentary election results and Andhra Pradesh legislative assembly results have proved that the political leaders should not neglect rural development.

References

Alagh, Y.K. (1999) : Indian Development Planning and Policy, Vikash Publishing House, Delhi.

Agrawal, A.N. (2000) : Indian Economy : Problems of Development and Planning, Vishwa Prakashan, New Delhi.

Brahmanand, P. and Vakil, C.N. (1956) : Planning for Expanding Economic, Vohra Publishing House, Bombay.

Dantwala, M.L. (1973) : Poverty in India : Then and Now (1870-1970), Macmillan, Bombay.

Gag Lama Chandra and Tindal Sahara (1989) : Rural Development : A Critical Appraisal, Natasha Publication.

Hick, Ursula K. (1961) : Development for Below, Oxford University Press, London.

Joshi, P.C. (1976) : Land Reforms in India, Allied Publishers, Bombay.

Prasad, Kama (1985) : Planning for Poverty Alleviation, Agricola Publishing Academy, New Delhi

Aryan, Jai Parkas (1959) : A Plea for Reconstruction of Indian Polity, A.B. Sarva Seva Sangh Prakashan, Rajghat Kashi (U.P.).

Panjwani, Vijay (1986) : Rural Development—A Hand Book, Oxford and IBH Publishing Co.

Prasad, B.K. (2003) : Rural Development : Concept, Approach and Strategy, Sarup and Sons, New Delhi.

Sen, Amartya (1981) : Poverty and Famines : An Essay on Entitlement and Deprivation, Oxford University Press, London.

Streeton Paul and Lipton Michael (1968): The Crisis of Indian Planning, London.

Subramaniam, R. (1988) : Rural Development : An Inside looked Problems and Prospects, Yatan Publication, Madras.

6

Indian Agriculture Towards Upliftment

SHABNAM PERWIN

India is world's leading producer of agriculture produce. Agriculture accounts for 9 percent of total exports and 5 percent of imports. EU is India's top market, followed by ASEAN, USA, Bangladesh and China. Under the price support policy, MSPs are set annually for basic staples to protect producers from sharp price falls, to stablise prices and to ensure adequate food stocks for public distribution. Subsidies on farm inputs include fertilizers, electric power and irrigation. Agriculture occupies a prominent position in Indian policy-making and it has made huge strides in developing its potential. Reforms introduced in India have greatly increased overall trade flows.

The leading forecasting institutions expect that India will play a bigger role in world markets in future. In a number of markets, it is expected to consolidate its position among the world's leading importers (vegetable oils) and exporters (rice).

Given the size of Indian agriculture, changes in its balance sheets for key commodities have a potentially large impact on world markets.

The Indian economy has seen high growth rates of more than 8% since 2003. In 2005 and 2006 GDP grew at a rate of over 9%. Globally India's growth is surpassed only by that of China. This is expected to continue with robust of growth 7% by 2015.

India is one of the fastest growing economies today and among the world's leading agricultural producers and yet its trade flows are relatively small. However given the size of Indian agriculture, even small changes in its trade have a potentially large impact on world markets. The average size of holding is just 1.4 hectares and 60% of the work force depends on agriculture for a living. Its agriculture and trade policy partly stem from its goal of self-sufficiency and have an impact on trade. The latest MAP examines India's agriculture trade with the EU and globally.

India is the third largest economy in Asia and the second fastest growing economy in the world. From 2003, its high growth rates of 8% were surpassed only by China. However, it is still ranked as a low income country, with an estimated GDP/capita around US $ 820 in 2006. The share of agriculture in India's GDP fell from 29% in 1991 to below 17.5% in 2006. Yet, around 60% of the labour force is still employed in the agriculture, compared to 70% in the early nineties. There are 116 million farmers in India, a large number of them managing small scale holdings, on average just 1.4 Ha in the late nineties.

India is one of the leading members of the G-20 within the DDA negotiations. Moreover, it has begun free trade agreement talks with the EU and ASEAN. And it also has a preferential trade agreement with the Mercosur since 2005. India has an overall trade deficit since the nineties but has been a small net exporter of agricultural products since 1990. In 2005, its agricultural trade generated a small surplus of just under $4 billions. Agricultural trade flows in India appear relatively modest compared with those of other main players on the world agricultural markets. Agriculture accounts for 9% of total exports and 5% of imports. This can be explained by the fact that although India is a leading world producer of agricultural products, it is also a major consumer.

The EU is India's top market, followed by ASEAN, USA, Bangladesh and China. Commodities represent around one third of agricultural exports. The single biggest export is milled rice, accounting for over 15% of the value of exports in 2003-05. Soyabean meal is the second most important export, accounting for 10% of sales while overall intermediate products represent around 25% of total value of exports. Final products, including cashew nuts, beef, coffee and tea account for the remaining 40% of total export value.

ASEAN is by far the biggest supplier of agricultural products to India, accounting for a massive 40% of India's imports in 2003-05. Argentine and Brazil rank second and third respectively. Intermediate products account for 56% of India's agricultural imports, reflecting the importance of vegetable oils. Palm oil imports, mainly from Indonesia and Malaysia, represent 29% of the total imports value.

The EU, as the top market for India, accounts for 16% of the value of agricultural export sales in 2003-05, down from 21% a decade ago. It imports 1.3 billion worth of agri-food products from India, equivalent to 2% of the EU's global agri-food imports. Overall 97% of imports from India enter the EU duty free or with a tariff lower than 30%. Meanwhile, the EU only has a 4% market share in India's agricultural imports valued at about 250 millions. Thus, India accounts for less than 0.5% of the EU's total agricultural exports. The average bound tariff for agricultural products in 2006/07 is 117.2% while the average applied tariff is 40.8%. In 2006, wheat was the EU's highest value export to India, worth one third of the value of exports. Exports of whiskies have grown four-fold from 1999 to 2006 and now account for 10% of export sales.

OECD and FAPRI both expect India to play a bigger role in world markets in the future. It is likely to remain a small net exporter of agricultural products, consolidating its position among the world's leading exporters of rice. For sugar, a big change is expected, with India forecast to switch from being a net importer to a net exporter. Turning to imports, India is forecast to remain a leading vegetable oils importer. It absorbs one quarter of world soyabean oil imports and 14% of palm oil imports. Combined with the recent hike in prices, this could lead to a doubling of India's vegetable oil import bill in 10 years. The World Bank predicts that the shift towards the service sector will continue at the expense of agriculture, whose share could decline by 30% by 2030.

Despite India's economic development, over 70% of the populations still live in rural areas. This compares with 44% in China (2002) and 21% in Brazil (2004). Indian agriculture policy is aimed essentially at improving food self-sufficiency and alleviating hunger through food distribution. Aside from investing in agricultural infrastructure, the government supports agriculture through measures including minimum support prices (MSP) for the major agricultural crops, farm input subsidies and preferential credit schemes.

Under the price support policy, MSPs are set annually for basic staples to protect producers from sharp price falls, to stabilize prices and to ensure adequate food stocks for public distribution. In the past, guaranteed prices have been below the prevailing market prices, according to the International Food Policy Research Institute (IFPRI) in 2007. At the same time subsidies on farm inputs including fertilizers, electrical power and irrigation water have led to inefficient use of inputs and indirectly subsidies income. IFPRI concluded that "support for agriculture (from 1985-2002) has been largely counter cyclical to world prices". OECD appears to reach a similar conclusion. Its 2007 monitoring report points out that the level of agricultural support (covering transfers from taxpayers and consumers) for India "would appear to be slightly below the OECD average but considerably higher than that of the emerging economies reviewed by the OECD". Furthermore, the instruments of support used are "the least efficient and the most trade distortive forms of support". The implication is that many of the very small farms are subsistence holdings, with low investment and little productivity growth. It is either the world leader or the second largest producer in eight out of its top ten products. Some of these are widely traded while others are more specialist products.

Reforms introduced in India in the early 1990s have greatly increased overall trade flows. However, it has consistently run a trade deficit unlike China and Brazil (US $

35 billion in 2004-05). The EU (27) ranks as India's largest trading partner accounting for about 21% of total Indian trade in 2005, ahead of the United States and China. Meanwhile India is the EU's tenth largest trading partner accounting for 1.8% of total trade. In 2005 its trade deficit with the EU was about 2 billion. India is one of the leading members of the G-20 within the DDA negotiations. It has a preferential trade agreement with Mercosur since 2005. It is also part of the South Asia Free Trade Agreement (SAFTA) covering seven nations (India, Bhutan, Nepal, Sri Lanka, Pakistan, Bangladesh and the Maldives) which came into effect in January 2006 with the aim of reducing tariffs for regional trade. And it is currently negotiating Free Trade Agreements with the EU and ASEAN. Turning our focus to trade in agricultural and food products; this accounts for a relatively small share of overall Indian trade. Agricultural exports represent 9% of the value of total exports while the share of agriculture in total imports is just 5%.

When compared with other main players on world markets and considering the size of the country, Indian agricultural trade flows appear relatively modest. As the key goal of agricultural policy since independence has been to achieve self-sufficiency, trade has been relatively limited. However, technological developments and macroeconomic policy reforms have brought increased liberalization, following the implementation of the Uruguay Round Agreement, and have contributed to changes in agricultural trade. Indian agricultural exports totaled $ 9.3 billion in the year 2005 while imports were worth roughly $ 5.5 billion.

Thus India is a net exporter of agricultural food products with a small surplus of just under $ 4 billion. Between 1993-95 and 2003-05, exports nearly doubled while imports grew almost threefold. The value of exports grew from $ 4 to $ 7.7 billion while imports rose from $ 1.8 to $ 5.2 billion within a decade. The balance of agricultural trade has always been in surplus though there were sharp fluctuations during the nineties. Since 2000, both imports and exports have grown steadily.

ASEAN is by far the biggest supplier of agricultural products to India, accounting for a massive 40% of its imports in 2003-2005. Argentina and Brazil rank 2nd and 3rd respectively while the EU only has 4% market share (down from 7% a decade ago), ranked at number six in 2003-05.

India's agricultural imports are focused mainly on intermediate products. These account for 56% of imports; final products are 31%, while the share of commodities is just 13%. The biggest growth has been in intermediate products which increased nearly fourfold over the period. India is forecast to consolidate its position among the world's leading exporters of rice (its top export), though the volume of exports has been erratic since the mid-nineties (depending on the size of the crop and on domestic consumption). Currently, it is the second largest rice producer after China and the third largest net-exporter after Thailand and Vietnam.

Indian buffalo beef exports are projected to grow as production rises faster than demand, with world market share for beef stable at around 11%. On the dairy side, net exports of butter and SMP will also grow. For butter although there is a strong increase in production, this is in response to surging demand growth, so India remains a small net exporter. On the other hand it becomes a significant net exporter of SMP, with its share of world trade rising from 4% to 6%. Turning to imports, in 2006/07 India became a net importer of wheat having been a net exporter for the 5 years previously. However, it is not expected to be a big net exporter in the coming decade. For dairy, there may be opportunities for EU in the future. If an EU-Indian FTA is agreed, then, given changing consumer habits, India is a potential market for EU exports of high quality processed milk products.

Last but not the least, India is projected to remain a leading vegetable oils importer, absorbing one quarter of world soyabean oil imports and 14% of palm oil imports. Although the share does not increase much over the projection period, this marks an increase in imports from 5 million tonnes to 6-8 million tonnes by 2016/17, given the expansion in world trade in vegetable oils. Indian consumption of vegetable oils has grown faster than production since the mid-nineties and the trend is expected to continue. Combined with the recent hike in prices, this could lead to a doubling of India's vegetable oil import bill in 10 years.

CONCLUSION

Agriculture occupies a prominent position in Indian policy-making, not only because of its contribution to GDP but also because of the large proportion of the population that is dependent on the sector for its livelihood. The growth in population and wealth has stimulated demand to the extent that domestic production has not always been able to keep up and there is increasing speculation that the Indian economy may be overheating leading to inflation. The downside of the increased import demand and the current commodity boom is that India's food import bill will rise sharply. However, it is clear that India's agricultural sector has made huge strides in developing its potential. The green revolution massively increased the production of vital foodgrains and introduced technological innovations into agriculture. This progress is manifested in India's net trade position. Where once India had to depend on imports to feed its people, since 1990 it is a net exporter of agri-food products. Its agriculture is large and diverse and its sheer size means that even slight changes in its trade have significant effects on world agricultural markets.

How India will develop is still a big unknown, with the picture changing rapidly. Questions have arisen about India's capacity to compete in global markets under the current farm structure and farm policy. As the service economy grows, the share of agriculture will diminish, which may also have implications for India's stance on trade and agriculture policy in the future.

Mapping the Contours of High Growth Trajectory for the Rural and Agrarian Economy

NAVLATA AND REKHA JHA

India has made rapid strides in the field of agriculture. Rural and agrarian development is one of the most important factors for the development of Indian Economy. But certain factors are hampering its growth. Irrigation facilities are inadequate. India's large agricultural subsidies are hampering productivity enhancing investment. It is opined to double the rate of growth in irrigated area, and focusing on soil quality, improving water management, rainwater harvesting and watershed development, diversifying into high-value outputs, fruits, vegetables, flowers, herbs, spices, medicinal plants, bridging the gap between knowledge and practice, providing easy access to credit at affordable rates, introduction of molecular biology and biotechnology so that Indian agriculture may enter a developed stage. These issues need to be addressed in all seriousness to develop Indian agriculture.

Development is a goal universally cherished by all individuals, communities, societies, states and nation. Rural Development implies physical, technological, economic, social, cultural, attitudinal, organizational and political change to uplift the living standard of common people in villages. India is to be found not in few cities but in its 7,00,000 villages.

Rural Development is a prerequisite for overall development and, hence, it deserves the highest priority in terms of allocation of resources. Indian economy is predominantly rural in character. Rural Development in India is one of the most important factors for the growth of the Indian economy. India is primarily an agriculture-based country. Agriculture contributes nearly one-fifth of the gross domestic product in India. The progress made by agriculture in the last four decades has been one of the biggest success stories of free India. Agriculture and allied activities constitute the single largest contributor to the Gross Domestic Product, almost 33% of it.

The planning commission contends that foodgrain productivity per hectare has to go up 100% to meet the growth in demand at the end of the 11th Plan period and up to 2020-21. But a new study from the National Centre for Agricultural Economics and Policy Research (NCAEPR) presents a grimmer picture of India's food scenario. It says the growth rate in overall domestic foodgrain production needs to accelerate three to four times to guard against an adverse impact on household food and nutritional security.

The study (*Economic and Political Weekly*, December 2007) has stated that the total demand for foodgrains would increase at 2% a year in the medium term, despite a slowdown in population growth (but not population *per se*), as also a phenomenal growth in the need for grain as feed and related purposes.

Meeting the projected demand for food grains would require 1.86% annual growth in food grain production during the 11th Plan. As compared to these growth rates, India's

Projected Household Demand for Food in India at 7% Income Growth

(million tons)

Commodity	*Annual household demand*				
	Year				
	1991	*1995*	*2000*	*2010*	*2020*
Foodgrains	168.3	185.1	208.6	266.4	343.0
Milk	48.8	62.0	83.8	153.1	271.0
Edible oil	4.3	5.1	6.3	9.4	13.0
Vegetables	56.0	65.7	80.0	117.2	168.0
Fruits	12.5	16.1	22.2	42.9	81.0
Meat, fish and eggs	3.4	4.4	6.2	12.7	27.0
Sugar	9.6	10.9	12.8	17.3	22.0

Source : TIFAC, Food and Agriculture : Technology Vision, 2020.

foodgrain production during the last 10 years (1997-98 to 2006-07) increased annually by a meager 0.48%.

PDS and consumer affairs ministry has chalked out a plan to consider a countrywide awareness campaign on impending skyrocketing food prices. That's quite different from the farm ministry, which smugly projected a Rs. 4,800 crore-odd NFSM-compatible 0.64 MT surplus against a demand of 77.3 MT wheat in 2011-12 and only a 0.79 MT deficit in rice against a demand of 98.7 MT for the same period. But even those projections acknowledge the urgent need for higher end-year stocks, up from the current 15 mt-odd to a higher 20 mt, at least, for rice and wheat.

One of the biggest success stories of independent India is the rapid strides made in the field of agriculture. From a nation dependent on food imports to feed its population, India today is not only self-sufficient in grain production but also has substantial reserves. Dependence of India on agricultural imports and the crisis of food shortage encountered in 1960s convinced planners that India's growing population, as well as concerns about national independence, security, and political stability, required self-sufficiency in food production. This perception led to a program of agricultural improvement called the Green Revolution. It involved bringing additional area under cultivation, extension of irrigation facilities, the use of improved high-yielding variety of seeds, better techniques evolved through agricultural research, water management, and plant protection through judicious use of fertilizers, pesticides and cropping practices. All these measures had a salutary effect and the production of wheat and rice witnessed quantum leap.

Several economic activities such as cottage and village industries, Khadi, handloom, handicrafts, small shops, petty traders and services such as transport, communication, banking and marketing of farm and non-farm products is to be given prime importance to enhance rural development and growth in India. The non-agricultural sector occupies an important place in India's economy as a source of Income and employment opportunities particularly for the landless. The micro and small enterprises (MSEs) account for 32% of the workforce and 29% of the value added in non-agricultural private unincorporated enterprises. The income generated from various non-agricultural activities is more evenly distributed than that generated in the large-scale manufacturing companies.

However, there are still a host of issues that need to be addressed regarding Indian agriculture. Indian agriculture is heavily dependent on monsoons. The monsoons play a critical role in determining whether the harvest will be rich, average, or poor. The structural weaknesses of the agriculture sector are reflected in the low level of public investment, exhaustion of the yield potential of new high yielding varieties of wheat and rice, unbalanced fertilizer use, low seeds replacement rate, an inadequate incentive system and post harvest value addition.

Slow agricultural growth is a concern for policy-makers as some two-thirds of India's people depend on rural employment for a living. Current agricultural practices are neither economically nor environmentally sustainable and India's yields for many agricultural commodities are low. Poorly maintained irrigation systems and almost universal lack of good extension services are among the factors responsible. Farmers' access to markets is hampered by poor roads, rudimentary market infrastructure, and excessive regulation.

The low productivity in India is a result of the following factors:

- According to World Bank's "India: Priorities for Agriculture and Rural Development", India's large agricultural subsidies are hampering productivity-enhancing investment. Overregulation of agriculture has increased costs, price risks and uncertainty. Government intervenes in labour, land, and credit markets. India has inadequate infrastructure and services. World Bank also says that the allocation of water is inefficient, unsustainable and inequitable. The irrigation infrastructure is deteriorating. The overuse of water is currently being covered by over pumping aquifers, but as these are falling by foot of groundwater each year, this is a limited resource.
- Illiteracy, general socio-economic backwardness, slow progress in implementing land reforms and inadequate or inefficient finance and marketing services for farm produce.
- The average size of land holdings is very small (less than 20,000 m^2) and is subject to fragmentation, due to land ceiling acts and in some cases, family disputes. Such small holdings are often over-manned, resulting in disguised unemployment and low productivity of labour.
- Adoption of modern agricultural practices and use of technology is inadequate, hampered by ignorance of such practices, high costs and impracticality in the case of small land holdings.
- Irrigation facilities are inadequate, as revealed by the fact that only 52.6% of the land was irrigated in 2003-04, which result in farmers still being dependent on rainfall, specifically the Monsoon season. A good monsoon results in a robust growth for the economy as a whole, while a poor monsoon leads to a sluggish growth. Farm credit is regulated by NABARD, which is the statutory apex agent for rural development in

the sub-continent. At the same time over pumping made possible by subsidized electric power is leading to an alarming drop in aquifer levels.

There is an urgent need for second green revolution in Indian agriculture and taking it to a higher trajectory of 4% to 4.5% of annual growth. The major areas which need to be rationalized to achieve this objective:

- Doubling the rate of growth of irrigated area;
- Reclaiming degraded land and focusing on soil quality;
- Judicious land use surveys;
- Improving water management, rain water harvesting and watershed development;
- Bridging the knowledge gap through effective extension services;
- Data improvement for better research, better results and sustainable planning;
- Diversifying into high value outputs, fruits, vegetables, flowers, herbs and spices, medicinal plants, bamboo, bio-diesel;
- Bridging the gap between knowledge and practice;
- Providing easy access to credit at affordable rates;
- Providing financial security to our farmers;
- Support for marketing infrastructure; and
- Export promotion

Landholdings in India are not only small in size but also widely scattered all over the countryside as such consolidation of landholdings needs to be addressed. The process of sub-division and fragmentation of landholdings continues unabated generation after generation, under the existing land inheritance laws. Small and fragmented landholdings are great obstacle to economical use of farm labour and machinery.

Liberalization has opened up new opportunities for Indian farmers to benefit from higher world prices for their produce and lower price for inputs. To export agricultural products, we need to implement modern cultivation innovations by integrating high technology for enhancing per acre output of agricultural products. We also need to assess and meet the credit demand for high-tech projects.

With uncertainties in global markets and hardening of the international prices of food, fuels and edible oils, domestic price stability and food security critically depend on growth of agricultural sector. This requires working out the forward and backward linkage to enhance productivity through balanced allocation and better utilization of all available resources at all levels of implementation and quantifying output per unit of resource used.

New initiatives in the form of National Food Security Mission (NFSM) with an outlay of Rs. 4,822 crores and Rashtriya Krishi Vikas Yojana (RKVY) with an outlay of Rs. 25,000 crores have been taken in 2007-08 to rejuvenate the agricultural sector. The sector will benefit immensely from these policy interventions.

Though, Agri Clinics and Agri Business Centers (ACABC) Scheme was launched in April 2002, to encourage unemployed agri-graduates to set-up agri-clinics and agribusiness centers, thereby, supplementing the efforts of public extension system and serving as supplementary sources of input supply and services to the needy farmers, it remains on paper. Through this process, the scheme provides gainful employment to agriculture graduates in the emerging areas in agricultural sector and capital subsidy to the extent of 25 per cent (33 per cent for North-east and hill areas and women graduates) and interest subsidy for first two years is provided to ACABCs through credit linked and back-ended form to banks though NABARD.

India is looking for rejuvenating its sagging agricultural production and productivity by integrating high technology space inputs for both irrigated and rainfed areas. The Earth Observations (EO) products today serve as major inputs to policy, planning and targeted interventions, contributing to building social capitals, natural resources assets and environmental gains on the long-term basis. The benefits are mostly indirect and often difficult to quantify in terms of money.

The enabling role EO products have been demonstrated in several projects especially those related to building physical and social infrastructure and also natural resources assets building. The cost effective role EO has played in the watershed development planning and implementation in India, including improving the livelihoods as well as natural resources assets building, is one success story worth emulating in many developing countries.

India's first operational Earth Observation Satellite IRS-1A, a 850 kg. satellite was launched into a 900 km polar orbit on 17th March 1988 by a Soviet rocket. In 1997, India used its own rocket PSLV to place IRS-1D into polar orbit. With the development of PSLV, India has the capability to place upto 1,200 kg. satellites into polar orbit.

There is a growing global interest in plants as potential sources of undiscovered drugs. "Satellite remote sensing will provide a tremendous boost to bio-prospecting", says Manju Sharma, DBT Secretary. "It will help speed up the search for novel biological resources. And speed is crucial in the increasingly competitive field of bio-prospecting".

Scientists involved in the DBT-DOS project are using IRS satellites to map India's richest zones of biological diversity, the eastern and western Himalayas and the Western Ghats. They are among the world's top 20 areas teeming with a rich diversity of plants and animals.

The country is on a very crucial threshold where it has to take important decisions. "We are entering the knowledge society and there will be always be demand of qualified and productive workforce," Dr. Kalam said while addressing the 7th convocation of the National Institute of Technology, Rourkela.

For these high-tech methods to be implemented we need:

- Reaching-the-Unreached, "Resource-Poor-Farmers", through Information Technology applications;
- "Land information system" in district and block levels;
- Strengthening "Agricultural Resources Information System" in all districts (regions) of the Country, "irrespective of past or future growth regions;
- Development of decision support systems on "production practices and systems" which need to be

adapted to respond to new market demands and export opportunities, poverty alleviation or growing labour shortages, depending on the agricultural production setting;

- Development of generic decision support systems (DSS) using databases and model bases for agricultural planning and management at micro watershed level; and also to establish GIS centers at block or panchayat level;
- Decision Support System on water allocation in an irrigation system to remove the existing disparities in the availability between the head-reach and tail-end farms and between large and small farms, to achieve "equity and social justice";
- Decision Support System on Land Resources development issues, given in the DSS section;
- Linkages to Development of National Water Database as envisaged in the World Bank aided National Hydrology Project to strengthen water resources management facilitating agricultural planning in districts;
- Development of Agrometeorology Database providing vital information of long-term and short-term objective in agricultural production, planning and management;
- National Agricultural Drought Assessment and Monitoring System (NADAMS) and also Agromet Advisory Services on NICNET;
- DSS on Water Bodies (Basin) based agricultural development, using Watershed and Agro-Eco Region Planning Concepts;
- Development of "metadata" standards and application of "Open GIS Model" on agricultural resources for Internet/Intranet access; and
- Involvement of Institutions viz., ICAR Institutions, State Agricultural Universities, Rural Development Institutes, NIC, DOS, NATMO, GSI, CGWB, Departments of Geography Research, etc., working on spatial data generation and application of spatial

theory for problem solving in respect to agricultural development, rural development and backward area development.

Scientists have already completed vegetation maps for five states in the North East region and three districts of Karnataka and Maharashtra. By analyzing maps of the same region over time researchers hope to evaluate threat to biodiversity caused by human activity.

There are several botanical and agricultural research centers participating in the bio-prospecting program. The images beamed down by the IRS satellite will be processed by the Scientists at the Indian Institute of Remote Sensing at Dehradun and the National Remote Sensing Agency at Hyderabad.

The technology adoption by farmers is also very encouraging, which has reached to more than 2500 hectare in 2005 from demonstration of systems approach in 2.4 hectare farmer's field in the year 1999. More than 3000 farmer families are benefited from the programme. Constant supply of input materials (seed, fertilizers, pesticides, etc.) has been met through people's participation in terms of creation of Agro-Service Centre and Seed Growers Association. Knowledge empowerment of farmers with improved cultivation technology was given a special thrust. During this period total 156 training camps were organized on different aspects of agriculture, which were attended by about 6700 farmers.

In national priority setting, the following recurring and emerging issues for sustainable agricultural development and poverty alleviation must be considered:

- Population pressure and demographic transition;
- Resource base degradation and water scarcity;
- Investment in agriculture, structural adjustment and impact on the poor;
- Globalization and implication on the poor;
- Modern science and technology and support to research and technology development; and
- Rapid urbanization and urbanization of poverty.

In addressing the above issues, a policy statement on agriculture must take note of the following uncommon opportunities:

- Conservation of natural resources and protection of environment.
- Vast untapped potential of our soil and water resources, and farming systems.
- Technology revolution especially in the areas of molecular biology, biotechnology, space technology, ecology and management.
- Revolution in informatics and communication and the opportunity of linking farmers, extension workers and scientists with the national and international databases.

References

Acharya, S. and A. Mitra (2000). "The Potential of Rural Industries and Trade to Provide Decent Work Conditions: A Data Reconnaissance in India", SAAT Working Papers, International Labour Organization, New Delhi.

Ahluwalia, M.S. (1978). "Rural Poverty and Agricultural Performances in India", *Journal of Development Studies*, Vol. 14, No. 3, April.

Basant, R., B.L. Kumar and R. Parthasarathy (1998). (edited). Non-Agricultural Employment in Rural India: The Case of Gujarat, Rawat Publications, Jaipur, India.

Gopalappa, D.V. (2004). "Rural Non-farm Employment in Karnataka", Unpublished report submitted by Agriculture Development and Rural Transformation Unit of the Institute of Economic and Social Change, Bangalore to the Ministry of Agriculture, GoI, New Delhi.

Government of India (1994). Report of the Technical Committee on DPAP and DDP, Ministry of Rural Development, New Delhi.

———, (2001). Report of the Task Force on Employment Opportunities, Planning Commission, July 2001.

———, (2002). Special Group on Targeting Ten Million Employment Opportunities Per Year, Planning Commission, May 2002.

———, (2004). Economic Survey, 2003-04, Economics Division, Ministry of Finance, GoI, New Delhi.

The Change of Agriculture in India's Rural Economy

RAJESH KUMAR

Commencing in 1960s, the First Green Revolution helped India in achieving the record agricultural produce for quite some year now. Now requirement is to initiate the Second Green Revolution. It will require use of genetically modified seeds to double per acreage production and technology, private sector to develop and market the usage of genetically modified foods. Agricultural diversification is pre-requisite to open new dimension in Indian agriculture and to raise the incomes of Indian farmers. Indian agriculture faces a far more complex set of problems in the new millennium.

Agriculture is one of the most important factors for the growth of the Indian Economy. India is primarily an agriculture-based country. Agriculture has been and will continue to be the life line of the Indian Economy. Agriculture is the main stay of the economy of any developing country of the world and the performances of the other sectors are largely dependent on the progress of agriculture. The agriculture constitutes the backbone of the Indian economy and shapes the life and culture of people of India. The agriculture plays a vital role in shaping the economy. It is engine of growth in Indian Economy. The life and culture of the Indian people depend upon it. Agriculture support means different things to different people.

India is the seventh largest in geographical area and second most populous country in the world scattered in 6.5 lacks villages where 70% of population directly or indirectly depend on agriculture and allied business and contributes 23% of Gross Domestic Product. A total of 329 million hectare land is available of which 143 million hectare area is cultivatable. India is sharing 2.4% of the world population.

Agriculture is the backbone of Indian economy in terms of gross national produce and proportion of population, which depends on it for their livelihood. In agriculture sector, 70% of total work force of the country depends and its share in gross domestic product is 22%. After independence, the growth process in agriculture was initiated with a planned endeavour. The various "five years plans" concentrated on growth in output for which several institutional changes like land reforms, restricting credit institutions, remodeling pachayati raj institutions were undertaken. These efforts have increased the production of foodgrains since independence from 51 million tons in 1950-51 to 217.3 million tones in 2007-08.

GREEN REVOLUTION

Green Revolution refers to transformation of agriculture. The term 'green revolution' was first used in 1968 by former USAID director William Gaud. Green Revolution Programme, started with help of US-based Rockefeller Foundation, was based on high yielding varieties of wheat, rice and other grains that had been developed in Mexico and the Philippines. There were three basic methods of the Green Revolution—First, continued expansion of farming areas, Second, doubled cropping of existing farmland. And third, using seeds with improved genetics. The goal of green revolution was to increase the efficiency for agricultural process so that the productivity of the crops was increased and could help developing countries to face their growing population needs.

THE FIRST GREEN REVOLUTION

The period of Green Revolution was 1970 to 1990. Commencing in 1960s it helped India in achieving the record agricultural produce for quite some years now. India is now producing more than 299 million tones of foodgrains every year. The green revolution has been the cornerstone of India's agricultural achievement, transforming the country from one of food deficiency to self-sufficiency through enhanced technology adoption, increased public and private investments and certain institutional innovations that have augmented production and productivity gains.

In the First Green Revolution, agriculture has undergone changes. Increased use of high yielding variety seeds, better quantity inputs, improved irrigation facilities, crop diversification, increase in the cropping intensity have helped increase the level of output. There has also been a marked increase in the employment elasticity as seen in the aggregate use of labour in agriculture due to increased crop intensity, multi-cropping and crop diversification induced by new technology and changing demand pattern.

THE SECOND GREEN REVOLUTION

The Green Revolution (1970-90) is to be strengthened, then a Second Green Revolution is to be initiated. The second green revolution is a high-end initiative as Central and State government are full participants. The second green revolution is a process of technological development of agricultural techniques. Addressing the nation on the eve of 54th Republic Day, President of India, and Dr APJ Abdul Kalam called for the second green revolution, "It is right line for India of embark upon the second green revolution, which will enable it to increase its productivity in the agricultural sector. The production of cereals needs to be increased for present 200 million tones to over 300 million tones by 2020 in view of population growth. But the requirement of land for the increasing population as well as for greater forestation and environmental preservation activities would demand that the present 170 million hectare of arable land would have to be brought down to 100 million hectare by 2020". He said the Indian Agriculture faced three main challenges in the time ahead; first, area under wheat and rice cultivation is estimated to come down to 100 million hectares by 2020, secondly, irrigation and water shortage and thirdly, decline in the number of people in farming.

The Second Green Revolution will also require—first, genetically modified seeds to double the per acreage production and technology, second, private sector to develop and market the usage of genetically modified foods, i.e., efficient marketing of the ideas and thirdly, linking of rivers as much as economically possible to bring surplus water of one area to others. The second green revolution will focus on water efficient irrigation system, environment friendly pesticides, bio-dynamic farming. It promotes the commercial farming, the farming of horticulture, floriculture, sericulture, plantation crops, medical crops, aromatic crops, spices, the local geographical and climate position, soil fertility and productivity and nature, water, human resource and infrastructure availability and cost of production, etc. It is expected to be careful towards prospective yields of supply price or cost of production of these crops so that productivity can increase. It would be launching of an action plan for massive crop diversification, multi-cropping and doubling or per hectare yield of crop. In the second green revolution, efforts will be made for achieving self-sufficiency in pulses and oilseeds. All our agriculture scientists and technologists have to work for doubling the productivity of the available land with lesser area being available for cultivation. The type of technologies needed would be in the areas of bio-technology, proper training to the farming, additional modern equipment for preservation and storage, etc. The second green revolution is indeed graduating from grain production to food processing and marketing as visualized.

The Second Green Revolution of boosting food grains output in India to 400 million tones in next 15 years is need of the day. Achieving it is not very difficult. Rather, it is achievable, if mindset on introducing newer technology is changed. India has to whole heartedly embrace the new technology. Private sector is better suited to deliver results than government managed schemes. Governments on the other hand can play a key role in expediting irrigation schemes and managing water resources.

DIVERSIFICATION OF AGRICULTURE

Agriculture diversification means opening of new dimensions to the traditional agriculture and to elevate the economic condition of farmers and thereby attempting to bring about desired socio-economic development in the country. Agriculture development should be considered as an inclusive concept for instances: animal husbandry, horticulture, dairy development, floriculture, poultry farm, fisheries, forestry and wildlife, plantation, soil and water conservation, food processing, storage and warehousing, drain and flood control, etc. All these impinge directly or indirectly on agricultural development. Diversification of agriculture should be viewed as part of the wider objective of rural diversification. Agricultural diversification can fulfil the growth targets of plan against the constraints of diminishing land resources, increasing biotic and abiotic stress, threatened loss of bio-diversify, shrinking natural resources, intensifying competition in the world trade

POLICY FOR AGRICULTURE

The general policy of government for agriculture development may be concluded in the three ways—

1. Supply of input like HYV seeds, fertilizers, pesticides at reasonable cost,
2. Supply of credit, electricity, canal, water at subsidized rate,
3. Fixing of minimum support price for important foodgrains and other crops along with procurement system for wheat and rice.

AGRICULTURE GROWTH

Agriculture is the foundation of our economy, which occupies a place of pride in the country's progress. It plays a pivotal role in providing livelihood, food, employment and ecological balance and anti-migrational force for rural population. Agriculture has its impact on the balance of payments of country, progress, development and employment generation which has increased several folds in last five decades since green revolution took place. Country has come out from the stage of "SHIP TO MOUTH" to self-sufficiency in food and fiber requirement of population. Indian agriculture witnessed a remarkable growth after independence, especially after "green revolution" in the mid 60's, which enabled to self-sufficiency level.

Some Important Figures of Indian Agriculture Chart

A.	Total Geographical Area	328.7	million hectare
B.	Gross Cropped Area [2000-1]	187	million hectare
C.	Net Cropped Area [2000-1]	141.4	million hectare
D.	Gross Irrigated Area	75.14	million hectare
E.	Net Irrigated Area [2000-01]	54.68	million hectare
F.	Drought Prone Area	260	million hectare
G.	Flood Prone Area	40	million hectare
H.	Fertilizer Consumption [N+P+K] 2003-04	16.80	million hectare
I.	Area Under High Yielding Varieties	116	
J.	Operational Holding [million Nos.]	1.4%	
K.	Contribution in GDP [2003-04]	23%	

Source : FAI Statistics, 2003-04.

Green Revolution led to accelerate growth in almost four decades. Foodgrains production, which was 50.8 million metric in 1950-51 has increased several folds as shown in Tables A and B.

TABLE A

Year	*Agriculture Production (% increase/decrease over the previous year)*	*Foodgrains Production (% increase/decrease over the previous year)*
1975-76	15.2	21.2
1980-81	15.6	18.1
1990-91	3.0	3.1
2000-01	-0.1	-6.2
2001-02	6.3	8.1
2002-03	-7.1	-18.2
2003-04	9.6	22.6
2004-05	1.1	-1.4

Source : *Economic Survey*, GoI, 2004-05.

TABLE B

(*Million tones*)

Year	*Foodgrains*
2000-01	196.8
2001-02	212.0
2002-03	182.6
2003-04	212.1
2004-05	204.6
2005-06	216.6

Source : *Economic Survey*, GoI, 2005-06.

India's self-reliance in food production can primarily be credited to 'green revolution' which has led to increase in cropping intensify, nutrient consumption per hectare. Increased crop yield per unit area through effective and scientific use of technology, judicious use of fertilizers, HYV seeds and irrigation has been the success story of crop production and development of agriculture. Fertilizers use in India started in 1920's and was in limited use. The ever first factory of single super phosphate started in 1906 at Ranipet (Tamil Nadu). The rapid growth of fertilizers is seen after mid-60's when green revolution started. There is ample scope for growth and development in agriculture.

Indian agriculture faces far more complex set problems in the new millennium. Pandit Jawahar Lal Nehru always used to say, "we have to run twice as fast as to stay where we are" which is true for the development of agriculture in India to run from green revolution to evergreen revolution. 400 million tones of foodgrains production as opposed to about 214 million tones in 2006-07 is the target of second green revolution. To achieve the foregoing amount of production a growth rate of 5 to 6% in agricultural sector has to be maintained over next 15 years. Current growth rate in this sector is stagnant or at best 2% (in last ten years). The latter has depleted the country's food stock and forced the government to negotiate imports of 5 million tones of wheat. With particularly no more land to farm and some depletion of the agricultural land, this miracle is not easy to achieve. Science and Technology has to play its big role. High productive seeds, private sector involvement and expenditure on long stalled irrigation schemes are key to achieving higher production.

Although major benefits of the green revolution were experienced in the north and north-west, the green revolution substantially increased production of foodgrains, mainly wheat and rice, catapulting the share of agriculture in GDP to 36.4% in 1982-83. The tempo of foodgrain production growth could not be maintained, due to decline in irrigated cultivated land and scarce rains. It added that in 1992-97, irrigated areas cultivating foodgrains registered a growth rate 1.74% against 1.24% in 1989-2007. Only 72% of the country's districts get normal rainfall annually. The survey said that around 362 million hectares irrigation potential has been created in 2005-07.

The economic Survey said the growth rate of foodgrains production decelerated to 1.2% in 1999-2007, lower than the annual growth of population pegged at 1.9%. The country reported an estimated foodgrains production of 217.3 million tones in 2006-07, missing the target by 2.7 million tones. In 2007-08 foodgrains production is expected to be 219.3 million tones against the target of 221.5 million tones.

SUGGESTIONS

1. To improve governance.
2. Raise educational achievement.
3. Control inflation.
4. Introduce a credible fiscal policy.
5. Liberalize financial markets.
6. Increase agricultural productivity.
7. Improve environmental quality.
8. Improve facility for proper storage.
9. Accelerate the advanced technology.
10. Solve the problem of standardization.
11. Improve the problem of transportation and communication.
12. Solve the lack of information.
13. Minimize the low productivity.

CONCLUSION

Agriculture in India is one of the most important factors for the growth of the Indian Economy. India is primarily an agriculture-based country. Agriculture contributes nearly 22% of the GDP in India while about 70% of the population is dependant on agriculture for their livelihood. The agricultural output, however, depends on monsoon, as nearly 65% of area shown, is dependent upon rainfall. The production of foodgrains during 2007-08 is 219.4 million tones. India has become self-sufficient in agricultural production due to green revolution in India. This increase in agricultural production has been brought about by bringing additional area under cultivation, extension of irrigation facilities, the use of improved high yielding variety of seeds, better techniques evolved through agricultural research, water management and plant protection through judicious use of fertilizers, pesticides and cropping practices. Agricultural diversification has emerged as an important alternative to attain the objectives of output growth, employment generation and natural resources sustainability in the developing countries. At last, India today is not self-sufficient in grain production only, but also has a substantial reserve.

References

Acharya, Shankar (2003), "Reform Agenda for Indian Agriculture". ICR on International Economic Relations, New Delhi.

Majumdar, N.A. (2006), "Centrally of Agriculture to India's Economic Development", *E&PW*, Vol. XLI, No. 5, January 7-15, pp. 28-35.

V.S. Vyas (2000-01), "Agriculture, The Second Round of Economic Reforms, *IEJ*, Vol. 48, Jan.-March, No. 3.

M.P. Shrivastava and S.R. Singh, "Prospects of Second Green Revolution", *Kurukshetra*, Vol. 53, No. 3, Jan., 2005.

Gulati, Ashok; Narayan, Sudha, "The Subsidy Syndrome in India Agriculture", Oxford Publication, 2003, New Delhi.

Shiva Vandana; Bedi, Gitanjali, "Sustainable Agriculture and Good Security", Sage Publication (2002), New Delhi.

Bhalla, G.S. and Singh, Gurmail (2001), Indian Agriculture : Four Decades of Development, New Delhi : Sage Publication.

Economic Survey, 2004, 2005, 2006, 2007, 2008, GoI.

The Hindu, TOI and Hindustan Times, News Papers.

World Report of FAO, Agriculture Statistics Report.

Globalization and Agriculture Marketing in India

SANDHYA RANI

Agriculture marketing is a link between farm and non-farm sectors. The present scenario of agriculture produce marketing is an integral part of agricultural farm activities. Surplus of agriculture is sold in Hats and Shanties, Mandies and sometimes through cooperative marketing societies. Storage, transport, proper gradation, increase in number of regulated markets, reduction in the role of middlemen and proper information about ruling prices are some of the measures suggested to improve the marketing of agriculture produce in India. Contract farming has considerable potential in India as it provides access to productive services and credit as well as knowledge of new technology.

INTRODUCTION

Indian agriculture marketing is facing several challenges

in current scenario due to shifting of economic policy to market driven economy. The Royal Commission on Agriculture (1928) while delineating various types of market disabilities stressed upon the government intervention in agricultural marketing system in the country. One of the most important aspects of government intervention was related to establishment of regulated markets. Again in 1937, "The Agricultural Produce (Grading and Marketing) Act" was introduced. However, the process of regulating agricultural produce marketing could be speeded up by the enactment of legislations by many state governments in their respective jurisdiction for establishment of regulated markets during sixties and these legislative provisions were introduced with the objective to secure the cultivators the better prices for their produce on the one hand and at the same time to protect the interests of consumers. The past forty five years have observed a phenomenal rise in the role and importance of agricultural marketing in India. It has been increasingly realized that a predominantly agrarian economy like ours cannot embark on rapid growth path without developing a full proof system for ensuring remunerative prices to the producer in the function of an efficient system of agricultural marketing.

Regulated markets occupy a place of pride in these institutions. From just 268 at the outset of the First Five Year Plan, the number of regulated markets in the country touched an all time high figure of 7062 as in March 1998 and by the end of March 2005, the number stood at 7,521. Besides, the country has 27,294 rural periodical markets and about 15% of which function under the ambit of regulation. However, the issues which need to be examined are mainly two-fold: first, the impact of market development programme on agricultural marketing efficiency and second, the right approach of market intervention policies in the light of the liberalization of agriculture trade.

The subject of agriculture marketing includes marketing function, agencies, channels, efficiency and cost price spread, and market integration, producers surplus, etc. In fact, agricultural marketing system is a link between farms and non-farms sectors. In the present society, there is an increasing awareness that it is not enough to produce a crop in the farm

- The model law on marketing has been formulated keeping these requirements in view. The Model Act provides for an institutional arrangement for registration of sponsoring companies, recording of contract farming agreement and indemnity to farmers' land, and lays down a time-bound dispute resolution mechanism.
- In view of the above, contract-farming arrangements need to be encouraged widely. While doing so, Government needs to protect the interest of both the farmers as well as the industry equitably. Registration of sponsoring companies and recording of contract farming agreements will be required to keep a check on unreliable and spurious companies. A dispute resolution mechanism needs to be set-up to quickly settle issues that might arise between the farmers and the company.
- Forward and futures markets have been identified as an important tool of price discovery and risk management in agricultural commodity markets. The commodity futures market is regulated under the provisions of the Forward Contract (Regulation) Act, 1952. In order to include some new features in line with the developments in the commodity markets, certain amendments have been proposed in the Act. Accordingly, the Forward Contract (Regulation) Amendment Bill, 2006 has been introduced in the Lok Sabha in March 2006. Various proposals relating to the Forward Market Commission (FMC), commodities to be traded, provision for use of options trading along with futures, registration of members and provision for investigation, enforcement and penalty in case of contravention of provision of the FCR Act, 1952 are under consideration.

CONCLUSION

On the basis of above discussed facts, it may be concluded that various reform measures have been initiated by the

Government in the agricultural marketing sector. These measures would encourage the private sector also to make massive investment in farm infrastructure and agro-processing industry but much has to be done in this field. Though Central Government circulated the Model Act for agricultural marketing reforms in 2003, yet a number of the State Governments have not amended their repressive Agricultural Produce Marketing Committee (APMC) Acts to accommodate the suggested reforms in toto. In order to accelerate the pace of agricultural marketing reforms, it is imperative that this subject should be brought to the Central list by making amendments in the constitution. Since corporate houses are also governed by Companies Act of the Central Government bringing Agricultural Marketing Act under the purview of the Central Government will ensure better synergy in operations.

References

Annul Report, 1998-99, Government of India, Ministry of Rural Areas and Employment, p. 86.

Acharya, S.S., "Marketing Environment for Farm Products", Presidential Address, 8th Annual Conference of Agricultural Marketing, 1994, p. 17.

Draft Ninth Five Year Plan (1997-2002), Vol. II, p. 450.

Mishra, Dr. P.K., "Agricultural Market Reforms for the Benefit of Farmers", *Kurukshetra*, Oct. 2007.

Pursell, G. and A. Gulati, "Liberalising Indian Agriculture—An Agenda for Reform", Working Paper, Policy Research Department, The World Bank, Sept. 1993.

High Growth Trajectory for the Rural and Agrarian Economy—Strategy and Interventions in Bihar

CHANDRIKA PRASAD

Various measures to uplift the rural and agrarian economy of Bihar have been suggested. Rural infrastructure, social overhead, good governance, land reforms, empowerment of women and weaker sections will help ameliorate the ills of rural areas in the State. As Bihar is predominantly agricultural, measures to the revitalize agriculture and increase the income of rural poor can transform the rural economy. Under the new dispensation, "winds of change" are blowing for the better, opines the author.

INTRODUCTION

The economy of Bihar is predominantly rural. It is characteristically a state of villages. The agriculture is its main stay. The per-capita income is the lowest in India. In the absence of vital infrastructure, it continues to lag behind in offering job and growth opportunities. Good governance and inclusive development are the two challenging tasks that are finding more and more emphasis among policy-makers today. The per capital income of Bihar is Rs. 6,227 whereas the per capita income of Delhi is Rs. 29,137 (2004-05, CSO estimates). So, it is one of the poorest state roughly five times behind in comparison of Delhi. The human development is lower than compared to the country level.

Poverty is, of course, a matter of deprivation. BPL (Below the Poverty Line) is estimated low. Prof. Suresh Tendulkar, Chairman of the Expert Group to review the methodology for the estimation of poverty observed that the consumption expenditure conforming to the new poverty line "is more than sufficient for purchasing food items that will provide the minimum prescribed intake of 2,400 calories to each individual." The committee estimated in Bihar that 54.4 percent live below the poverty line whereas the Chief-Minister, Mr. Nitish Kumar, said that about 75 percent of the people live below the poverty line according to the study of N.C. Saxena. According to the report of the State Rural Development Department, the number of BPL families are 1,25,55,110 at present in Bihar, which was 1,11,89,824 in the year 2007 according to the survey. So, 57.22 percent of the rural people live below the poverty line. Tendulkar Committee also estimated that 54.4 percent live BPL in 2004-05. This basket of minimalist needs includes access to nourishment, shelter, clothing, education, protection from disease and ability to be mobile so as to have meaningful social interaction. The rural areas have continued to lack basic facilities like water, agriculture know-how, education, health, etc. The rate of growth of the rural economy continued to be relatively slow in this state. Consequently, the benefits of development and growth did not seem to be reaching all layers of the society, particularly the poorer sections. Increasing emphasis has, therefore, been laid in the successive Five Year Plans of the State on the progressive reduction of inequalities in income and removal of poverty through specially designed policies and programmes of both self-employed and wage employment, depending upon the nature, abilities and skills of the target population. Some developmental programmes are supplement to it and some which preceded it, were conceived essentially with this object of securing growth consistent with social justice.

In this state, strong caste feelings stand as stumbling-blocks in the way of organizing community efforts. It is the major and the biggest caste in every village that arrogates to itself the responsibility of speaking on behalf of its entire populace. Most officers belong to that caste and monopolize the schemes, subsidies and co-operative and bank loans. The three alarming problems staring Bihar in its face are poverty, unemployment and inflation. The rural areas in the state are more unfortunate in comparison to the urban. The ability to raise resources is sharply limited. There is huge migration of farm labourers from Bihar to other states due to lack of gainful employment. Land revenue in Bihar has often remained suspended because of floods and droughts or was cancelled on holdings of smaller sizes.

BIHAR : AT GLANCE

It is situated on Latitude—24° 20′ 10" to 27° 31′ 15" North and Longitude 33° 19′ 50" to 88° 17′ 40" East. There are 94,163 sq. km. in which rural areas is on 92,358.40 sq. km. and urban areas is on 1804.60 sq. km. There are 45,077 villages, 8471 Panchayats, 533 Blocks and 38 Districts in this state. According to the 2001 census, the total population is 8,28,78,796 in which number of males are 4,31,53,964 and females are 3,97,24,832. The total land is 93.60 lakh hectare in which cultivated land is 80.26 lakh hectare. Forest areas spread up to 6.87 lakh hectares and useless land is 5.93 lakh hectare. Irrigated area is on 35.20 lakh hectare land, etc. The state is divided into two parts-North Bihar and South Bihar. The Ganges is divine-line. The plain-land of Gangetic region is very fertile. Soil is alluvial, sandy and tall-land is full of clay. The "winds of change" have been blowing and have affected the village-dweller in most areas of the state.

Table 8
Position of Crop Production in Bihar

	Rice	*Wheat*	*Maize*	*Other crops*	*Pulses*	*Total*	*Oil seeds*
(1)	*(2)*	*(3)*	*(4)*	*(5)*	*(6)*	*(7)*	*(8)*
Year 2001-02							
Wet land (lakh-hectare)	36.56	20.68	6.21	0.56	7017	71.18	1.54
Production (lakh-hectare)	54.44	44.36	14.97	0.58	6.22	120.59	1.31
Productivity (quintal/hectare)	14.89	21.46	24.11	10.37	8.67	16.94	8.51
National Productivity (quintal/hectare)	19.27	27.42	18.06	10.10	5.53	16.38	7.38
Year 2004-05							
Wet land (lakh- hectare)	31.67	20.55	6.23	0.48	6.51	65.4	1.393
Production (lakh-hectare)	25.69	34.26	14.23	0.42	5.04	79.70	1.155
Productivity (quintal/hectare)	8.11	16.88	22.94	8.75	7.75	12.12	8.29

Source : Directory of Statistical and Evaluation Deptt., Bihar Government, Patna.

The table shows the position of crop-production in the year of 2001-02 and 2004-05 which is below the average production of national level. The natural calamities also are the major factors of low production. On account of poor irrigation facilities, agriculture in Bihar has to rely largely on natural rainfall. If rains did not fall, agricultural production suffered badly. The long periods of drought has affected badly.

THE STATE ECONOMY STARTS MOVING IN THE RIGHT DIRECTION

At present, the economy has started moving in the right direction on the basis of increasing government investment and the sustained fiscal stimulus provided for three years. Although Banks are not giving loans to the rural people according to their target, Rs. 8738 crore was given in 2006-07 whereas target was Rs. 10,000 crore and Rs. 8738 core loan was given but target was Rs. 21,128 crore in current financial year. In spite of Bihar's GDP grew by 11.03% between 2004-05 and 2008-09, much more than the national average of 8.49% and ranked only second to Gujarat (11.05%). These are good indicator for future development of the state economy. The state deputy Chief Minister, Sushil Kumar Modi said, "Even for the current fiscal, we have targeted a plan expenditure of over Rs. 16,000 crore, Earlier, before the NDA government took over, the annual performance was dismal, to say the least. On an average, it could spend between Rs. 1,500-2,000 crores". Drawing a comparison between the RJD government which managed to spend Rs. 25,000 crore in its 15 years tenure till 2004-05. Mr. Modi said the NDA government has spent nearly Rs. 36,000 crore on development over the past four years. "The level of plan expenditure will easily scale up to Rs. 51,000 crore if the estimate of the annual plan of 2009-10 is taken into account". "On the road alone, we have targeted an investment of Rs. 5,000 crore and on education Rs. 10,000 crore in the current fiscal", Mr. Modi added. But, opposition leaders of the ruling government objected on GDP's growth rate. So, there is need for inclusive growth. But, the potentiality of development is very high. The significance of agriculture development can not be underscored. It is not only basic for the development of rural areas but also of the industrial sector as it supplies the major and necessary raw-material for many industries. Rural Development is broader concept which covers the maximum areas and maximum people. It is comprehensive and multidimensional concept.

PROBLEMS AND SUGGESTIONS

There is a need to create an enabling environment for the people by developing infrastructure and social overhead, raising the strength of good governance, providing job opportunities, adopting the new policy of land reform, increasing the empowerment of weaker sections and women from various methods.

(1) Today, nearly four decade after our green revolution, our agriculture sector produces on an average 14 Kg. of rice and wheat per person per annum or slightly over a kilogram a month, and this meagre production is growing at the rate of 0.5% year on year. Land issues are the most important hindrance. At least, consolidation of land-holding should be implemented at present. Secondly, unregistered cultivators face difficulties in accessing institutional credit and other facilities available to farmers with land titles. Once priority is to record and register actual cultivators including tenants and women cultivators, and provide pass-books to them to ensure that they gain access to institutional credit and other inputs. For this, there should be strong willingness among political leaders.

(2) There should be interconnections of economic growth and public support. It should be geared to facilitate wide participation of the population in the process of economic growth. This can be done particularly through widespread promotion of skills and education and the maintenance of maximum employment opportunities. In addition, state policies have crucial role in promoting growth itself. The masses can gain a share in general opulence not only

through the increase of private incomes, but also through wide-ranging public provisioning.

(3) *Maximization of good-governance*: The good-governance including decentralization of power on the village level and maintaining law and order play a vital role in the various disputes and corruptions. The empowerment of Panchayati Raj is very suitable for macro-economic progress of the rural areas.

(4) *The strengthening of the co-operative movement*: The co-operative has failed to make desired impact. But it is instrument to development. It will create enlightened membership and right type of leadership will emerge to take care of the interest of the society. It will be useful to dispel the myth that one village will have only one co-operative society. There are many groups in the village. At the initial stage each group may form its own society and when each society becomes fairly advanced it may constitute a multi-purpose society as Japan has done. These small group societies may federate at Block level or district level in order to take advantage of scale. The prospective members must be aware of what co-operative is, what are its principles and methodology, what are its potentials, etc.

(5) Provision of good quality infrastructure is a crucial prerequisite for sustainable growth. It is a true "Engine of Growth" and can provide the much needed impetus to the economy in this time of economic slow down. The pattern of inclusive growth of the economy projected for the Eleventh Plan, with GDP growth averaging 10% per year can be achieved only if this infrastructure deficit can be overcome and adequate investment takes place to support higher growth. There are also many areas where these facilities are badly lacking.

(6) Transforming the rural non-farm economy. Non-farm production includes all economic activities other than production of primary agricultural commodities including mining, manufacturing, utilities construction, commerce, transport, the transforming

raw agricultural products by milling, packaging, transporting, etc. These play an important role in the economic transformation. They, in turn, are contributing to growth in the demand for diverse rural outputs.

(7) Microfinance is not simply banking, it is a development tool. Microfinance refers the provision of financial services on a small scale to the rural and urban poor including the self-employed. The self-help group (SHG) is the dominant microfinance methodology. The operation of 15-25 member SHGs are based on the principle of revolving the members over savings. NABARD has facilitated and extensively supported a programme which entails commercial banks, Co-operative Banks and Regional Rural Banks lending directly to SHGs. But, the lowest share, both in terms of cumulative numbers of SHGs and loans sanctioned is in Bihar. It is tended to provide finance to the poorest sections of rural population and particularly women groups which should be increased. This leads to self-exploitation and reduces the potential employment opportunities. On the other hand, if credit facilities increase in the production, then the repayment capacity of the debtor will increase and his creditworthiness will be enhanced.

(8) *Minimum wages*: In Bihar, the average daily earnings of men is less than the minimum wage fixed by the respective state government. In most of the progressive states, the actual wages are higher than the minimum wages which is the important cause of labour migration in other state. It should help NREGA in generating employment *vis-a-vis* community assets. It gives 100 days of guaranteed employment to a rural every household whose adult member volunteer to do unskilled manual work. But, it is seen that bungling of this programme is found in the newspapers. There is need of perfect evolution. A very good monitoring system should be adopted.

(9) *To review critically the rural health scenario*: The human development is the lowest in the world. Health is multi-dimensional. Our prime goal should be to improve the "Quality of life" of the rural people in terms of employment, occupation, literacy, purchasing power, living standard including housing, water supply, sanitation, communication, etc. and assertive power (organization) to maximize the gains from investment in health care and *vice-versa*.

(10) *Development of Rural Marketing*: Even today, middlemen exploit rural people on agriculture prices. Till date, most rural products are marketed through temporarily set-up rural hats. Provision of permanent marketing centers in villages will help the rural artisans and producers to promote the marketing of their wares; it will meet the daily needs of the villagers along with boosting the socio-economic development of the area. A complete food market reform programme should be undertaken with a multi-directional integrated approach to take up problem-solving and purpose-oriented research for vertical and horizontal integration of agricultural marketing at the top and consumer services/ satisfaction at the other end, by conducting surveys of farmers, milkmen, fishermen, wholesalers, retailers. Women traders can be assisted by the provision of adequate market facilities. Practical demonstration of improved marketing methods and provision of management training to the women folk will be of great assistance. There should be modern storage structure, so that post-harvest losses can be eliminated.

(11) There is poor performance of our live-stocks. The main problems facing the dairy industry are governmental policies, unorganized sector, poor productivity of cattle and ignorance of farmers about animal health care.

(12) Water available for irrigation is likely to decrease in future. A diagnostic analysis of several irrigation

projects needs to be carried out to find out why the gap exists between potential and utilization. Natural calamities like flood and drought present an opportunity for new innovations. Agro-forestry, that is, cultivation of trees together with crops can help farmers cope with several of the adverse consequence of climatic change. Planting of trees between the crops and in the boundaries around crops can help prevent soil erosion, restore soil fertility and provide shade for other crops. Interdisciplinary research is essential on water resource management starting from dams to field application including watershed.

(13) Rural Electrification and Non-conventional Energy: Problem of electrification is serious. Steps shall be undertaken in a right direction to improve the power situation. There is need to the growth of biogas, biomass, solar energy, wind energy, small hydropower, geothermal energy and other emerging technologies. The new and renewable energy technologies will make a great revolution mainly in isolated areas, where it is difficult to provide electrical energy through grid.

CONCLUSION

In this way, by addressing these issues, multi-dimensional efforts will undoubtedly help in the element of inclusive growth and the livelihoods of the majority of people will improve. Apart from crop sector, higher growth in horticulture, livestock, poultry and fisheries is needed to achieve at least 4 per cent growth in agriculture for high growth trajectory through public-private partnership project in Bihar. It will be appropriate to refer to the emerging scientific progress on the farms as an "even-green revolution". The productivity advance is sustainable over time since it is rooted on the principles of ecology, economics, social and gender equity and employment generation.

REFERENCES

The Hindustan News Paper (Hindi) (for different information), Patna.

Prasad, K.N., Problems of Indian Economic Development, Sterling Publishers, Pvt. Ltd., New Delhi, 1983, pp. 361-69.

The Economic Times, Monday, 4 January, 2010 , pp. 13, 17.

S. Mahendra Dev, Inclusive Growth in India, Oxford University Press, New Delhi, Published 2008, p. 69

Jha, Ugra Mohan, Rural Development in India, Anmol Publication Pvt. Ltd., New Delhi, Reprint 2000, pp. 16-17, *Kurukshetra*, Vol. 57-58, October 2009, Nov. 2009.

Self-Help Groups and Rural Development in India

SHABNAM VERMA AND RITESH KUMAR

The promotion of SHGs in India began formally in 1992 with the launch of SHG-Bank Linkage Programme by NABARD. Government of India merged various credit programmes together and launched SGSY. Now, the programme has grown to enormous size and is empowering women and building their confidence and self-esteem. It has reduced vulnerability of the poor through asset-creation, income generation and consumption smoothening, provision of emergency and giving them assets.

Learning from the experiences abroad, India took tentative step towards microfinance in the early nineties with the National Bank of Agriculture and Rural Development (NABARD), experimenting with a new and innovative idea of Self-Help Groups (SHG) to deal with the problem of providing access to banking services for the poor on a sustainable terms by leveraging the vast banking network spread across the country. They tried out a pilot project which was a success and debunked most of the myths associated with the rural poor. This led to the implementation of the SHG-Bank Linkage Programme on a full-fledged basis.

The SHG was envisaged as a microbank, meeting both the savings and credit needs of its member on their own terms. Thus, in one stroke, transaction cost both for the bank and the clients was reduced considerably. Majority of them consists of female members. Slowly SHG-Bank Linkage Programme has become a movement. The country has witnessed a rapid growth of self-help groups in the last decade or so. The SHG growth which is almost assumed the form of movement represents a massive grassroots levels mobilization of poor rural women into small informal associations capable of forging links with formal systems to help access financial and other services needed for their socio-economic advancement. Basically, SHGs are being promoted as a part of the microfinance interventions aimed at helping the poor to obtain easily financial services like savings, credit and insurance.

The promotion of SHG in India began more formally in 1992 with the launch of SHG-Bank Linkage Programme by NABARD. This program's main aim was to improve rural poor's access to formal credit system in a cost effective and sustainable manner by making use of SHGs. A self-help group has been defined as a small and informal association of poor having preferably similar socio-economic background and who have come together to realize some common goals based on the principles of self-help and collective responsibility. SHGs become relevant because of these reasons. First, a SHG working on the principle of solidarity helps the poor to come together to pool their savings and access credit facilities. A SHG by tapping Social Capital like trust and reciprocation helps in replacing physical collateral, a major hurdle faced by the poor in obtaining formal credit. Next, through the principles of joint liability and peer pressure, a SHG ensures prompt loan recovery from the members. In the process, a SHG helps poor, especially women, to establish their creditworthiness.

It also helps in empowering the rural women. The participation in SHG and the access obtained to savings and credit play transformation role for women both socially and economically. By access to savings and credit, women members take care of consumption and production needs of the family members. The continued participation in SHG will enhance the awareness, skills, etc. of women which builds the individual self-esteem.

Studies available indicate that members, by participating in SHGs, have been able to accumulate significant savings. In Andhra Pradesh, for instance, SHG members have accumulated individual savings worth up to Rs. 1800. In mature SHGs the average individual savings has been as high as Rs. 10,000. Thus, SHGs have helped the poor the access to savings and credit. Own savings can be useful in many ways. SHGs have helped development of thrift. Evidences suggest that women, by dint of their accumulated savings, have been able to meet many life cycle needs like housing, education and marriage.

SHG helps women access to credit by leverage to savings. Savings mobilized by members are used to lent small loans internally. A large member of SHGs meets the urgent consumption and social credit needs by internal lending. Bigger credit requirements for production purposes are met by borrowings from banks and SHGs federations. Thus, members get access to formal credit system. The SHG is the dominant microfinance methodology in India. The operations of 15-25 member SHG are based on the principle of revolving the member's own savings. External financial assistance—by MFIs or banks augments the resources available to the group operated revolving fund. Savings thus precede borrowings by the members. In many SHG programs, the volume of individual borrowing is determined by the volume of member's savings or the savings of the group as a whole. Some NGOs operate microfinance programmes by organizing federations of SHGs to act as a MFI which obtains external loan funds in bulk to be channeled to the members via SHGs. NABARD refinances the loans of commercial banks to SHGs.

Microfinance has evolved over the past quarter century across India into various operating forms and to a varying degree of success. One such form of microfinance has been the development of self-help groups. The result from these self-help groups are promising and have been a focus of intense examination as it is proving to be an effective method of poverty reduction. During the International Year of Micro-credit, 2005, significant policy announcements from the Government of India and Reserve Bank of India have served as a shot in the arm for rapid growth. SHGs have spread rapidly due to their ease of replication. Today, it is estimated that there are at least over 2 million SHGs in India. In many states, SHGs are networking themselves into federations to achieve institutional and financial sustainability. Cumulatively, 1.6 million SHGs have been linked with cumulative loans of Rs. 69 billion. In 2004-05 alone, almost 800,000 SHGs were bank-linked.

The post-nationalization period in the banking sector, circa 1969, witnessed a substantial amount of resources being earmarked towards meeting the credit needs of the poor. Later, initiatives were underway that were institution driven which attempted to converge the existing strengths of rural banking infrastructure and leverage this better serve the poor. NABARD, which came up in 1980 conducted a series of research studies independently and in association with MYRADA, a leading NGO from Southern India which showed that despite having a wide network of rural bank branches servicing the rural poor, a very large number of the poorest of the poor continued to remain outside the field of the formal banking system.

In 1999, the Government of India merged various credit programmes together, refined them and launched a new programme called Swarnjayanti Gram Swarojgar Yojana (SGSY). The mandate of SGSY is to continue to provide subsidized credit to the poor through the banking sector to generate self-employment through a self-help group approach and the programme has grown to an enormous size.

In the early stages, NGOs played a pivotal role in innovating the SHG model and in implementing the model to develop the process fully. State Governments established revolving loan funds which were used to fund SHGs. By the 1990s, SHGs were viewed by State Government and NGOs to be more than just a financial intermediation but as a common interest group, working on other concerns as well. The agenda of SHGs included social and political issues as well.

SHG federations are formal institutions while the SHGs are informal. Many of these SHG federations are registered as societies, mutual benefit trusts and mutually aided cooperative societies. SHG federations resulted in several key benefits including:

- Stronger political and advocacy capabilities,
- Sharing of knowledge and experiences,
- Economies of Scale, and
- Access to greater capital.

A SHG is usually association of similar class and region, which come together to form savings and credit organizations. The movement creates an ethic that focuses on savings first.

SHG BANK LINKAGE

A most notable milestone in the SHG movement was when NABARD launched the pilot phase of SHG bank linkage programme in Feb. 1992. This was the first instance of mature SHGs that were directly financed by a commercial bank. The informal thrift and credit groups of poor were recognized as bankable clients. Soon after, the RBI advised commercial banks to consider lending to SHGs as part of their rural credit operations thus creating SHG bank linkage. The linking of SHGs with the financial sector was good for both sides. The banks were able to tap into a large market, namely, the low-income households, transaction costs were low and repayment rates were high. The SHGs were able to scale up their operations with micro-financing and they had access to more credit products.

THE STATE OF SHGs IN INDIA

The Table 1 indicates the number of SHGs and amount of financing they received through SHG Bank Linkage during the 12 month period ending March 31, 2005 (NABARD, 2005).

TABLE 1

(in millions of Rs.)

	No. of new SHGs provided with bank loan during 2004-05	*No. of existing SHGs provided with repeat bank loan during 2004-05*	*Cumulative No. of SHGs provided with bank loan up to Mar. 31, 2005*	*New Customer Bank loans during 2004-05*	*Repeat Customer Bank loan during 2004-05*	*Cumulative Bank loan up to Mar. 31, 2005*
(1)	*(2)*	*(3)*	*(4)*	*(5)*	*(6)*	*(7)*
Northern Region	33,622	3,381	86,018	927	145	2,395
North-Eastern Region	21,960	125	34,238	815	3	1,020
Central Region	107,391	24,557	265,628	2,101	477	5,183
Western Region	41,451	5,837	96,266	1,319	223	2,951
Southern Region	264,585	2,18,761	9,38,941	10,221	11,461	52,421
Grand Total	5,39,365	2,58,092	1,618,456	17,266	12,676	68,985

The financial management of SHGs has found to be ranging from weak to average. Specifically, internal controls at SHGs and SHG federations are lacking. The achievement of women members to form common interest groups to help themselves is remarkable. NGOs have been particularly important towards the success stories of many SHGs. The loans that SHG members receive are intended to improve their livelihood so that they can receive greater and steadier cash flows. In rural areas, livelihoods range agriculture farming, animal husbandry, dairy and various other goods and service activities. Experience have shown that SHGs have improved to the extent of providing the leveraging needed to start enterprises. Of course, the outreach of financial services to the poor through SHGs has been good in South India. However, the outreach has been limited in the rest of the country.

One of the key benefits of SHGs is women empowerment. The role of SHGs is both important as an inspiration and as a financer. Impoverished women develop greater language and financial skills through the SHGs which provides the building blocks for higher level of confidence to engage the world. Before 1990s, credit schemes exclusively for rural women were almost negligible. The financial banking sector always demands rigid discipline in collateral security.

It has played valuable roles in reducing the vulnerability of the poor through asset creation, income generation and consumption smoothing, provision of emergency assistance and empowerment and emboldening women by giving them control and assets and increased self-esteem and knowledge.

However, state of SHGs identifies key weaknesses which undermine the sustainability of SHG movement. Financial management, governance and human resources range from weak to average quality for a majority of SHGs. While the spread of movement is impressive, these are key areas that need to be addressed. In South India, significant improvements in fertility rates, female literacy, participation in development programmes and economic independence are evident. Now, women are able to fight for their rights and entitlements and have emerged as a force to be reckoned with.

CONCLUSION

SHG require external help to continue to grow and have greater outreach and impact to the civil society. It is expected that with the increased momentum of SHG movement, women will usher in a new era of more responsible politics and public life.

The need for livelihood support is critical to SHGs development. The support of livelihoods is increasingly being seen as an important area related to microfinance. The need of SHGs varies from the introduction of new livelihoods to providing support such as market linkages or procurement techniques to refine existing livelihoods. Large scale investment is required to build infrastructure, roads and bridges. Sustainability of SHGs is linked to their financial sustainability.

References

Sharma, Abhijit (2006) : Microfinance : Hope for the Poor, *Yojana*, Dec. 2006.

Shylendra, H.S. (2008) : Role of Self-Help Groups, *Yojana*, Jan. 2008.

Koul, Divy Ninad and Mohan, Garesh (2009) : Women Self-Help Groups and Micro Finance, *Kurukshetra*, Feb. 2009.

Rajesh, S. and Venkatamma, G. (2009) : Microfinance Institutions in India, *Kurukshetra*, Nov. 2009.

12

Rural Development Programmes in Pre-Independence India

Anil Kumar Singh

Metcalfe's observation that villages are "little republic" was reflected in Indian villages with the prevalence of subsistence economy in pre-independence period. Several pioneering experiments were made by eminent persons of the country to develop socio-economic conditions of our villages. In this connection, Shri Niketan experiment of Bengal by Ravindranath Tagore, Spencer Hatch experiment of 1921, Gurgaon experiment of 1927, Baroda experiment of 1932, Itawa experiment of 1941, Village Swarajya Movement by Mahatma Gandhi in 1942, Firka experiment (Madras) of 1946 and Nilokhery experiment of 1947 were notable movements which served as beacon-lights for rural development during alien rule.

India can not boast of any development unless she develops her villages where about 70% of her population lives. The development of villages is a pre-condition for balanced economic development, accelerated economic growth and industrial advancement. The basic requirement for economic growth, viz., saving and investment and expanding market for industrial product ultimately depend upon the rural development.

Specialists have defined the term rural development in many ways. According to Giriappa, 'Rural development involves developing the rural economy, so as to raise the standard of living of those rural people who are poor and require upliftment. Ensminger says, that "Rural development seeks to involve a process of transformation from traditionally oriented rural cultures towards an acceptance and reliance and on science and technology." Lale defines Rural Development as "improving the living standards of the mass of low income population residing in rural areas and making the process self-sustaining". In fact rural development involves a process in which the rural society, at large, moves from one step of the economic ladder to the next, thereby enhancing its social and economic status. However, the gist of all the definitions of rural development filters down to a primary goal of providing an opportunity for decent living to the mass of the low income population residing in rural areas on a self-sustaining basis.

The Indian village Community has been recognized as a unique entity differing widely from the villages of west Europe, the Mir of Russia, the German mark or the Chinese village. Karl Marks, Baden Powell and others assume a semi-autonomous or independent structural significance for village in India. C.T. Metcalfe's observation that "village communities are little republics, having nearly everything that they want within themselves, and almost independent of any foreign relations" has become a classic formulation. Although critics like Louis Dumont had challenged the view of Metcalfe, but more and less it can be said that in pre-British India, villages were self-sufficient based on subsistence economy. Prior to the advent of Britishers, village economy was neither developed nor under developed in modern sense. Its economic structure was traditional based on agriculture and some sorts of small scale industries. Political disturbances and changes of dynasty did not alter the basic economic nature of Indian village in pre-British period.

But this self-sufficiency and isolation of Indian villages suffered a crippling blow during the British rule. The new-comers belonged to capitalist and industry-oriented society which was very different from the semi-feudal society of India. For the development of industry in Britain, they needed a plenty of raw materials and in this background, the exploitation of Indian village communities started. Due to the growth of market-economy, the self-sufficiency and isolation of Indian villages ended. Commercialization of agriculture, high rate of land revenue, introduction of Zamindari system—these all were like thunderbolt for Indian farmers. The three main phases of the growth of economy in British-India. 1. The Commercial Age, 2. The Industrial Capitalist Age, and 3. The Finance Capital Age—were in favour of British economy, and the Indian economy which was basically village-economy at the time, was exploited badly. For providing raw materials to factories in U.K. and securing markets for their products, the alien rulers deliberately strangulated the flourishing village cottage industries. Due to reduced agricultural output, curtailed means of livelihood, high population growth and heavy debt burdens, the bulk of the villagers gradually became victims of low productivity, reduced income, utter misery and poverty. Although 'Morise-de-Moris' deny that the poverty of India was due to British rule, but there is no disagreement on the fact that people lived on the verge of starvation. "India's economic backwardness and poverty were not due to the niggardliness of nature. They were man-made. The natural resources of India were abundant and capable of yielding, if properly utilized, a high degree of prosperity to the people. But as a result of foreign rule and exploitation and of a backward agrarian and industrial economic structure—in fact, as the total outcome of its historical and social development, India presented the "paradox of a poor people living in rich country."

Before Independence, several pioneering experiments regarding rural development have been made by many eminent persons in this country towards the end of the 19th century. The British became increasingly concerned with rural development in India. This is evident from the creation of District Boards, and agriculture, health and education departments. In 1904, the first All India Co-operative Act was passed in order to promote Co-operative Credit Relief Works.

Rabindra Nath Tagore started the Sri Niketan experiment in Bengal in 1921. The main objectives of Sri Niketan experiment were moral and economic rehabilitation of rural people. In this experiment, Co-operative Societies were formed among the villagers to meet the challenge of natural calamities like Malaria, Plague, etc. Emphasis was given on village crafts such as poultry-farming, Apiculture, growing new vegetables and other craftsmanship. For educational development, certain boardings were started for boys and girls. Training programmes were introduced among boys and girls such as poultry farming, Dairy project and sports and games were organized.

Another important experiment regarding rural development was initiated by Spencer Hatch in 1921. This was five sided programme like development of spirit, mind, body, economy and society. This experiment was based on the principle that self-help is the best. In this experiment people of every community were included and priority was given to the poor people. Comprehensive economic programme such as poultry-farming, Apiculture, Cottage Industry, etc. were adopted. Emphasis was given to train the people for self-development. For the implementation of the scheme, various clubs were organized.

Gurgaon experiment was initiated by Mr. F.L. Branye in 1927 the then Dy. Commissioner of Gurgaon. The main objective of the experiment was to provide amenities and create conditions for the development of the life of the rural poor in the district. Under the scheme some institutional centers like: The School of rural economy, Domestic school of economy, Health Association, etc. were opened for the development. Rural sanitation work and Agricultural Rural Development Programmes were adopted. Arrangement was made for providing improved seeds, latest techniques of cultivation, etc. Under this scheme,. the villagers were encouraged to make propaganda against—social evils such as—parda system, child marriage, etc. There was marked progress in various schemes of Gurgaon experiment but this had no lasting effect on villagers and the main difficulty was the transfer of officials, inadequacy of infrastructure, etc.

In 1932, Baroda Experiment was initiated by V.P. Krishnamachari. Under this experiment, the first Rural Reconstruction centre was started for the rural development of the area. The main objectives were the improvement of the different aspect of the rural life and improvement of cultivation and increasing the yields. Various programmes like the development of subsidiary occupation, Co-operative societies, Village Panchayats, educational and moral programmes were encouraged.

Itawa Experiment was launched in 1941. Initially, 64 villages were selected for experiments and within three years, 300 villages were covered. The scheme was initiated in 1941 which was an impact of the enlightened interim Government formed in U.P.

The project aimed at making improvement over productive and social conditions of villages. The inherent principle of this experiment was to make a combined efforts of people, Government, voluntary workers and others. Systematic planning of the different schemes, self-measurement and correction of every scheme was the guiding principle of the scheme.

Under this scheme, various programmes like application of improved varieties of Seeds, Fertilizers, Irrigation, Plant Protection, Horticulture, Animal Husbandry, Soil Conservation, Co-operative Societies, Marketing and supply, Health Services, Maternity and Child Welfare Service, Social Education. Adult Education, Training Programmes for the villagers were adopted. Later on, the programme was merged with Community Development Programme.

In 1942, our beloved national leader Mahatma Gandhi, who was very much conscious for rural development gave the idea of 'village-swaraj' and under sarvodaya scheme the emphasis was being given on the improvement of the rural people, specially the persons belonging to Harijan, (Scheduled Caste and Scheduled Tribes). He wanted to provide complete republic in village life. On the principle of Sarvodaya, the experiment was made by the Govt. of Bombay and certain schemes were started for Rural Reconstruction. In our constitution, philosophy of Sarvodaya was adopted. Under the impact of advanced communist thought, the Sarvodaites were thinking of an ideal society without classes, without the state, a society based on the principle 'from each according to his capacity, to each according to his necessity.'

Firka Experiment was started in Madras in 1946 with 34 firkas. The main objective of the experiment was the attainment of Gandhian idea of village swaraj and efforts were being made to make the villagers become self-reliant and self-confident. It helped rural communities, formed panchayats, ensured water supply, etc. Certain projects were taken for making the villagers self-sufficient. Especially development of Khadi, Handloom and Cottage Industries were of special importance. For implementation of the schemes, Firka development committees were constituted. This experiment brought certain remarkable improvement in the standard of living of the villagers. Later, this scheme was merged with the Community Development Programme during 1952-53.

Nilokheri Experiment was launched by S.K. Day in 1947. Through this programme, 7000 displaced persons were settled on 1100 areas of land which later on took the shape of township. The main principles of this experiment were—right to live, right to work for living and right to receive what is earned. Co-operative societies were established and 6 acres of land were given to a head of a family for cultivation and their livelihood.

References

Anker, D.L.W., Rural Development: Problems and Strategies.

Pranab, K. Bardhan, Land, Labour and Rural Poverty,

C.S. Baker, An Indian Rural Economy.

W.C. Neale, Economic Changes in Rural India.

Giriappa, Urganism and Rural Development.

A.R. Desai, Rural Sociology in India.

S.K. Sen, Studies in Economic Polity and Development of India.

B.H. Baden-Powell, The Land Systems of British India.

Daniel and A. Thornier, Land and Labour in India.

Amit Bhaduri, Evolution of Land Relations in Eastern India under British Rule.

K.N. Chaudhary, Economy and Society in India.

Bipin Chandra, Nationalism and Colonialism in Modern India.

V.B. Singh (ed.), Economic History of India (1857-1956).
B.R. Tomilson, Political Economy of The Raj.
R.C. Dutta, Economic History of India.
J.J. Spengler, Economic Growth.
E. White Combe, Agrarian Condition in the Northern India.
Peter Robb, British Rule and Indian Improvement.
A. Achunpeter, History of Economic Analysis.
Omkar Goswami, Evolution of the Indian Economy.
Rajni Pam Dutta, *India Today*.
S.C. Dube, India's Changing Villages.

Alternative Agriculture for Bihar

MIRA MRIDUBHASHINI AND KUMKUM NARAIN

Agricultural diversification should be cornerstone of agriculture policy in the state of Bihar. There is subsistence agriculture in the state. The Seed Replacement Rate (SRR) in the state is among the lowest in India. To diversify the agriculture, fruits, vegetables, sugarcane, jute, aromatic and medicinal plants should be grown along with traditional rice and wheat system. This will ensure sustainability and profitability of agriculture. Agriculture requires holistic approach so that it becomes a remunerative occupation for the farmers. Cash crop, horticulture, livestock, fisheries, agro-forestry, watershed-based soil and water management and social capital formation should be incorporated to accelerate the agricultural development.

The State of agricultural development is both the bane as well as the hope for the State of Bihar. On the one hand, nine-tenths of the population depends on agriculture for their livelihood while on the other, the abundant natural resources such as fertile soil and easy availability of water promises exponential progress in the agricultural sector. A more coherent policy should be adopted. It is the argument of this paper that the State should emphasize agricultural diversification as the cornerstone of its agricultural policy in order to maximize gains from this sector.

NATURAL ENDOWMENTS OF BIHAR

The geographical area of Bihar is 93.6 million hectares of alluvial plain and comprises of three agro-climatic zones:

(i) *The Northwest Zone*—This comprises 13 districts whose average annual rainfall ranges between 1040-1450 mm. The soil is mostly sandy loam.

(ii) *Northeast Zone*—This zone comprises 8 districts whose average annual rainfall ranges from 1200-1700 mm. The soil is mostly sandy loam and clay loam.

(iii) *South Zone*—This is the largest zone comprising of 17 districts which is sub-divided into the eastern and western zones. The eastern sub-zone has 6 districts while the western sub-zone has 11 districts including the capital, Patna. This zone receives 990-1240 mm of annual rainfall and has a variety of soils—sandy loam, clay loam and clay.

For Bihar as a whole the average annual rainfall is 1098 mm, though there is considerable variation across years and districts. Forests are limited in extent and comprise just 6.64% of the geographical area. Barren and uncultivated land is even less at 4.46% of the area in 2005-06, land put to non-agricultural use comprises 17.5% of the area while the land under tree crops comprises 2.5%. The total uncultivable land is 40.6% (2005-06) while the net sown area is 59.3%. This shows that the soil of Bihar is very fertile. The cropping intensity has increased from 1.41 to 2.06.

Production

Farmers in Bihar produce a large number of crops-cereals, pulses, oilseeds, fibre crops, fruits and vegetables. The average levels of production of major crops in Bihar are 43.7 lakh tons (rice), 36 lakh tons (wheat) and 14.9 lakh tons (Maize). The total production of cereals is 95.4 lakh tons (2007-08). The total production of foodgrains is 100.3 lakh tons (2007-08). Bihar produced 11.8 lakh tons of potato, 10.1 lakh tons of cauliflower, 9.2 lakh tons of tomato and 11.2 lakh tons of Brinjal in 2006-07. In 2006-07 the state produced 13.1 lakh tons of mango, 2.1 lakh tons of litchi, 2.5 lakh tons of guava and 11.3 tons of banana.

The fact that agriculture is basically subsistence based is evinced by the fact that 95% of the area under major crops is devoted to foodgrains. In this category, the share of cereals production has increased from 87.2% in 2001-02 to 94.2% in 2007-08 while the share of area under pulses has deceased from 8.77% in 2000-01 to only 1.42% in 2006-07. For Fibres, the share of area has remained stagnant at 2.3%. Figures in this paper are from various volumes of Economic Survey of Bihar, Government of Bihar, Finance Department.

Productivity

The productivity of crops has varied across the years. The average productivity of rice is 1287 kg/hectare. The productivity of wheat is higher at 1749 kg/hectare but the highest productivity is of maize at 2367 kg/hectare. The productivity of pulses varies between 929 kg/hectare in the kharif season and 738 kg/hectare in the rabi season. There is considerable difference in the yield by district. The productivity of rice, for example, varies from 2080 kgs/hectare in Bhabua to 522 kg/hectare in Sheohar while in the case of wheat productivity ranges from 2789 kgs/hectare in Samastipur and 698 kgs/hectare in Araria.

The State should produce more of pulse, oilseeds, jute, tobacco, fruits, flowers, livestock, diary products, fisheries, medicinal and aromatic plants. There is scope for introducing coconut, oil palm, cashew nut production successfully in this region. Farm-based waste such as paddy straw should be used for Mushroom Culture, Vermiculture and multiple use of waste water should be taught to our farmers. At present, area under floriculture is much less compared to its potentiality. There is need to encourage farmers to produce flowers in large quantities like Marigold, Chrysanthemum, lotus, roses, rajnigandha, etc. The districts of Patna, Nalanda, Bhagalpur and Siwan are suitable for floriculture and ready demand for decorative flowers exists in this region itself. Programmes for promoting litchi in Muzaffarpur, Mango in Darbhanga, Spices in Samastipur, Makhana in Madhubani should be taken up immediately as there is huge potential of success. Tobacco and jute are two crops which can be grown easily by our farmers, only assured marketing facilities are required.

The average productivity of rice and wheat is much below the national average in Bihar. Therefore,there exists tremendous scope for raising output by improving technology through enhanced cropping intensity, changes in cropping pattern, improvement in quality of inputs, adopting better cultivation practices and providing post-harvest facilities.

Irrigation

Irrigation facilities are necessary to free agriculture from the uncertainties of the monsoon. Between 2001-01 and 2007-08 the total irrigated area increased by 14.3% from 28.2 lakh hectares to 32.3 lakh hectares. Tube-well irrigation is the most important source accounting for 83.8% of the irrigated area in 2007-08. The share of tube-well has actually increased from 81.9% in 2000-01 to 83.8% in 2007-08 while the share of others, like canals, tanks and wells has either stagnated or decreased.

Year	*Canal Surface MI*	*Tank*	*Tube-well (private and public)*
2000-01	29.22 (1.0)	332.56 (11.8)	2310.06 (81.9)
2001-02	23.25 (0.8)	332.56 (11.8)	2308.71 (82.0)
2002-03	28.69 (1.0)	332.56 (11.1)	2474.77 (82.9)
2003-04	34.88 (10.5)	332.56 (10.5)	2650.38 (83.7)
2004-05	17.56 (0.5)	431.21 (13.3)	2664 (82.2)
2005-06	19.86 (0.6)	332.56 (10.5)	2643.21 (83.4)
2006-07	29.34 (0.9)	332.56 (10.3)	2710.5 (83.6)

Source : Economic Survey of Bihar.

The state government has prepared a road map for agriculture which visualizes creation of additional irrigation capacity through several projects.

Agricultural Inputs

Agricultural development requires supply of adequate and quality inputs such as seeds and fertilizers.

(i) *Seeds*—The Seed Replacement Rate (SRR) in Bihar is among the lowest in India though recent efforts by the state government has improved the situation. Among the kharif crops, the SRR for paddy in 2007-08 was 19% compared to only 12% in 2006-07. In the case of arhar, and moong, the increase in SRR is only marginal. Among rabi crops the SRR for two crops has seen significant improvements between 2006-07 and 2007-08 from 60 to 74% in the case of maize and from 40 to 73% in the case of mustard. For other crops such as wheat and gram the increase in SRR is only moderate.

(ii) *Fertilizer*—The consumption of chemical fertilizers has risen steadily—by 62% over the last 4 years. The consumption per hectare is 155 kgs. Consumption is higher in the rabi season. Urea comprises of half of the fertilizer consumption.

(iii) As regards animal husbandry, cows and buffalos are most important. There is substantive number of goats and poultry but they are in subsistence character for our farmers.

This Table depicts of operational holding size of Bihar. Almost 60% of the total cropped area is under 0.75 hectare as against all India average of 1.41 in 2005. The situation is likely to worsen in coming generations if land inheritance policy is not changed. According to a recent national sample survey, about 42% of our farmers want to opt out of farming for a better option to urban sectors.

To overcome the above quoted problems, selective crop diversification including cultivation of legumes, vegetables and

Distribution of Operational Holdings by Size Class in Bihar

Size Category	*% total number of holding*	*% share in total operated area*
Less than 1 ha	82.9	40.8
1-2 ha	9.6	19.0
2-4 ha	5.7	23.1
4-10 ha	1.7	14.3
Above 10 ha	0.1	2.8
Total	100.0	100.0

Source : Economic Survey, 2006-07.

other high value crop is essential to tackle the problems of soil, weeds, disease and human nutrition.

Crop diversification shows lots of promises in alleviating these problems through fulfilling the basic needs and regulating farm income, with standing weather aberrations, controlling price fluctuating, ensuring balance food supply, conserving natural resources, reducing the chemical fertilizers and pesticide loads and creating employment opportunity.

Diversification in Agriculture, a paradigm shift from traditional crop to another will being desirable change in the existing pattern towards more balanced cropping system to meet ever increasing demand for cereals, pulses, oilseeds, fibres, fodder and grasses, horticulture crops and fuel, etc. for burgeoning population. It aims to improve soil health and agro-ecosystem with socio-economic improvement of the people. In other words, agricultural diversification means producing crops and live stock that are not being produced so far, and production should be larger than that at the current rate. It takes into account higher economic return from different crops and other allied farming activities of the state. The traditional farming should be replaced gradually and the farmer's should show keen interest to diversify their farming to create regular and constant source of income for the small holders, to generate additional employment, to conserve natural resources and to supply larger basket for the consumers.

In the present era, farmers are adopting new schemes under the guidance of technical expert such as use of sprinkler irrigation, drip irrigation, underground pipeline instead of flood irrigation to conserve water resources. They are adopting poultry, goat and piggery farming for additional income, mushroom cultivation and cultivation of medical and aromatic plants, fishery and bee-keeping in their spare time. To increase fertility of soil, they are taught to prepare compost and farm yard manure (FYM), and green manuring. Directorate of cropping system research of Modipuram, Meerut (U.P) has identified around 30 scientific cropping patterns for India. These are rice-wheat, rice-rice, rice-chick pea, rice-mustard, rice-groundnut, rice-sorghum, cotton-sorghum, cotton-chick-pea, maize-wheat, maize-gram, sorghum-groundnut.

Farmers along with soil scientist should adopt crop diversification to enhance the productivity and profitability by conserving soil-nutrients and to conserve water-resources. The soil scientists are educating farmers to prevent formation of hardpan because of puddling, appearance of new bio-types, insect-pests and diseases. For diversification, several options are available which are more productive than rice-wheat system and ensure conservation of resources and safe results. In Bihar, fruits, vegetables, sugarcane, jute, aromatic and medicinal plants should be grown along with traditional rice and wheat system. Thus, region specific crop diversification is one of the potential options for sustainability and profitability of our agricultural production.

ADVANTAGES OF DIVERSIFICATION

The advantage of diversification in agriculture can be summated as follows:

To Increase farm income: In Bihar, 80% of the farmers are having less than 0.75 hectares of land and practice traditional agriculture. To enhance their income they must shift to high value crops such as fruits and vegetables, pulses and oilseeds in their cropping system along with crop production. They should adopt dairying, poultry, live stock, fisheries bee-keeping, Sericulture, cultivation of medicinal and aromatic plants. Luckily for Bihar the soil and weather conditions allow production of sweet smelling rice such as Basmati and sonachur and katarny.

To withstand weather aberrations: The state is visited by floods and droughts regularly and agricultural output is always uncertain. Agriculture must adhere to crop diversification through inter-cropping, mixed cropping, cultivating high lands and low lands to mitigate the risk of crop production to complete failure.

Control price fluctuation : Dependence on monoculture in two seasons increases the viscosity of excess and shortage scenario and hence diversification can make our farmers tolerate ups and downs in price of various farm products and it may ensure economic stability of farming income.

Ensure balanced food supply : The adoption of pulses, oilseeds, livestock, vegetables and horticulture with cropping will ensure the balanced food supply for good health and resource conservation for the future.

Conservation of natural resources: Indiscriminate use of natural resources and their over exploitation have resulted in a series of problems. Crop diversification helps in rotational use of basic resources like land, water, vegetation and climate (air, temperature, rainfall) in such a way that it may serve the objectives of accelerated growth, employment and eco-system protection.

Reduce chemical, fertilizers and pesticide loads: The chemical, fertilizers and pesticide loads in crop production can be reduced substantially by following an efficient crop diversification plan. Crop rotation reduces the menace of weeds, pests and diseases resulting less use of pesticides. Similarly, introduction of legumes in different cropping sequence in inter/mixed cropping improves the soil fertility.

Environmental safety: Continuous cropping of rice, wheat with heavy doses of fertilizers are posing threats to environmental pollution and affecting the soil micro-flora discernibly. Likewise, No. 3-N concentration in drinking water, entrophication of water bodies, methane emission and other greenhouse gases pose serious problems. By diversification, the inclusion of cowpeas as fodder in rice-wheat system and replacement rice with pigeon-pea not only increase the total system productivity and nutrient use efficiency but also help in trapping the No. 3-N occurring in rice-wheat cropping system.

Create employment opportunities: By adopting and shifting to fruits, vegetables, floriculture, bee-keeping, sericulture, fisheries, aromatic and medicinal plants, etc. will ensure employment vistas. Their cultivation is labour-intensive and also requires physical cleaning, grading and packing in routine manner during marketing.

Thus, diversification in agriculture plays a major role in increasing the production of the crop diversification as suggested with greater profitability for the farmers.

CONCLUSION

A holistic system-based approach is needed simultaneously to enhance productivity, profitability, equity and environmental sustainability through synergistically integrating crop, cash crop, horticulture, livestock, fisheries, agro-forestry, watershed-based soil and water management, social capital formation, agro-processing and marketing at the end in order to accelerate agricultural development.

Agriculture and Rural Development in Assam

JAGADISH DEKA

Measures to improve agricultural scenario in the state of Assam and to ameliorate the condition of the poor in its rural areas have been outlined. Production process of crops of Assam like tea, rice, jute, ginger, fruits and vegetables and sericulture of the state needs major revamp and revitalization to modernize its backward economy. Transfer of sizeable population from agriculture to industry, transport and trade has been advocated to develop the rural economy. Rapid industrialization would be necessary.

Assam is situated at the North-East Himalayan sub-region of India. Assam is clearly the gateway to the North-East, neighbouring Myanmar, China, Bangladesh, Nepal and Bhutan making it positively viable for the trade with ASEAN countries. There is a strong potential to be a future international trading hot spot. Business opportunities also exist for information technology enabled services as it has a large pool of educated population.

The major portion of the total population in Assam (88.8%) are living in rural areas. Thus priority must be given to the development of rural areas which requires development of agriculture, implementation of land reforms measures and the development of co-operatives. The economy of the Assam is mainly depending on agriculture, as it plays a major role in the economy of the Assam and as it is the mainstay of large majority of the population of the state. More than 70 percent of the total population in the Assam gets its means of livelihood from agriculture sector. As per census 1991, 64 percent of the total workers in Assam are agricultural workers. In recent years (1990-91) agriculture alone contributed 36 percent to the total state domestic product. According to population census 2001, about 53 percent of the total working force of the state was engaged in agricultural activities. The share of this sector in the Net Demotic Product was 31.19 percent in the recent years. Therefore, it is also called the "backbone of the Economy of Assam". Thus agriculture sector occupies a very important place in the economy of the state and forms the major sources of occupation of the people of the Assam. The soil, topography, rainfall and climate in Assam is quite suitable for cultivation of rice crop which occupies about 70 percent of gross cropped area and more than 90 percent of the total area under foodgrains. Agriculture in Assam is mainly depending on rainfall. On an average the state receives rainfall in different seasons as follows:

Winter (December to February)	90 mm
Summer (March to May)	640 mm
Monsoon (June to September)	1460 mm
Post-monsoon (October to November)	140 mm.

Moreover, most of the farmers use very old and primitive methods of cultivation in agricultural sector and only a very small number of farmers have undertaken commercialized farming in the state. As contrary to the traditional agriculture, relying heavily on indigenous inputs, such as simple wooden plough and other primitive agricultural tools, animals power etc.; the modern agriculture makes use of better techniques of production, chemical fertilizers, improved verities of seeds called HYVs, pesticides, agricultural machines, extensive irrigation, and diesel and electricity as power. These resources or form of inputs are produced outside the agricultural sector. On the other hand, once modernization of agriculture is adopted successfully, the new technologies lead to continuous expansion in the area under crops, total production and productivity. These become possible with the help of "mechanization of agriculture" instead of depending fully on human and bullock power and "commercialization of agriculture" with shift in agricultural production from food crops to cash crops. These types of technological changes in agricultural sectors have been able to generate a very little influence on the agricultural activities and the economy of the rural people of the state. Moreover, though there has been some transformation in the pace of development in agricultural sector due to priorities assigned to it in the successive plans, much more still remains to done to bring the situation compatible with other developed states of the country.

The importance of agriculture in the economy of Assam can be exaggerated. It is the very backbone of her economic system. The place of agriculture in Assam's economy is clearly brought out by the following facts:

- It is considered major source of livelihood for the majority population of Assam.
- Agricultural income contributed to the State of income.
- Agriculture plays an important role and the only major source of food supply to the increasing population of the state.
- Agriculture is the major sources of supply of the raw materials for various small and medium agro-based industries of Assam.
- Agriculture is also an important sources of revenue of the state government.
- It also plays an important role in reducing economic inequalities.

- Agriculture is the source of employment generation of the state of Assam.

Agricultural sector of Assam has also a great commercial importance. Most of the traded items of Assam come from agriculture. Tea, rice, jute, ginger, fruits, vegetables, etc., are some of the most important trade items of Assam. These agricultural products have developed ample scope for the promotion of trade and commerce within and outside the state as well as the country as a whole. Textile products produced by sericulture units have also great commercial importance inside and outside of the State. Thus, Agriculture plays the major role in the economic functioning of the state. It is rightly termed as the backbone of Assam's economy. Development of Assam's

TABLE 1

Sl. No.	*Crops*	*1980-81*	*1990-91*	*2001-02*	*2002-03*	*2003-04*
1.	Rice	76.2	76.6	72.5	74.0	80.5
2.	Wheat	3.4	2.5	2.1	2.0	2.2
3.	Other Cereals	0.8	1.0	0.8	0.8	0.9
4.	Pulses	3.8	3.4	3.3	3.2	3.6
	Total Foodgrains	84.2	83.6	78.7	80.1	87.3
5.	Oil seeds	7.8	9.7	10.4	9.0	9.7
6.	Jute	3.8	2.9	1.9	2.0	2.0
7.	Cotton	0.1	0.1	0.1	0.1	0.1
8.	Mesta	0.4	0.2	0.1	0.1	0.2
9.	Sugarcane	1.6	1.1	0.8	0.7	0.8
10.	Potatoes	1.3	1.7	2.5	2.4	N.A.
11.	Others	0.9	0.8	5.5	5.6	N.A.
	Total Non-foodgrains	15.8	16.4	21.3	19.9	12.7
	Grand Total	100.0	100.0	100.0	100.0	100.0

Sources : Compiled from Statistical Handbook 2004 and previous issue and Economic Survey, Assam, 2005.

economy depends grossly on the development of agricultural sector of the state. Therefore, the government should make every effort to improve the agriculture in the state so that it can help in developing the economy in a faster rate.

Percentage Change in Area under Different Crops in Assam since 1980-81 (in 000 hectares) (see Table 1).

From the Table 2 it can be said that, the farmers of Assam have not been in a position to bring a radical change in the cropping pattern in their cultivation. In other words, crop diversification has not been taken place in a remarkable scale to bring about changes in the crop position in the state. Some minor fluctuations in the percentage share of area under different crops are discernible, which are due to the influence of various factors in this regards.

TABLE 2
Index Number Area, Production and Productivity for Foodgrains, Non-Foodgrains and all Commodities in Assam

Period	*Types of index*	*Foodgrains*	*Non-foodgrains*	*All commodities*
2003-04	Area	110.00	117.11	111.63
	Production	169.77	161.82	165.68
	Productivity	141.69	110.11	124.98
2004-05	Area	103.58	112.34	105.59
	Production	152.42	154.06	153.27
	productivity	135.79	112.56	123.37
2005-06	Area	104.18	106.46	104.71
	Production	155.24	148.27	152.61
	Productivity	135.41	107.24	122.51

Sources : Compiled from Statistical Handbook, 2007, Assam.

Rural Development—(Through Eradication of Poverty)

The development of an economy is fruitless until and unless the rural sector of the economy is improved. Poverty can be defined as a socio-economic phenomenon in which a section of people in the society lives without getting most of their basic necessities of life. This section of people in the society is deprived of the minimum level of living and continues to live at a bare subsistence level, a characteristic features found most frequently in the third world countries, although pockets of poverty exists even in the developed countries of Europe and America.

In the study "poverty of India" Dandekar and Rath estimated the incidence of poverty on the basis of minimum nutritional needs from the NSS Consumer expenditure data of 1960-61 and found that about 48 percent of Assam's population was below the poverty line (BPL). The extent of poverty in Assam aggravated during 1970-71. During that period, the price level in Assam was about 20 percent higher than that of all India level. Thus, cut-off norms of poverty line, which was estimated at Rs. 40 for all India Level (as per Planning Commission's approach documents), correspondingly become Rs. 48 at Assam's prices. Taking Rs. 48 as the cut-off norms of poverty line, the number of persons living below poverty line become 112.65 lakhs (73.67%), out of which 5.53 lakhs (40.14%) lived in urban areas and the rest of 107.12 lakhs (77.38%) lived in the rural areas of the state.

Although poverty has been persisting since the inceptions of Five Year Plans, or even before that, but some serious programmes have been undertaken to eradicate it only in the recent years. Poverty alleviation has been accepted as one of the main objectives of the planning since the Fifth Five Year Plan. It was during the seventies that some anti-poverty programmes, like Small Farmer's Development Agency (SFDA), Marginal Framers and Agricultural Laborers Development Agency, Drought Prone Areas Programme (DPAP) and Food for Work Programme (FWP) were introduced. It was aimed at uplifting the economic conditions of the poverty-ridden farmers and the agricultural labourers through these programmes. Later on, the Integrated Rural Development Programme (IRDP) was lunched in 1980 with an objective of generating self-employment by developing assets through the financial support from the government in the form of subsidy and from the financial institutions in the form of rural credit. In order to provide wage employment to the rural poor, the National Rural Employment Programme (NREP) and

Rural Landless Employment Guarantee Programme (RLEGP) were introduced in Assam along with other states during the Sixth Plan. Later, on April 1, 1989, NREP and RLEGP were merged into a single wage employment programme under Jawaharlal Rodger Yojana (JRY) with a view to generate additional gainful employment for the rural unemployment men and women and to generate productive socio-economic assets so as to improve overall quality of life in the rural areas. Other programme like Training of Rural Youth for Self-employment (TRYSEM), Employment Assurance Scheme (EAS) and Prime Minister's Rojgar Yojana (PMRY) were introduced in 1979, 1993-94 and 1994-95 respectively. In 1995-96 the Prime Minister Integrated Urban Poverty Eradication Programme (PMIUPEP) was launched with a specific objectives of effective achievement of social sector goal, community empowerment, shelter and skill up-gradation as a multi-pronged strategy. Again on 15th August 1995, the National Social Assistance Programme was announced. The Government of Assam has introduced the vocational training programme under "Assam Vikash Yojana" from the year 2008-09 through DICC to every district in the state. The vocational courses offered by the Government are—Computer training, Mobile Repairing, Video Editing, Screen Printing, Scooter/Motorcycle Repairing, Beautician Courses, Tailoring and weaving, etc. Under that programme, each trainee will be provided a stipend of Rs. 500 (five hundred) and selected training institute will get Rs. 1000 (one thousand) against each trainee for the period of one month only. Under this scheme, it is believe that it will help the educated youth to encourage them for their self-employment. On the other hand, from the year 2008-09, Government of India have introduced "Prime Minister Employment Generation Programme" (PMEGP) for the North-East states to develop the educated youths through self-employment and encourage them for entrepreneurship.

CONCLUSION

Agricultural and rural developments are two sides of the same shield. Rural development in Assam can not be thought of without development of agriculture on proper lines. But excessive dependence on agriculture again is the cause of the rural poverty of the state. Without transferring sizeable population from agriculture to industry, transport and trade rural development is simply impossible. A rapid industrialisation particularly the development of medium and small scale industries would be necessary to solve the problem of economic development of the state. This means that we shall have to tackle the problem of unemployment and under-employment in the rural sector through diversification of occupation. There is enough scope for enterprises like crop-cultivation, Horticulture, Sericulture, Animal husbandry, Poultry keeping, Bee-keeping and Fishery can be suitably integrated to make each farm unit viable for both generation of income and employment. This means that concept of planning shall have to be oriented towards the rural sector.

References

Dr. Prasen Daimary, Economic Development of Assam, Published by EBH Publisher, 2008.

D. Bhorali, Economic Development of the North-eastern Region, Published by United Publishers, 1988.

P.K. Dhar, The Economy of Assam, Published by Kalian Publisher, 2001.

Banking Sector Reforms and Agricultural Sector of India

SHIWANI SINGH

Commercial banks as the 'creators' of bank credit influence significantly community's money supply. 'Service Area Approach' was adopted as a new strategy for rural lending by the banks. Microfinance is another approach to 'banking with the poor' in which bank credit is provided to the poor through the SHGs. Banks can play more meaningful role through more concerted efforts towards meeting credit available to the agriculture sector and rural population.

INTRODUCTION

Banking Sector Reforms covers the entire gamut of issues ranging from capital adequacy, bank mergers, and the creation of global sized banks, recasting bank boards and revamping bank legislation. Since independence, the Government of India and the Reserve Bank of India have made concerted efforts to provide the poor with access to credit. The recommendations of Narasimhan Committee, 1991 aimed at transforming the highly regulated and directed public sector banking system into one characterized by openness, competition, prudential and supervisory discipline.

INSTITUTIONAL CREDIT : HISTORICAL PROSPECT

The inadequacy of agricultural credit has had more than a century of tortuous history. The entire finance required by agriculturalists was supplied by money lenders and the cooperatives and other agencies played a negligible role. The Reserve Bank of India since its inception was very active in continuing the attempt to reinvigorate the co-operative credit movement through a variety of initiatives. Besides providing financial accommodation to the co-operative movement RBI built co-operative credit structure one for short-term credit and another for long-term credit. Despite all the efforts the provision of credit through co-operatives remained only 3.3 percent and 0.9 percent from commercial banks. The Report of the All India Rural Credit Survey, 1954 observed agricultural credit fell short of the right quantity, was not of the right type, did not serve the right purpose and often failed to go to the right people. A new act was passed in 1972 giving legal recognition to credit societies and the like the *MacLagan Committee* on Co-operation in India issued a report in 1915 advocating co-operatives which got established in almost all provinces by 1930. Thus giving rise to the 3-tier co-operative credit structure.

REGIONAL RURAL BANKS

Agricultural growth is crucial for alleviating rural poverty. Access to more farmers and appropriate quantity and quality of agricultural credit are crucial for realizing the full potential of agriculture as a profitable activity. Recognizing the crucial role of credit the Government of India promoted regional rural banks through the RRB Act of 1976. Their equity is held by the Central Government Concerned State Government and

Sponsor bank in the proportion of 50 : 15 : 35. There were 196 RRBs with over 14,000 branches by 2003. Their deposits rose from Rs. 4,035 crore in 1990-91 to Rs. 48,346 crore in 2003 while their share in the total agriculture credit at the national level has remained at 8 to 9 percent right from its inception. There were 156 RRBs in profit in 2003, with 97 having wiped-off their losses and built up collective reserves of Rs. 2,300 crore. They have collectively earned a relatively slim margin varying between 0.8 percent and 1.4 percent annually. This is caused by factors such as limited area of operation, narrow client, base, high cost of servicing, numerous small accounts, poor human resources of RRBs and their ineffective boards. The RRB mandate has to continue, even as they need to be restructured into viable financial institutions, retaining their regional character and rural focus.

COMMERCIAL BANKS

Commercial banks as the 'creators' of bank credit influence the community's money supply significantly.

TABLE 1

Flow of Institutional Credit to Agriculture from 1999 to 2005

Institutions	*1999-2000*	*2000-01*	*2001-02*	*2002-03*	*2003-04*	*2004-05*
Co-operative Banks	18,363	20,801	23,604	24,296	26,959	24,471
Share (Percent)	40	39	38	34	31	28
Regional Rural Banks	3,172	4,219	4,854	5,467	7,581	9,176
Share (Percent)	7	8	8	8	9	11
Commercial Banks	24,733	27,807	33,587	41,047	52,441	52,038
Share (Percent)	53	53	54	58	60	61
Total	46,268	52,827	62,045	70,810	86,981	85,686
Percent Increase	26	14	17	14	22	32.5

Source : NABARD.

Institutional Structure Agricultural and Rural Credit in India

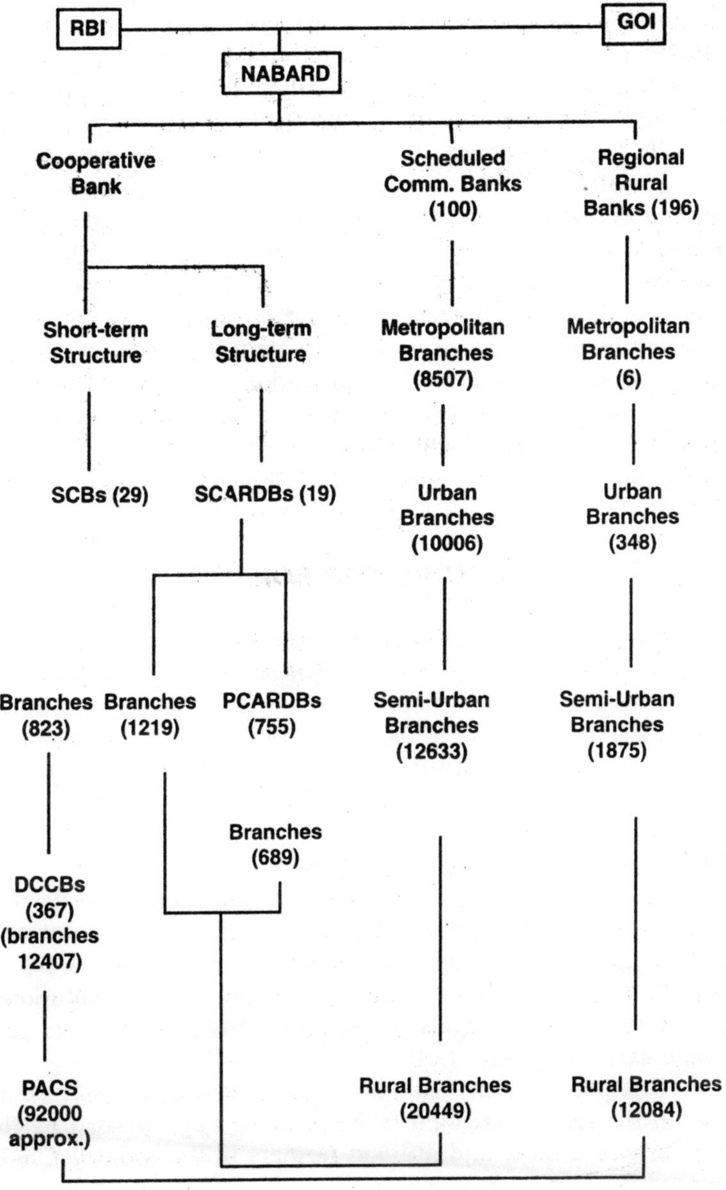

Commercial banks urged a well defined role in delivering credit for agriculture in specialized areas. The social control and the subsequent nationalization of major Commercial banks in 1969 and 1980 as a catalyst in providing momentum to the efforts of leveraging the commercial banking system for extending agricultural credit. The outreach of the banks was enlarged considerably within a relatively short period of time. Despite all these efforts, the flow of credit to the agricultural sector failed to exhibit any appreciable improvement due mainly to the fact that commercial banks were not tuned to the needs and requirements of the small and marginal farmers. *Shri M. Narasimhan* in 1991 provided the blue print for carrying out overall financial sector reforms during the 1990s which resulted in setting up of various committees, working groups, task forces to look into their operations such as "The High Level Committee on Agricultural Credit through Commercial Banks" (R.V. Gupta, 1998). 'Task Force to Study the Functions of Cooperative Credit System and to Suggest Measures for its Strengthening" (Jagdish Kapoor, 1999).

DEPOSITORS AND BORROWERS

Given chart clearly emphasizes the agricultural credit system as a product of both evolution and intervention and symbolizes the systems response to the stimuli from continuing dissatisfaction with credit delivery. In India, a 'Supply Leading Approach' to the institutional development for agricultural credit has been followed which led to its failure.

Shortcomings of Institutional Credit

The share of various sources in rural credit reveals that hold of money lenders has bounced back to 70 percent and PSU banks and co-operative banks have trailed behind at merely 19 percent. This shows the failure of the institutional credit to meet the needs of farmers, landless labourers and wage earners in rural India.

Briefing in short, the shortcoming of institutional credit lies in the vastly extended facilities being appropriated by the top 30% of middle and affluent farmers in the country. Credit

TABLE 2
Share of Different Agencies in Rural Credit, 2004
Agency Share in Total Credit (%)

Agency	*Share in Total Credit (%)*
Money lenders	70
Public Sector Banks	10
Co-operative Banks and Societies	9
Government Loans	1
Self Help Groups (SHGs)	1
Others	9
Total	100

Source : Table 2.
Hindustan Times—IIEF Study (2004).

facilities created for marginal and small farmers and economically backward classes do not reach the target groups but are misappropriated by affluent farmers through collusion with Government Officials and Politicians. Little is being done for the weakest of the rural population, bonded labourers, landless agricultural labourers, tribals, scheduled castes and tribes. They continue to be cruelly exploited by the high class money lenders and landlords. This has led to extensive suicides by farmers in all over the country, especially in Andhra Pradesh and Karnataka.

Service Area Approach : New Strategy for Rural Lending

A new strategy for rural lending 'Service Area Approach' was adopted under which each semi-urban and rural branch of commercial bank was assigned a specific area comprising of a cluster of villages within which it would operate, adopting a planned approach for its economic growth. The rationale of this approach was to avoid duplication of efforts and scattered lending over wider areas. The compactness in the area of operation will make it easy for the clientele approach of the bank for credit.

However problems occurred while implementing the SAA regarding Allocation of Villages, Under-Utilization of Bank Staff, Tribal and Hilly areas and Organizational problems.

The SAA strategy can succeed only if (a) a time-bound programme for its success was worked out by all banks, with full support of RBI and the Government of India, and (b) banks were compelled to switch over to the new approach completely instead of granting partial or full freedom.

Micro Finance

Micro finance is a novel approach to 'banking with the poor' in which bank credit is extended to the poor through Self Helf Groups (SHGs), Non-Government Organizations (NGOs), Credit Unions, etc. Micro credit attempts to combine lower transaction costs and high degree of repayment. This is essentially because of the involvement of potential beneficiaries of rural credit in the credit-delivery system. The SHG bank linkage programme, introduced and encouraged by NABARD is now being implemented vigorously by more than 30,000 branches of Commercial Banks, RRBs and Cooperative banks in over 520 districts in 30 states and union territories.

TABLE 3
SHG Bank Linkage : Cumulative Progress

As on March 31	*No. of SHGs (Cumulative)*	*No. of SHGs Financed by banks*	*Bank Loans disbursed (Cumulative Rs. Crore)*
1999	33,000	33,000	57
2001	2,63,830	1,49,000	480
2003	7,17,360	2,55,000	2,050
2004	10,79,090	3,61,730	3,900

Source : RBI—Trend and Progress of Banking, 2003-04.

Micro Finance initiatives have shown that banking with the poor is a viable proposition. Micro credit has been hailed as the best method of creating additional employment and removing poverty. NABARD has been playing a catalytic role in terms of promotional support to NGOs and also in nurturing quality SHGs.

Despite significant progress of Micro-finance nearly 70 percent of poor families are yet to be covered. Only in four States A.P., T.N., Karnataka and U.P., 30% of SHGs were linked to bank credit and 80% of bank loans. Most states in the Country have not yet encouraged the organization and promotion of SHG-bank credit link.

Ninth Plan

The focus of the Ninth Plan was on 'Growth with Social Justice and Equality'. The Ninth Plan focused on accelerated growth recognizing a special role for agriculture for its poverty reducing and employment generating efforts. The institutional credit flow to agriculture during the 8th Plan (1997-2002) was Rs. 2,30,000 crores for the 5 year period, the average credit flow per annum was Rs. 46,000 crores.

Tenth Plan

The Tenth Plan (2002-07) however projected a substantial increase in institutional credit flow to agricultural sector to the tune of Rs. 7,36,600 crores and the annual average credit flow would be Rs. 1,49,120 crores.

AGRO-DIVERSIFICATION AND FOOD PROCESSING

Rising incomes, Urbanization and Globalization have opened new ground for diversification of agriculture. India is the worlds second largest producer of food. The food processing industry ranks fifth in size in the country and contributes over six percent to GDP. It accounts for 13 percent of the country's exports and 6 percent of the total industrial investment.

India fares poorly in terms of value addition to its raw produce in food processing, accounting for only seven percent of raw produce. The industry is dominated by small scale and unorganized sectors with inadequate access to modern technology and network.

A National Food Processing Policy was formulated on January 3, 2005. Development and promotion of area specific Agro Food Parks for processing the products grown in those localities, creation of units processing a cluster of trans-seasonal produce, harmonization of laws and standards and administering them through a single authority, rationalization of task structures, fiscal incentives and promotion of both direct and foreign investments.

In context of Bihar, Darbhanga faces acute flood problems and water logging. So Makhana production should be centralized over there. Adjoining areas of Patna should concentrate on vegetables production. Muzaffarpur should specialize in lichi production and land with lot of fertility on multiple cropping. States which have concentrated on agro-diversification have developed.

To conclude with :

> Indian agriculture faces both opportunities and challenges with liberalization of domestic and global markets. There is a need to develop a new strategy for the agriculture sector. There are several gaps in the agricultural credit system like inadequate provision of credit to small and marginal farmers, paucity of medium and long-term lending and limited deposit mobilization and heavy dependence on borrowed funds by major agricultural credit purveyors.

To conclude with, a simple paper work could be devised for execution by the beneficiary and banks can take the help of model projects on numerous agri-business activities keeping in view the borrower's requirements and profile. A regular complaint against bank is that they don't sanction more loans even when the demand is genuine and when the borrower has run into a fit of trouble due to seasonality of the cash flows. This attitude on the part of the banks has led to the failure of many agri-business projects despite having god prospects. To offset, banks should workout 'flexible credit line', higher time limit of peak credit requirements and lower limits.

There could be initial teething troubles but all these possibilities should not inhibit exploring newer ways of advancing loans.

References

Ballad, G.S. (1994), Economic Liberalization and Indian Agriculture. Institute for Studies in Industrial Development, New Delhi.

Gupta, K.R. (1980), Issues in Indian Agriculture, Atlantic Publishers & Distributors.

Dot and Sandarac, R. (2005), Indian Economy.

Singh, Karat (2002), Cooperative, Emerging Challenges and Coping Strategies, *Kurukshetra*, Vol. 51, No. 1, Nov.

Agarwal, A.N. (1980), Indian Agriculture Vikas Publishing House Pvt. Ltd.

Rao, Hanumantha, C.H., July (1990), Government of India Report of Expert Committee on Review of Methodology for the Cast of Crop Production Committee, Ministry of Agriculture, New Delhi.

NABARD (2005), Annual Report.

RBI December (2004), Bulletin.

Economic Survey (2004-05), Annual Report.

16

Social and Political Dividends from NREGA

Rajesh Kumar Pandey

The writer pinpoints social and political dividends from MGNREGA and makes Bhilwara (Rajasthan) Social Audit Report as a pointer towards the importance and relevance of this scheme in socio-economic development of rural areas. This novel scheme has benefited poor people of this region and increased their bargaining power, thus improving their lives. In the final analysis, what makes any NREGA social audit worth all the pain and effort is the awareness it creates among poor beneficiaries.

It is a measure of the hard labour that awaits NREGA activists in other States that a social audit conducted under blazing lights, and with so much official support, such as the one in Bhilwara in Rajasthan, could run into so many roadblocks. Virtually all of the Rajasthan Government (in September) Rajasthan became the second Government after

Andhra Pradesh to set-up a Directorate of Social Audit was at the disposal of the Bhilwara audit team which also had the full backing of C.P. Joshi, Union Minister for Rural Development, elected to Parliament from Bhilwara.

Mazdoor Kisan Shakti Sanghatan activists Aruna Roy and Nikhil Dey said they chose Bhilwara for the audit exercise because they wanted to see if the Minister could face up to an NREGA audit in his constituency; after all, there was no knowing what the audit would reveal. Yet a question arises : Would Mr. Joshi have shown interest in the Bhilwara audit had he not been its MP? Secondly, what happens to NREGA work in States that lack men and women of the calibre and commitment of Ms. Roy, Mr. Dey and other MKSS activists? Can a programme's success be made dependent on a few individuals? What will happen when the government shows no interest which is the case in most States?

Mr. Dey argued that the MKSS social audit had visibly and strongly demonstrated the positive effects of civil society-government collaboration. The unity of purpose shown in Bhilwara by social auditors, government, media and the office of the Comptroller and Auditor-General was replicable in other States. Indeed, if Minister Joshi took the trouble to watch over the audit in his constituency, it only showed that there was huge political capital to be made from pushing NREGA.

Through the audit the Bhilwara team was inundated by calls from people impressed by its work in the district. And a day after the gargantuan exercise wound up, Congress MP from Alwar, Jitendra Singh, turned up in Bhilwara asking that the MKSS organize in NREGA audit in his constituency.

The Rajasthan experiment is itself based on the Andhra Pradesh government's success while conducting NREGA audits. The A.P. government was the first to institutionalize social audit by means of a Social Audit Directorate. Since then the state government has gone a further step with a committed budget for social auditing and provisions to host audit results on its NREGA website.

At a meeting the Bhilwara audit team had with Rajasthan government officials and other experts, Sowmya Kidambi, an MKSS activist deputed to work with the A.P. government, strongly advocated bringing audit results into the public domain via computerization, arguing that this had greatly increased transparency in Andhra Pradesh.

In the final analysis, what makes any NREGA social audit worth all the pain and effort is the awareness it creates among poor beneficiaries, who slowly but surely learn to hold the programme's managers to account. A quick survey by *The Hindu* in a cross-section of Bhilwara's villages showed that the village people had fully internalized their rights and entitlements. But because of the patriarchal, dominating nature of the panchayat set-up, most of them lacked the courage to speak up. This situation would gradually change if accountability was built into the system.

Accountability could also impact social evils like untouchability, which the audit team found as widely prevalent in NREGA sites. In many panchayats, Scheduled Caste and Scheduled Tribe NREGA beneficiaries were given separate utensils and prevented from accessing common resources.

The social and economic spin-offs from even partial implementation of NREGA were only too evident in Bhilwara, NREGA beneficiaries were unanimous that the programme had improved their lives. For years the Bhil tribal community in Malanas in Gram Panchayat Jindras had battled hunger and poverty, traveling out of the State in search of work. Today, most Bhil wives are employed under NREGA, bringing stability and assured incomes to families that were until recently desperately poor. NREGA also made valuable contributions in times of drought which was the case in Rajasthan this year. Though poor, few families in Bhilwara seemed on the brink of starvation. Besides, as many villagers pointed out, the minimum wage of Rs. 100 a day under the NREGA had increased wage levels across the private sector, benefiting both families that could not avail NREGA work and families that had completed the NREGA quota of 100 work days per family. As MKSS activist Shanker Singh remarked : "NREGA has greatly increased the bargaining power of poor people. They are no longer willing to work cheap".

POVERTY REDUCTION POTENTIAL

One has only to look at the funds the NREGA has placed in the hands of local administrators to understand its poverty reduction potential. Bhilwara alone drew Rs. 330 crore from the NREGA budget in 2009-10. Assuming the programme is properly utilized, NREGA can change the complexion of poor India.

Yet the Bhilwara social audit also revealed that funds can easily get into the wrong hands. Indeed, even as the MKSS team deservedly takes credit for the massive Bhilwara social audit, it must know that it can hardly rest on its laurels. On the concluding day of the audit, a Rajasthan Minister suggested that while sarpanchs caught with their hands in the deal must be made to refund the misappropriated funds, they ought not to be punished. This is exactly what the sarpanchs demanded at the various *jan sunwais* (public hearings). If this point was conceded, the social audit would lose its purpose, irreversibly damaging NREGA. Other dangers include threatened official amendments to a job programme hailed far and wide as progressive and empowering.

Even with all these ifs and buts, the Bhilwara exercise is worth emulating by other States. For as the audit and the responses to it showed, there is political dividend to be had from investing in NREGA. If politicians can use NREGA to win elections that will surely be the job guarantee programme's best guarantee for survival.

Which politician would not like that?

SECTION C

Inclusive Growth Strategy and Holistic Development

Microfinance : A Tool for Inclusive Growth

DINESHWAR KUMAR SINGH AND
BAKSHI AMIT KUMAR SINHA

Lack of access to financial services represents the most serious impediment in capacitating the rural households to attain their full income potential and to improve their livelihoods. Rangarajan Committee observed that 51% of farmer households are financially excluded from both formal and informal sources and 73% of farmer households do not have access to formal sources of credit. The poverty lending approach is unsustainable on large scale. Recently, banks have come up with strategies to reach the excluded through Banking Correspondents (BC) and Banking Facilitators (BF). The inclusive growth model takes a long-term perspective, as the focus is on productive employment rather than on direct income redistribution. The paper focuses on the financial inclusion and the role of SHGs to extend growth process within the poverty arena.

1. INTRODUCTION

Globalization and present growth trajectory brought about new challenges of widening inter-personal and inter-regional disparities with greater rural-urban divide in India. The United Nations declared 2005 as the International Year of the micro-credit to alleviate the poverty. In order to address these challenges and achieve balanced development, Financial Inclusion[1] (FI) and Self Help Groups (SHGs)[2] are emerging as viable strong alternatives, which could be possible only through the use of microfinancing. The Indian economy has been growing at a steady rate of 8.5% to 9% during the quinquennial 2006-07. The growth potential in the primary sector is enormous. Limited access to financial assistance from services such as savings, loan, remittances and insurance services by the vast majority of the rural population and unorganised sector is acting as a constraint to the growth impetus. Easy accesses to affordable financial services especially credit and insurance, widen livelihood opportunities and empower the poor to take charge of their lives. Such empowerment brings social and political stability. Apart from these benefits, Financial Inclusion imparts formal identity, provide better access to the payment system and also to saving safety net like deposit insurance. Hence, microfinance can play a major role for economic, social and cultural development.

This paper attempts to discuss implications of microfinance to achieve inclusive growth. This presents the model of inclusive growth which may be attained with the help of the microfinance because the growth does not touch the poor and the rural people. It believes that financial services are the key tools for enabling the low-income Bharat to allocate resources most productively, allowing them to play an active role in country's growth. Despite many steps taken to improve financial access for more people during the last five decades, (like, the Nationalisation of the Commercial Bank System, the introduction of Local Area Banks, Regional Rural Banks and Cooperative Banks) and evidence that financial access can lead to sharp reduction in poverty, the majority of the population remains even without minimum access to financial services and remain financially excluded.

In our view, lack of access to financial services represents the most serious impediment in capacitating the rural households to attain their full income potential and to improve livelihood. Lack of financial access for low-income households sharply reduces their ability to invest in skill building and education to make optimal occupational choices and to benefit from and contribute to the national growth process.

2. APPROACHES OF THE PAPER

This paper adopts two approaches to extend the growth to all the sectors and all regions particularly, to the poor and low-income people. The first approach is the *poverty lending approach* which primarily focuses on reducing poverty through credit that are funded by donors and patrons, government and other concessional dispensations. The other is however, the *financial system approach* which focuses on commercial financial intermediation for the active and willing poor who offer themselves for easy access to credit at a reasonable and affordable cost.

However, it has to be noted that the primary goal of both the poverty lending approach and the financial system approach is providing financial services to the people, who are under the poverty ring.

I. What is Microfinance? : Booster of the Economy

Microfinance can act as a booster of the economy by strengthening economically, and socially deprived people. The Reserve Bank of India[3] has defined microfinance as provision of thrift credit and other financial services and products in very small amount to the poor in rural, semi-rural and urban areas for enabling them to raise their income levels and improve their living standard. Microfinance institutions are those that provide these facilities. Micro credit is one way of reaching the poor and has already demonstrated its effectiveness. A major concern of microfinance is to increase penetrative outreach so that credit can be institutionalised and a large number of people can benefit through improved access to credit for enabling them to come out of the poverty net.

DIAGRAM 1

Entity Relational Diagram : Role of Group Corps

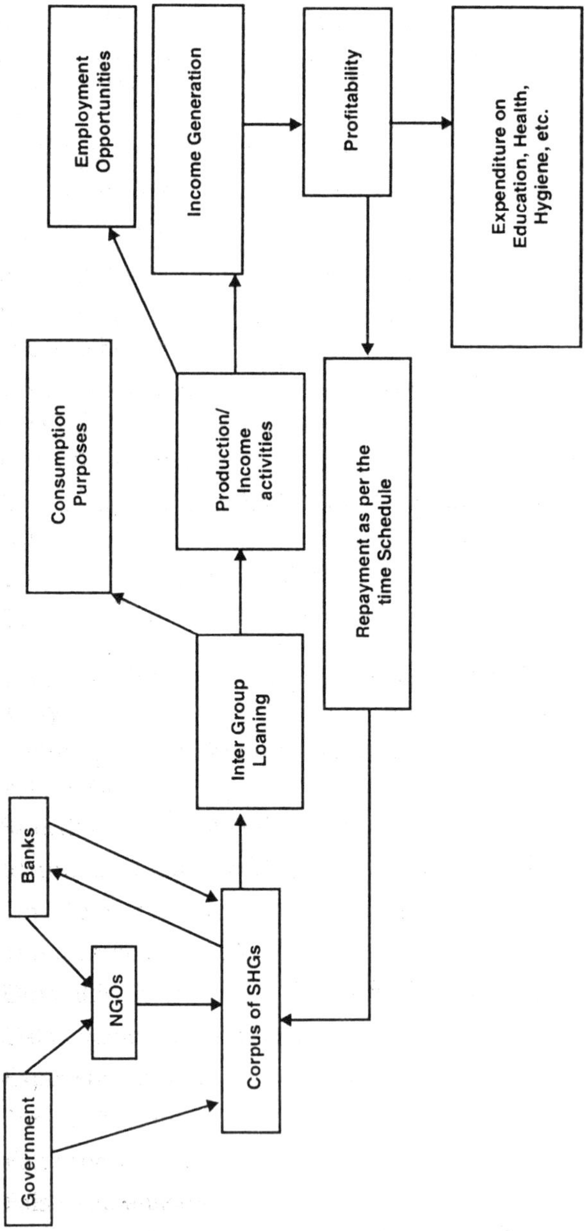

Government

NGOs

Banks

Corpus of SHGs

Inter Group Loaning

Consumption Purposes

Production/ Income activities

Employment Opportunities

Income Generation

Profitability

Expenditure on Education, Health, Hygiene, etc.

Repayment as per the time Schedule

2. Microfinance Institutions : The Source of Microfinance

Sustainable Microfinance is carried out by institutions that deliver financial services to the economically active poor at interest rate that enable the institution to cover all costs and risks and generate a profit. Such institutions include banks, credit cooperatives and other Non-Banking Financial Companies (NBFC's). Microfinance institutions are different from informal commercial money lenders who lend money for profit. In subsidized formal microfinance a regulated institution such as a nationalised bank, government or donor provide funds to borrowers at subsidized interest rates as also from unregulated institutions like NGOs which lend money to the borrowers obtained from the subsidized donor or government.

3. Interest Rates : Encouragement to Investment

Microfinance institutions charge higher rate of interest than the normal lending rate of commercial banks. The reason is that microfinance institutions are labour-intensive. Still the interest rates are higher than the bank rates; it is very alluring to poor borrowers because the interest rate is only a small fraction of the rate normally charged by commercial money lenders.

TABLE 1

An Overview of the Interest Rate being Charged by Various Segments

Sector/Segment/Scheme	*Rate of Interest*
NABARD to Banks (Refinancing Scheme)	6.5% for loans up to Rs. 25000 and 6.75% for above
Banks to SHGs	10 to 12%
Banks to VA/Self Help Promotion Institution (SHPI)	9 to 10%
Voluntary Agency (VA)/SHPI to SHGs	A maximum of 2 to 3% spread over the Bank's lending rate
SHGs to members	As decided by the SHGs

Source : V.S. Somanth, "Microfinance Redefining the Future", p. 114.

4. Services of Microfinance Institutions : Provide Friendly Credit and Deposit Facilities

Microfinance institutions provide both saving and credit services to the poor. The credit is made available to the poor borrowers who have the ability and willingness to repay a small loan at the interest rate required for institutional self-sufficiency. The savings are designed to the demand of low income households, the opening balances are low and a minimum balance is required to be maintained.

3. MICROFINANCE : INCLUSIVE GROWTH MODEL

This paper presents as to how microfinance can and shall redefine the future of the Indian economy and will go a long way in alleviating poverty and also create a win-win situation for all the players in the microfinance viz., the poor, borrowers, the banks, the NGOs, the federations, the SHGs and the country's economy as a whole. The idea of this model is when we make opportunity for the deprived and marginalized people to accelerate their growth then the growth automatically becomes inclusive because the rest of the population is already in the growth process.

This paper introduces two approaches for this model which are poverty lending approach and financial system approach which are portrayed through the microfinance:

"Microfinance is one of the practice development strategies and approaches that should be implemented and supported to attain the bold ambition of world poverty by half". Investing in development, UN Millennium Project.

1. Poverty Lending Approach : Encourage to Breaking the Poverty Cycle

Although India has been one of the fastest growing economies in the world in the last two and half decades, its per capita income in purchasing power parity term still lies among the bottom third countries. Low per capita domestic product implies low average absolute productivity, low productivity, in turn, is caused by inadequacy or total lack of access to human and physical capital. This paper would, therefore, avail this opportunity to reflect on the role of microfinance in the

Diagram 2
Flow Chart of the Growth Model

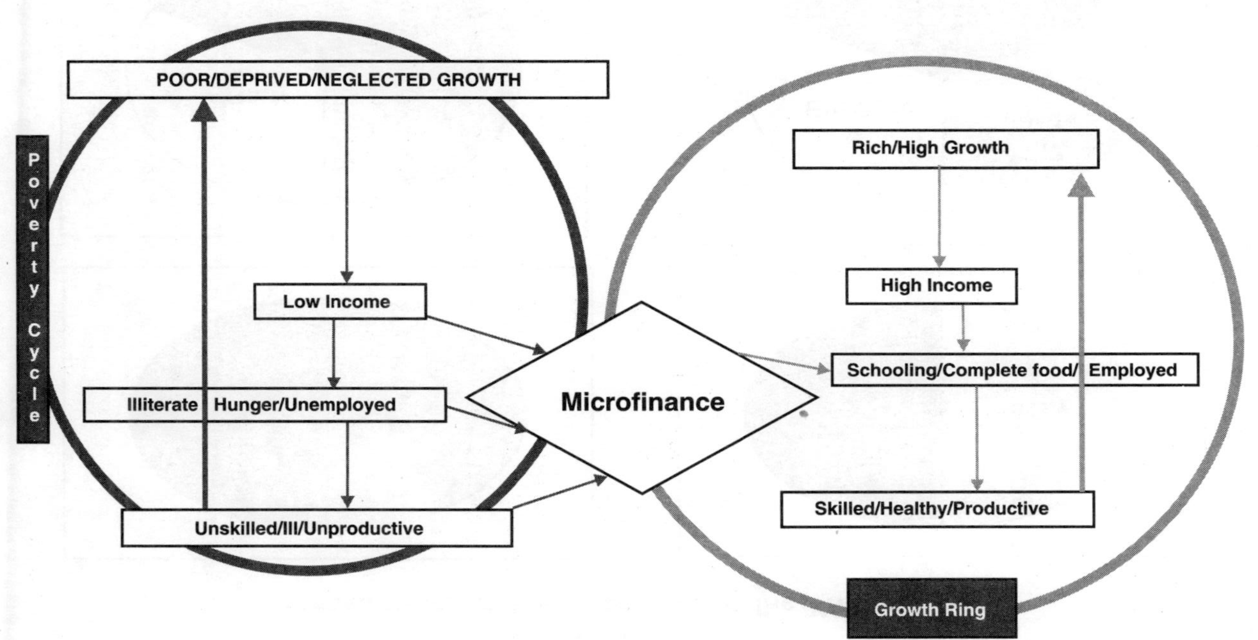

GRAPH 1

Characteristics of the Client are in the Whole World

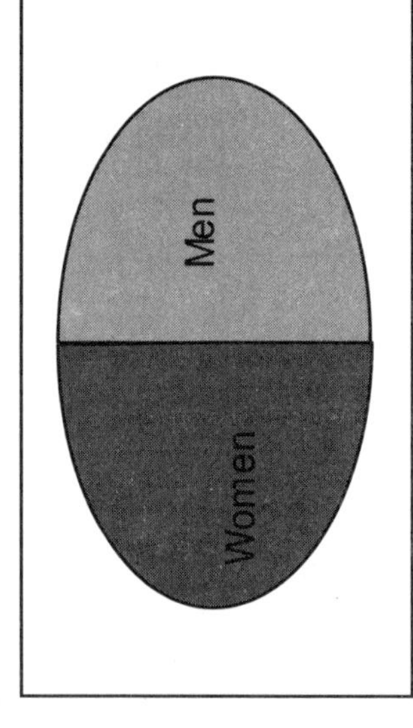

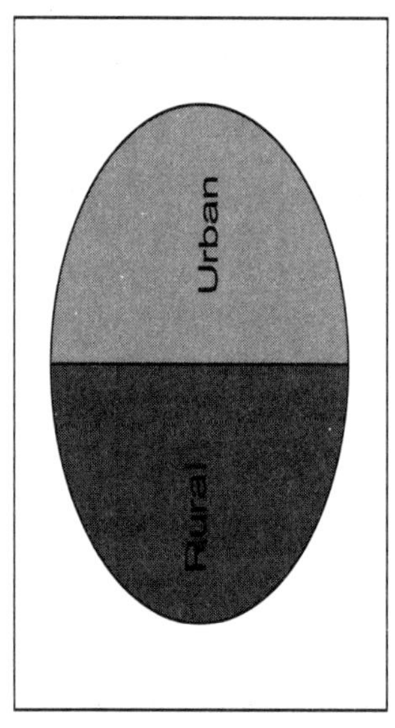

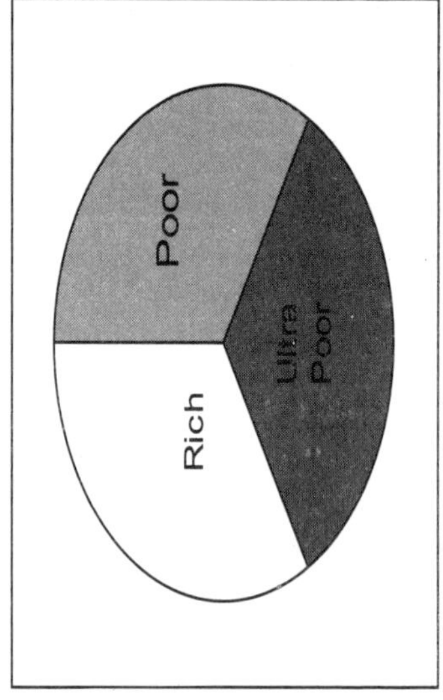

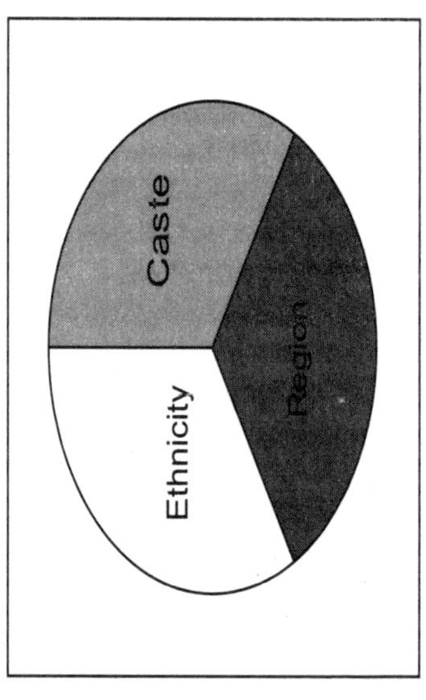

alleviation and eradication of poverty and flag certain problems for consideration in the context of theme of the 'inclusive growth'.

This approach is mostly concentrated to strengthen those people who are outside the growth ring. Microfinance matters a lot in a poor economy because it enhances the self-esteem and self-confidence of poor households by helping them to realise their dreams as also improve, expand and diversify their micro-enterprise, obtain a larger income and consequent higher return on investment, to learn more about effective and better management controls, to deposit the excess liquidity in safe and sound investment, to move away from the exploitation of local money lenders and to conduct their business and life with dignity and pride. Once the quality of life of the poor improves; there is a marked improvement in their health, housing and other standards of infrastructural living. Children are sent to schools. Medical care is provided to the elders at home. There is no child labour and there is a paradigm shift in their improved living conditions. They create larger and sustainable employment opportunities. The Government is benefited because it need not subsidise the credit programmes, and the resultant savings can be used for direct poverty alleviation programme for the poorest of the poor, and the economies of the country benefit from increased production. Last but not the least, large scale sustainable microfinance help create an enabling environment for the growth of political participation and democracy.

I. Government Driven Schemes/Programmes : Lending to Poor Approach

Government of India had initiated Integrated Rural Development Programme and Development of Women and Children in Rural Areas (DWCRA) for reaching the poor with credit facilities. Later, it was found that these programmes failed to reach the needy due to various reasons. Therefore, the government launched some other development programmes, viz. RMK, PMEGP, SJSRY, SGSY, etc.

(a) Rashtriya Mahila Kosh (RMK)

The National Credit Fund for women was set-up on 30th

March, 1993 with the corpus fund of Rs. 31 crore with the major objective of meeting the credit need of poor women, particularly in the informal sector. RMK provides short-term loan (15 months for up to Rs. 4000 per borrower) and medium-term loan (2-5 years for up to Rs. 6000 per borrower).

TABLE 2

Sanctioned and Disbursed Loan, No. of NGOs, No. of SHGs and Benefited Women in India

Year	*Loan Sanctioned (Rs. Lakh)*	*Loan Disbursed (Rs. Lakh)*	*No. of NGOs/ Others*	*No. of SHGs*	*No. of Women Beneficiaries*
Up to 2006-07	18714.84	14987.72	1244	55434	549641

(b) *Pradhan Mantri Rojgar Yojana (PMRY)*

This programme was first introduced on October, 1993 to provide sustainable self-employment opportunities to 1 million educated unemployed youth in the country during the 8th Plan period. Rs. 1 lakh for business sector and Rs. 2 lakh for other activities are provided by bank for all economically viable activities under this scheme.

(c) *National Rural Employment Guarantee Act, 2005 (NREGA)*

Guarantees 100 days of employment in a financial year to any rural household whose adult members are willing to do unskilled manual work. The Act has come into force with effect from February 2006 in 200 districts initially and later on extended to all the rural districts of India from the financial year 2008-09. It involves rural participatory planning and implementation of the scheme through (i) proactive role of Gram Sabha, (ii) rigorous and continuous monitoring by way of social audit, and (iii) involvement of ordinary people at the grass-roots level. It addresses (i) chronic poverty, (ii) drought, (iii) deforestation, (iv) soil erosion, etc. It also aims at (i) generating productive assets, (ii) protecting the environment, and (iii) empowering rural women, and (iv) arresting rural-urban migration.

GRAPH 2

Target and Achievement under the PMRY Scheme in Bihar : 2001-02 to 2007-08

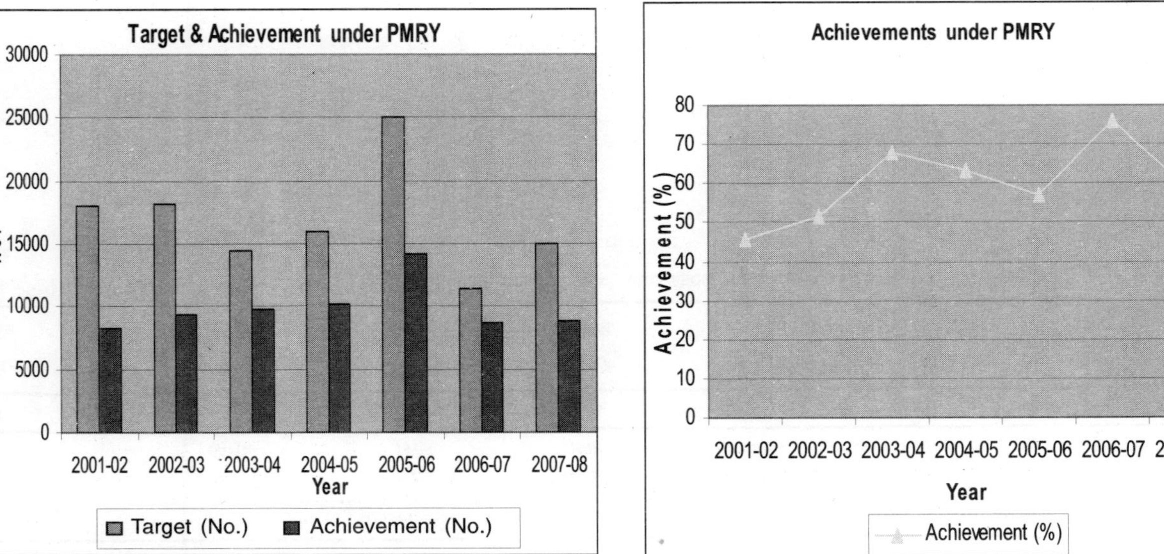

TABLE 3

Overview of NREGA : 2009-10

States	*No. of Households (in lakh)*			*Percentage of Households (in %)*		
	Issued Job cards	*Demanded Jobs*	*Provided Jobs*	*Demanded Job/ Issued Job Cards*	*Provided Job/ Issued Job Cards*	*Provided Job/ Demanded Job*
(1)	(2)	(3)	(4)	(5)	(6)	(7)
Bihar	121.65	30.28	30.27	24.89	24.89	99.99
India	1089.51	436.63	433.98	40.08	39.83	99.39

Source : 'http://nrega.nic.in/netnrega/mpr_ht/nregampr.aspx', accessed on 4th Jan., 2010 on 12:34.

(d) Prime Minister's Employment Generation Programme (PMEGP)

Prime Minister's Employment Generation Programme (PMEGP) is a credit linked subsidy programme of Government of India. It has been introduced by merging the two schemes, namely, Prime Minister's Rojgar Yojana (PMRY) and Rural Employment Generation Programme (REGP). The scheme was launched on 15th August, 2008.

TABLE 4
Target and Achievement under PMEGP

Year	*Target (No.)*	*Achievement (No.)*
2008-09	5367	—
2009-10 up to Sept., 2009	5367	125

Source : State Level Bankers' Committee.

(e) Swarnjayanti Grameen Swarojgar Yojana (SGSY)

A new programme was introduced which includes all aspects of self-employment such as organizing the poor to form SHG, training loans, technologies, basic infrastructure and marketing, etc. in 1999, (SGSY). The prime objective of this scheme is to ensure uplifting the beneficiaries above the poverty line through the sustainable growth in their income. While physical targets of SHGs were over-achieved in 2006-07 and 2007-08, it was below in 2008-09.

TABLE 5
Target and Achievement Under SGSY (SHGs)

Performance	*2006-07*	*2007-08*	*2008-09*	*2009-10 Up to Sept. 2009*
Target (Nos.)	9726	15040	19626	22836
Achievement (Nos.)	12230	18499	17463	10308
Achievement (%)	126	123	88.98	45.14

Source : State Level Bankers' Committee.

TABLE 6
Summary of the Physical and Financial Performance under SGSY in Bihar

	2006-07		2007-08		2008-09		2009-10 Upto Sept. 2009	
	No.	Amount (Rs. Crore)	No.	Amount (Rs. Crore)	No.	Amount (Rs. Crore)	No.	Amount (Rs. Crore)
(1)	(2)	(3)	(4)	(5)	(6)	(7)	(8)	(9)
Target	137805	354.41	188000	469.99	196260	490.78	228360	570.85
Proposal Received	119927	—	85460	—	75015	—	26198	—
Proposal Sanctioned	104893	281.95	79951	212.1	69027	183.4	25241	109.38
Proposal Disbursed	101965	231.98	76720	187.87	68156	170.16	24874	105.51
Achievement in % (Achievement/Target)	79.55	79.55	42.53	45.32	35.17	37.37	11.05	19.16
Achievement in % (Disbursement/Target)	74	65.46	40.81	40.14	34.73	34.67	10.89	18.48
Proposal Returned/Rejected	13897	—	5509	—	4991	—	304	—
Proposal pending for Disbursement	1137	—	3231	—	997	—	653	—

Source : State Level Bankers' Committee.

(f) Swarnjayanti Shahari Rojgar Yojna (SJSRY)

Is a unified Centrally Sponsored Scheme on a basis of 75:25 between the centre and state launched a fresh in lieu of the erstwhile Urban Poverty Alleviation Programmes viz., Nehru Rojgar Yojana (NRY), Prime Minister's Integrated Urban Poverty Eradication Programme (PMIUPEP) and Urban Basic Services for the Poor (UBSP). This scheme introduced in 1997 seeks to provide gainful employment to the Urban Poor through encouraging setting up of self-employment ventures or provision for wage employment.

TABLE 7

Summary of the Physical and Financial Performance under SJSRY in Bihar

	2009-10 Upto Sept. 2009	
	No.	*Amount (Rs. Crore)*
Target	—	—
Proposal Received	550	—
Proposal Sanctioned	531	2.39
Proposal Disbursed	531	2.39
Achievement in % (Achievement/Target)	—	—
Achievement in % (Achievement/Target)	—	—
Proposal Returned/Rejected	0	—
Proposal pending for Disbursement	19	—

Source : State Level Bankers' Committee.

2. Financial System Approach : Shifting of 'Goalpost'

The inclusive growth model takes a long-term perspective, as the focus is on productive employment rather than on direct income redistribution, as a means of increasing incomes for excluded group. So, it is commendable that, of late, the policy-makers and banking institutions have to come forward to address the issue of banking exclusion. It is estimated that globally over the two billion people are excluded from access to financial services, of which one-third is in India. This approach focuses on the financial inclusion and role of the SHGs to extend growth process within the poverty arena.

DIAGRAM 3

The Best Indicator of the Impact of the Microfinance is a Change in Clients' Finance

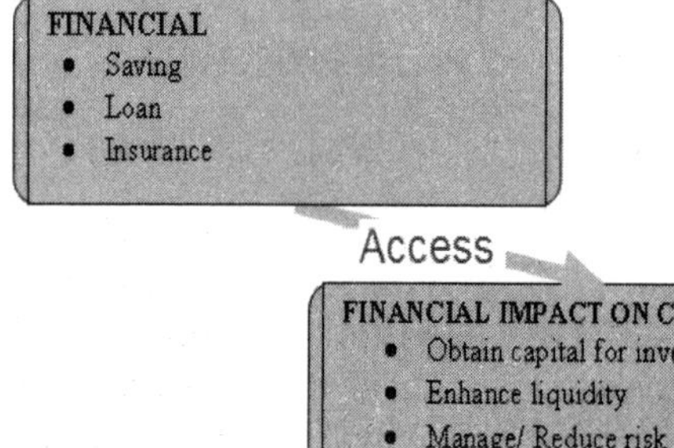

The committee on financial inclusion (Rangarajan Committee) observed that in India, 51% of farmer households are financially excluded from both formal and informal sources and 73% of farmer households do not have access to formal sources of credit. To be specific, those excluded are marginal farmers who happen to be women who are further excluded right from the first stage of perception.

Financial inclusion is a complex issue and not so simple. There are issues in outreach. When the excluded section approaches the formal financial institutions they are confronted with problems of accessibility, timeliness, inadequacy of credit. For one reason or other, they are compelled to approach the informal agencies to meet their credit demands as is known to all. The process of Financial Inclusion is shown through the flow diagram:

DIAGRAM 4

Concept of Financial Inclusion

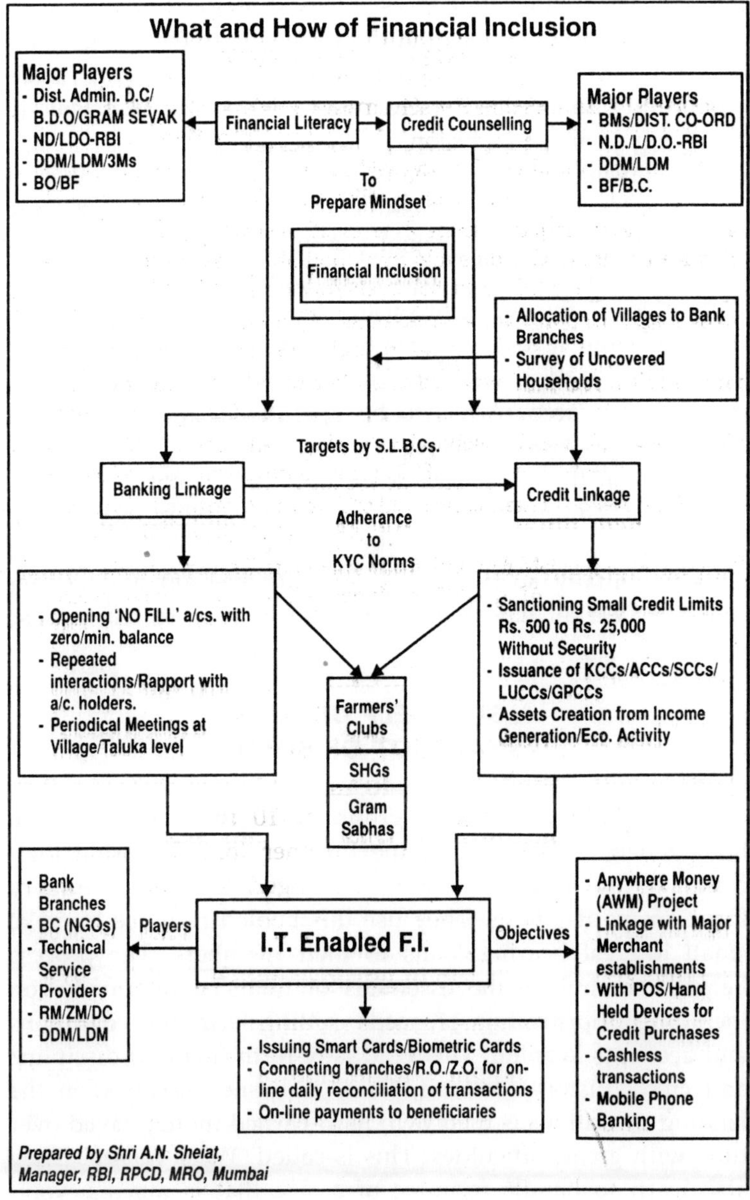

Moreover, recently banks have come up with strategies to reach the excluded through Banking Correspondents (BC) and Banking Facilitators (BF) Model. This strategy to make use of the informal channel to reach the poor is very encouraging for a larger outreach. It is high time for the banks and NGOs community to make the schemes to work the best way in achieving financial inclusion.

Financial inclusion means that, at least one member of family is having a bank account. It is a drive that wants the poor to get linked with formal banking institutions. However, there are several issues that need attention. Opening bank account is not the end of financial inclusion. It will be better for the household if that one member with formal access to bank account is a woman. Mere opening of an account is not enough. The account has to be operational too. The use of technology to increase access is invaluable and if this involves women then there are definite empowerment outcomes.

In fact, the inclusion is a continued banking relationship which cannot reset until the poor households become environmentally sustainable, financially well-off and gender sensitive. We all have significant role to play to reach those excluded.

4. SELF HELP GROUPS : SNAPSHOT OF BIHAR

Self Help Group is a group of 10 to 20 people from homogeneous class, who come together for addressing their common problems. They are encouraged to make voluntary thrift on regular basis. They use this pooled resource to make small interest bearing loans to their members. The process helps them imbibe the essentials of financial intermediation including prioritization of needs, setting term and conditions and accounts keeping. This gradually form financial discipline and credit history for themselves, as money involved in the lending operations is their own hard-earned money saved over time with great difficulties. This is called *'Warm Money'*. They also learn to handle resource of a size that is much beyond their individual capacities. The SHGs members begin to appreciate the fact that resources are limited and involve a cost. Once the group shows this matured financial behaviour, banks are encouraged to make loan to the SHGs in certain multiples of the accumulated saving of the SHGs. The bank loans are given without any collateral and at market interest rates. Banks find it easier to lend money to the groups as the members have developed the credit history. This is called *'Cold Money'*. This 'Outside (Cold) Money' gets added to the own 'Warm Money' in the hands of the groups, which have become structured, which are able to enforce credit discipline among the members. The members have experienced the benefits of credit discipline by being able to save and borrow regularly without much hassle. The group continue to decide the terms of loans to their own members. The peer pressure ensures timely repayments and acts as the 'Collateral' for the bank loans.

TABLE 8
SHGs Linkage and Loan Disbursement Progresses up to Sept. 2009

Year	*Linkage of New SHGs*	*Amount of Credit (Rs. Crore)*
Up to 2004	16246	51.82
2004-05	11769	37.42
2005-06	18206	31.2
2006-07	26517	82.54
2007-08	49738	240.99
2008-09	25696	211.44
2009-20 up to Sept. 2009	10919	104.66
Total	159091	760.07

Source : State Level Bankers' Committee.

Graph 3
Trend of the Credited Amount with Respect of New SHGs Linkage

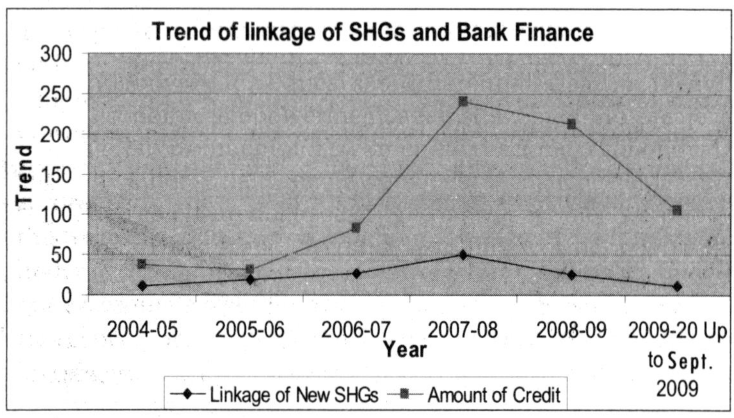

Table 9
Cumulative Number and Growth of SHGs Linked in 10 Major States of India

State	*2004*	*2005*	*2006*	*2007*	*2008*	*Growth rate in 2008*
Assam	10706	31234	56449	81454	10798	31
Bihar	16246	28015	46221	72339	93410	29
Gujarat	15974	24712	34160	43572	46526	07
Jharkhand	12647	21531	30819	37317	42605	14
MP	27095	45105	57125	70912	83336	18
Maharashtra	38535	71146	131470	225856	326425	45
Orissa	77588	123256	180896	234451	307591	31
Rajasthan	33846	60006	98171	137837	173192	26
UP	79210	119648	161911	198587	236929	19
West Bengal	51685	92698	136251	181563	228395	26
Total	363532	617351	933473	1283888	1549207	28
Percentage growth	59	68	51	37	28	

Sources : Microfinance, India 2008.

SUMMING UP

When poor will have strong desire and will to overcome poverty then poverty can be eliminated by the government running anti-poverty programmes. This is particularly applied with the Bihar where these poverty elimination programmes help only a fraction of poor. In this Scenario, microfinance is a key alternative for poverty alleviation. To succeed, microfinance should combine an innovative credit delivery mechanism that insures viable financial services for the needy with a realistic assessment of the micro-enterprise opportunity in the state. However, creating adequate awareness among the potential beneficiaries for this is the first prerequisite for the success of any such programme. The Self Help Groups (SHGs) and the SHGs-Bank linkage programme, implemented by commercial banks, regional rural banks and cooperative banks, have emerged as the major microfinance programme in not only Bihar but all over the country.

The poverty lending approach is unsustainable on large scales, so the commercialization of microfinance is inevitable. Although the purpose is the same to provide financial services to the large number of poor, and try to make them self-dependent. The poverty approach aims to serve the poorest while the commercial approach serve larger amounts of poor and is doing better in providing saving and credit services. In light of certain views of whom to be helped, poverty approach still has a role to play, although not a main role.

As mentioned in this paper, the performance of poverty approach needs improvement. More transparent implementation and efficient supervision are needed, and I also think that it should be made clearer that the priority should go to the extremely poor. Meanwhile, donors and government can help promote the financial system approach by help building self-sufficient commercial.

Still, questions remain in this field. It's difficult to tell whether the extremely destitute need micro credit or other financial services. And a comparison of these two approaches' ability to select the economically-active but currently extremely poor clients are missed. Therefore, 1st approach is helping poorest of the poor and the 2nd is about upper side of the poor.

Notes and References

1. Financial Inclusion (FI) refers to person or households accessing institutional credit from Commercial Banks, Cooperative Banks, Regional Rural Banks, National Bank for Agriculture and Rural Development—SHGs (Self Help Groups) linkage and other Non-Government Organisations (NGOs) and Micro Credit Institutions.
2. Self Help Groups (SHGs), the most common microfinance institution in India, are 'small voluntary association of poor people from the same socio-economic background who come together for the purpose of solving their common problems through SHGs and mutual help'—(NABARD, 2000).
3. Reserve Bank of India, "A Lifeline for the Poor".

References

Somanath, V.S., 'Microfinance Redefine the Future', Excel Book Publications.

Bhatnagar, Amitabh, 'Rural Microfinance and Microenterprise, Informal Revolution', 2008.

P.J. Christabell, 'Women Empowerment through Capacity Building, The Role of Microfinance', 2009.

Microfinance India Summit, Conference Report—'The Poor First Livelihood India', 13 Nov. 2008, New Delhi.

Srinivasan, N., 'Microfinance India: State of the Sector Report', 2008.

ICICI Foundation—Strategies for Inclusive Growth'.

http://books.google.co.in/books?id=luaAHdTKMM8C&printsec=frontcover&dq=poverty+lending+approach&source=gbs_similarbooks_s&cad=1#v=onepage&q=poverty%20lending%20approach&f=false, Accessed at 3:12 on 5th Jan., 2010.

http://books.google.co.inbooks?id=vsZvFKcFkJ4C&printsec= frontcover&dq=poverty+lending+approach&source=gbs_similarbooks_s&cad=1#v=onepage&q=poverty%20lending%20approach&f=false, Accessed at 1:12 on 5th Jan., 2010.

http://books.google.co.in/books?id=yXbtwV-_A3sC&printsec= front cover&dq=poverty+lending+approach&source=gbs_similarbooks_s&cad=1#v=onepage&q=poverty%20lending%20approach&f=false, Accessed at 10:12 on 7th Jan., 2010.

http://books.google.co.in/books?id=gn5vnT_SEZ0C&printsec=frontcover&dq=poverty+lending+approach&source=gbs_similarbooks_s&cad=1#v=onepage&q=poverty%20lending%20approach&f=false, Accessed at 12:12 on 8th Jan., 2010.

www.microfinanceindia.org

www.rbi.org.in

www.google.co.in

www.undp.org

www.mospi.gov.in

www.nabard.org

APPENDIX I

The basic differences between these Two Approaches are at a Glance

Dimensions	*Poverty-lending Approach*	*Financial System Approach*
Mission	Achieving depth of outreach	Achieving greater outreach specially breadth of outreach
Focus	Reaching the poorest	Financial sustainability
Mode of operation	Not for profit	For profit
Sources of finding	Donors, subsidied public sector funding	Private commercial agents
Perception of target group	Beneficiaries	Clients
Impact Assessment Measure	Impact on Beneficiary	Performance of the institution

APPENDIX II

Combined Programmes Running by Government of India and Government of Bihar for Rural Development

(Rs. In crore) (up to Oct. 2009)*

Schemes under DRDA	*Year*	*NREGA*	*SGSY*	*IAY (NEW and UP)*	*IAY (C&S)*	*IAY (5%)*	*IAY (Flood 2004 Affected)*	*IAY (Kosi Flood 2008)*
(1)	(2)	(3)	(4)	(5)	(6)	(7)	(8)	(9)
Financial Target	2007-08	2000.26	284.84	1417.93	—	—	—	—
	2008-09	2411.54	336.74	1984.94	—	—	—	143.75
	2009-10	3258.94	345.32	3843.00	—	—	—	—
Spillover from	2007-08	795.35	171.22	613.96	7.72	2.63	82.17	—
	2008-09	638.30	210.03	777.28	5.07	0.96	62.81	—
	2009-10*	912.79	292.94	1392.96	3.82	0.28	18.46	71.87
Share of Government of India (Released)	2007-08	544.79	105.21	1054.12	0.00	0.00	0.00	—
	2008-09	1369.03	240.75	2187.24	0.00	0.00	0.00	53.91
	2009-10*	420.72	96.83	994.98	0.00	0.38	0.00	0.00

(Contd.)

APPENDIX II (Contd.)

(1)	(2)	(3)	(4)	(5)	(6)	(7)	(8)	(9)
Share of Government of Bihar (Released)	2007-08	74.18	44.75	369.43	0.00	0.00	0.00	—
	2008-09	144.28	35.11	494.79	0.00	0.31	0.00	17.97
	2009-10*	65.09	65.00	534.98	0.00	0.13	0.00	0.00
Total (Government of India and Government of Bihar)	2007-08	618.97	149.96	1423.55	0.00	0.00	0.00	
	2008-09	1513.31	275.86	2682.03	0.00	0.31	0.00	71.88
	2009-10*	485.81	161.83	1529.97	0.00	0.50	0.00	0.00
Other funds	2007-08	58.57	2.11	0.00	0.00	0.00	0.00	—
	2008-09	25.96	4.06	29.68	0.00	0.00	0.00	0.00
	2009-10*	73.96	0.40	19.59	0.10	0.00	0.39	0.00
Total funds available	2007-08	1472.89	323.29	2037.51	7.72	2.63	82.17	—
	2008-09	2177.57	489.95	3488.99	5.07	1.27	62.81	—
	2009-10*	1472.56	455.17	2942.52	3.92	0.78	18.85	71.87
Total Expenditure	2007-08	1053.35	151.74	1453.89	3.26	2.10	52.53	—
	2008-09	1305.85	199.75	2131.24	1.73	0.54	20.50	—
	2009-10*	924.69	120.90	1795.17	0.14	0.22	4.59	10.62

% of Exp. against fund available	2007-08	71.52	46.94	71.36	42.23	79.85	63.93	—
	2008-09	59.97	40.77	61.08	34.12	42.52	32.64	—
	2009-10*	62.79	26.56	61.01	3.53	27.88	24.36	14.78
% of Exp. against target	2007-08	52.66	53.27	102.54	—	—	—	—
	2008-09	54.15	59.32	107.37	—	—	—	—
	2009-10*	28.37	35.01	46.71	—	—	—	—

(Contd.)

APPENDIX II (Contd.)

(Rs. In crore) (up to Oct., 2009)*

Schemes under DRDA	*Year*	*IAY (Kalazar 2006 Affected)*	*IAY (Kalazar 2008 Affected)*	*IAY (Aapki sarkar Aapke Dwar)*	*IAY (Naxal 2008)*	*Hariyali (DPAP and IWDP)*	*DRDA (Admin.)*	*Total*
(1)	*(2)*	*(10)*	*(11)*	*(12)*	*(13)*	*(14)*	*(15)*	*(16)*
Financial Target	2007-08	—	—	—	—	—	—	3703.03
	2008-09	—	255.99	99.00	368.93	—	—	5600.89
	2009-10	—	—	—	—	—	—	7447.26
Spillover from	2007-08	16.05	—	0.00	—	30.99	7.76	1727.85
	2008-09	4.95	—	0.00	—	23.67	3.88	1726.95
	2009-10*	2.46	96.00	17.81	138.35	23.52	1.41	2972.67
Share of Government of India (Released)	2007-08	1.63	—	0.00	—	1.18	10.41	1717.34
	2008-09	1.58	96.00	0.00	138.35	7.32	13.62	4107.80
	2009-10*	0.00	0.00	0.00	0.00	5.71	8.79	1527.40
Share of Government of Bihar (Released)	2007-08	0.54	—	0.00	—	0.57	5.06	494.53
	2008-09	0.53	—	99.00	—	0.79	4.64	797.42
	2009-10*	0.00	32.00	0.00	23.36	0.53	3.44	724.52

Total (Government of India and Government of Bihar)	2007-08	2.17	—	0.00	—	1.75	15.47	2211.87
	2008-09	2.11	—	99.00	—	8.11	18.26	4670.87
	2009-10*	0.00	32.00	0.00	23.36	6.23	12.22	2251.92
Others funds	2007-08	0.00	—	0.00	—	0.06	1.61	62.35
	2008-09	0.00	—	0.00	—	0.10	2.89	62.69
	2009-10*	0.00	0.00	0.00	0.00	0.05	1.28	95.77
Total funds available	2007-08	18.22	—	0.00	—	32.80	24.84	4002.07
	2008-09	7.06	—	99.00	—	31.88	25.03	6388.63
	2009-10*	2.46	128.00	17.81	161.71	29.80	14.92	5320.35
Total Expenditure	2007-08	12.62	—	0.00	—	10.85	18.75	2759.09
	2008-09	4.58	—	51.07	—	8.33	21.45	3745.04
	2009-10*	0.02	22.68	10.43	111.18	3.56	13.04	3017.24
% of Exp. Against fund available	2007-08	69.26	—	—	—	33.08	75.48	553.64
	2008-09	64.87	—	51.59	—	26.12	85.70	499.38
	2009-10*	0.75	17.72	58.56	68.75	11.96	87.42	466.07
% of Exp. agaist target	2007-08	—	—	—	—	—	—	208.47
	2008-09	—	—	51.59	—	—	—	272.43
	2009-10*	—	—	—	—	—	—	110.10

Inclusive Growth : Opportunities Ahead

MRIDULA KUMARI

Inclusive growth refers to growth strategy designed to reduce poverty and focus on bridging the various divides that fragment our society. Non-agricultural employment should increase at over 6 percent per annum during the 11th Plan. Major section of the population, now excluded from basic health and educational services needs focused attention. Manufacturing should grow at the rate of 12 percent per annum. For faster inclusive growth, provision for adequate physical and social infrastructure should be made. Development process has failed to bridge the gap between haves and have nots, urban and rural India and divide along gender line. Growth should also be environmentally benign.

INTRODUCTION

One and a half decade has passed since our economy had

entered into the arena of globalization, privatization and liberalization through economic reforms. Now, our economy is in a much stronger position than it was a few years ago. After slowing down to an average growth rate of about 5.5% in the 9th Plan period (1997-98 to 2001-02) it has accelerated significantly in recent years. The average growth rate in the last four years of 10th Plan period (2003-04 to 2006-07) is likely to be a little over 8%, making the growth rate 7.2% for the entire 10th Plan period. Below is the 10th Plan target of 8% which is the highest growth rate achieved in any Plan period.

Following macroeconomic indicators shown in the table reflect the strengths of our economy.

		9th Plan	*10th Plan*
1.	GDP growth in %	5.5	7.2
	(a) Agriculture	2.0	1.7
	(b) Industry	4.6	8.3
	(c) Services	8.1	9.0
2.	Gross Domestic Savings	23.1	28.1
3.	Gross Domestic Investment	23.8	27.5
4.	Current account balance	-0.7	0.7
5.	Combined fiscal deficit (of states and centre)	8.8	8.4
6.	Foreign Exchange Reserves (in US $ billion)	54.2	165.3
7.	Rate of Inflation	4.0	4.9

Source : Approach to 11th Five Year Plan.

The 11th Plan provides an opportunity to restructure policies to achieve a new vision based on faster, more broad-based and inclusive growth. Inclusive growth refers to the growth strategy designed to reduce poverty and focuses on bridging the various divides that continue to fragment our society. It is to create productive employment at a faster rate than before, and targets robust agricultural growth at 4% per year.

It is to reduce disparities among regions and communities by ensuring access to basic physical infrastructure as well as health and education facilities to all. Inclusive growth aims to recognize gender as a cross-cutting theme across all sectors and commit respect and promote the rights of the common person.

Despite having claim to many strengths which provide a sound base for the inclusion of marginalized and unprivileged class in the society, several challenges remain before our economy.

CHALLENGES

Decelerating Agricultural Growth Rate

One of the major challenges for inclusive growth is to reverse the deceleration in agricultural growth from 3.2% observed between 1980 and 1996-97 to a trend average of around 2.0% subsequently. This deceleration is the root cause of the problem of rural distress that has surfaced in many parts of the country and reached crisis level in some. Low farm incomes due to inadequate productive growth have often combined with low prices of output and with lack of credit at reasonable rates, to push many farmers into crippling debt. Even otherwise, uncertainties seem to have increased (regarding prices, quality of inputs and also weather and pests) which, coupled with unavailability of proper extension and risk insurances have led farmers to despair. This has also led to widespread distress migration, a rise in the number of female headed households in rural areas and a general increase in women's work burden and vulnerability. In 2004-05, Women accounted for 34% of principal and 89% of subsidiary workers in agriculture, higher than in any previous round of the National Sample Survey.

A measure of self-suffering is also critical for ensuring food security. A second green revolution is urgently needed to raise the growth rate of agricultural GDP to around 4%. This is not an easy task since actual growth of agricultural GDP including forestry and fishing is likely to be below 2% during the 10th Plan period. The challenge therefore is at least to double the rate of agricultural growth and to do so, recognize demographic realities particularly the increasing role of women.

Off-farm Employment Opportunities

An overall growth of 9% will further increase income disparity between agricultural and non-agricultural households unless around 10 million workers currently in agriculture find remuneration on agricultural employment. To make this possible and absorb all new entrants into the labour force, non-agricultural employment would have to increase at over 6% per annum during 11th Plan. This poses a major challenge not only in terms of generating non-agricultural employment but also in matching its required location and type. The inadequacy of widely dispersed and sustainable off-farm productive employment opportunities is a basic cause of most divides and disparities. Jobless growth can neither be inclusive nor can it bridge divides. All avenues for increasing employment opportunities, including those that can be provided by micro and small enterprises need to be explored. If we fail to do so, the demographic dividend can turn into a demographic nightmare. Thus, employment generation and raising employability is another major challenge providing essential public services to the poor.

Increasing Accessibility to Essential Services of Unprivileged Groups

Large parts of our population are still excluded from essential health and education services. Education is the critical factor that empowers participation in the growth process, but our performance has been less than satisfactory, both overall and in bridging gender and other divides. Overall literacy is still less than 70% and rural female literacy is less than 50% with corresponding rates even lower among the marginalized groups and minorities. While Sarva Shiksha Abhiyan has expanded primary school enrolment, it is far from providing quality education. In the area of health, there continue to be large gaps in the most basic services such as mother and child care, clean drinking water and access to basic sanitation facilities. The poor do not have even minimum access.

Although education and health services are available for those who can afford to pay, quality service is beyond the reach of the common people. Even where service providers exist, the quality of delivery is poor.

Increasing Global Competitiveness

Although growth in manufacturing sector has accelerated, compared to 9th Plan, it is unlikely to exceed 8% in the 10th Plan. This is unacceptably low. If we want our GDP to grow at 9% we have to target a 12% growth rate for this sector.

India's performance in IT enabled and other high end services is clearly a source of strength that must be built upon. However, India can not afford to neglect manufacturing. We meet most of the requirements for attaining a double digit growth rate in this sector. We have a dynamic entrepreneurial class in this sector. We have a dynamic entrepreneurial class that has gained confidence in its ability to compete. We have skilled labour and excellent management capabilities although this is an area where supply constraints will soon emerge. There are, however, some important constraints which limit our competitiveness, specially, in labour-intensive manufacturing.

Providing Adequate Infrastructure

Other major constraint in achieving faster and inclusive growth is the inadequacy of our physical infrastructure. Our roads, railways, ports, airports, communication and above all power supply, are not comparable to the standards prevalent in our competitor countries. This gap must be filled within 5 to 10 years if our enterprises are to compete effectively. In the increasingly open environment that we face today, our producers must compete aggressively not just to win export markets, but also to retain domestic markets against competition from imports. Indian industry recognizes this and no longer expects to survive on protection. But they do expect a level playing field in terms of quality infrastructure. Development of infrastructure is, therefore, to be accorded high priority in the 11th Plan.

Skill Development

There are emerging signs that rapid growth can result in shortage of high quality skills needed in knowledge intensive industries. One area of concern is that we are loosing our edge on the tracking of pure sciences. To continue our competitive edge and ensure a continuous flow of quality manpower, we need large investments in public sector institutions of higher learning. Our industries require skills in specific trades but we are still lagging behind in the area of technical/vocational training. Even today insolvent rating in Industrial Training Institutes (ITIs) and other vocational institutes, including nursing and computer training schools are only about a third of that in higher education. Vocational training institutes need to be expanded not only in forms of persons they train but also in the number of different skills and trades for meeting industry requirements as well as creating opportunities for self-employment.

Keeping the Growth Green

Environment has been the major issue of concern. While in the short-run, there may seem to be a trade-off between environmental sustainability and economic growth, in the long-run, we must take recourse to the complementarities between environmental sustainability and human well-being. Misuse of our natural resources like water, forest, mines, etc. has devastating effects on our future generations.

Good Governance

Ensuring good governance and transparency in the implementation of public programmes is the major challenge of inclusive growth.

Corruption has become endemic in all spheres of life. To reduce the scope of corruption, better design of projects and implementation mechanism and procedures are needed. Government must be ready to respond to the demands of people for improved governance through the Right to Information Act. Delayed and expensive dispensation of justice excludes poor and downtrodden from getting it. Speed and affordability are the two major challenges of good governance.

Disparities and Divides

There are many divides which the process of development failed to bridge rather it has sharpened some of them. The foremost divide is between rich and poor. There is no doubt that poverty is declining (NSS, 2004-08). Consumption poverty has declined in recent years from 36.0% to 27.8%. It is a very slow rate. There is also a divide between those having access to basic civic amenities like health, education, safe drinking water, sanitation, etc. and those who do not have.

Gender divide is another important rather most important divide which needs to be tackled with sincerity. Gender divide begins with the declining sex ratio, literacy differential between girls and boys, etc. Education differentials lead to heavily biased economic empowerment against women. To create an enabling environment for women to become economically, politically and socially empowered, is a challenge. Measures are needed to ensure that society recognizes women's economic and social worth, and accounts for the worth of women's unpaid work.

The divide between urban and rural India has become a truism of our times. There are large gaps in rural information, road connectivity, housing, water supply, electrification, telephony, primary health services, elementary education, etc.

Regional divide pertaining to growth and development is another important issue. Differences among states have always been a cause of concern but there exists imbalances within states as well. The spread of Naxalite movements in some parts of the country is the direct fallout of the failure of the state machinery to create an environment where the bulk of the people reap the benefits of development.

Strategy

The above described challenges need to be addressed through well chalked out broad policy measures. Rapid growth in previous plans has increased the size of the pie which needs to be combined with policies to help achieve the objective of growth with justice and equity. The transition towards faster and more inclusive growth calls for significant new initiatives in many sectors.

Agriculture

The crisis of stagnation in agriculture needs urgent attention. This sector still provides livelihood to 60% of our people and remains vital for food security. To ensure a better life for women and men engaged in agriculture, it is necessary to double the growth rate achieved in 10th Plan and put agriculture on a growth path of around 4%. To do this and at the same time maintain prices and profitability, a corresponding increase in demand for agricultural output matched with the supply side response based on productivity improvements is required.

As pointed out by National Commission on Farmers, we need a new deal that rebuilt hope about farming. Apart from larger public resources that this requires, state Governments. need to identify critical areas of support and reform that will instill confidence in farmers to undertake more investment.

Increasing Demand for Agricultural Output

Agricultural product prices have to keep pace with overall inflation and production costs to maintain farm profitability. Agricultural growth is the key to more inclusive growth. To increase agricultural demands, agricultural exports need to be increased. At domestic front increased incomes of the poor through program like MGREGP will help boost up demand in agriculture sector. Improved connectivity envisaged through the Bharat Nirman programme can also trigger growth of an integrated national market where rural people can meet each others demand. Rural trade is likely to create demand support in agriculture sector.

Renewed Focus on the Minimum Support Prices (MSP)

MSP policy needs to be strengthened; especially ensuring coverage of relevant crops and of new areas where production increase is likely to take place. A clearer understanding of best practices to adjust import tariff to insulate farmers from collapses in international prices need to be evolved. For this purpose, commission for agricultural costs and prices should develop subsequent policies regarding tariff revision.

Increase in Supply

Region-wise and crop-wise analysis is necessary to identify the specific constraints and policy distortions that have resulted in these yield gaps.

Growth strategy for agriculture sector in 11th Plan must have following elements in it :

Improvement in water management, rain water harvesting and water shed development:

- Double the rate of growth of irrigated area.
- Bridging the knowledge gap through effective extension activities.
- Diversification of agriculture into high value outputs such as fruits, vegetables, flowers, herbs and spices, medicinal plants, bamboo, bio-diesel, etc., but with adequate measures to ensure food security.
- Increased accessibility to credit at affordable rates.
- Promotion of animal husbandry and fishery.
- Improved marketing structure.
- Refocus on land reforms issues.
- Reclamation of degraded land and focus on soil quality.
- Agricultural research.
- Larger private investment.

Industry

Some major industries have shown a marked increase in global competitiveness. However, there are numerous constraints that limit industrial performance particularly of labour intensive manufactures, and these need to be addressed urgently. Organized sector, despite producing 67% of total manufacturing value, employ 12% of all workers in manufacturing. Stagnant labour productivity in unorganized manufacturing is another problem. The strategy for industrial sector must include increase in employment in organized sector and to improve labour productivity in unorganized sector. For this purpose, proposed strategy must have following elements:

- Enhancing labour flexibility.
- Special emphasis on infrastructure development and skill formation.
- Enhanced participation of women as equals in industrial growth.
- Provision of facilities like creches, toilets, maternity benefits, hostels, etc.

- Taxes and duties should be made non-distortionary and internationally competitive.
- Technological modernization.
- Single window clearance of application for establishment of industrial units.
- Required changes in the labour laws.
- Special care to the needs of micro, small and medium enterprises like removal of credit barriers, upgradation of technology and provision of marketing support.

Services Sector

The services sector accounts for 54% of GDP and is currently the fastest growing sector of the economy growing at 9 percent per annum since mid-1990s. But, industry leaders have been highlighting the emerging skill constraint. Many graduates not only from the humanities but also from the engineering and science streams need further training to acquire usable skills. India needs to ensure that the number of professionals turned out keeps increasing and even more importantly there is no slackening of standards in education.

Infrastructure

Infrastructural inadequacies in both rural and urban areas are a major factor constraining India's growth. To achieve the growth target of 9%, investment needs to be increased by 6 percentage point which should be in infrastructure. Since public sector resources are scarce, an aggressive effort at promoting public-private partnership in infrastructure development is required.

Roads

Road connectivity will not only bring India's villages into market economy but it will also help to tackle social sector problems like illiteracy, high IMR and MMR because while roads connect villages to markets, they also connect them to schools and hospitals.

The problems of development of roads network are diverse and require substantial resources. Hence, public-private partnership based on Build Operate and Transfer (BOT) model should be emphasized.

Energy

GDP growth is not possible without a commensurate increase in supply of energy, electricity coal, oil and gas and other fuels. Supply of commercial energy to all is essential for empowering individuals, especially women and girls who have the back-bending, time consuming and un-healthy task of collecting and using non-commercial fuels that remain the primary source of energy for cooking in over two-thirds of the households. Provision of clean fuels or at least wood plantation within one kilometer of habitation and dissemination of technology for use of clean fuels is vital for good health. Renewable sources of energy like solar wind and hydro energy need to be exploited. These can be set-up in a short time, especially solar powered units and can contribute to meeting peak demands. Exploiting non-traditional renewable sources of energy will also contribute in lessening the burden on environment.

Ensuring efficient distribution of energy between different regions to make expansion financially viable is another important strategy in this sector.

Environment

Rapid growth is need of the hour but it can also intensify environmental degradation. Hence, we must also ensure that rapid growth is environmentally benign. The 11th Plan must integrate development planning and environmental concerns, providing the use of economic instruments based on polluter pays principle, supplemented by command and control policies where these are more appropriate. Programmes and policies should be devised to support the existing ones and augment the quality and technology in the field of :

- Improvement in air and water quality.
- River cleansing
- Treatment of sewage and industrial effluents.
- Solid waste management.
- Preservation of wildlife and Bio-diversity.

- Mitigating land degradation.
- Increasing green cover.
- Improving the quality of green cover.
- Social afforestation with active involvement of PRIs.

Social Sectors

Protecting Childhood: We must ensure that our children do not lose their childhood because of work, disease or despair. The ICDS programme is working in this field. This programme covers supplementary nutrition, immunization, monitoring of weight and height and in some cases, creche facilities for a limited period. ICDS programme is to be universalized to bring in its ambit the left out children of 0-3 years age group.

Education and Training

Providing elementary education to all children in the age group of 6-14 years and reducing dropout rates for both boys and girls needs attention in 11th Plan. Mid day meal scheme can help not only in increasing attendance but also in improving children's nutritional status. Child mental health is a much neglected area in our country. According to the ICMR, at any given time, 7-15% of Indian children suffer from mental disorders. It is thus vital to provide counseling services for children in all schools to ensure their well-being. To rehabilitate street children, trafficked children of sex workers, HIV affected children and juvenile delinquents adoption, rescue, shelter homes counseling and medical aid, etc. are to be provided.

A set of national testing standards will be created and a chain of institutions that test and evaluate children according to set norms is to be established. This will help to monitor and improve the quality of learning. Sufficient resources are needed and strategies are required to significantly expand the number of places in secondary schools. It must be modernized and their numbers need to be expanded substantially to cater to the ever expanding skilled job market.

Health

To improve the primary health care system, the 11th Plan must lay emphasis on integrated district health plans and second on block specific health plans. These plans will ensure involvement of all health-related sectors and emphasize partnership with NGOs. The NRHM has already been launched to ensure quality health care in rural areas. In fact, we need a comprehensive approach which encompasses individual health care, public health, sanitation, clean drinking water, access to food and knowledge about hygiene and feeding practice.

The NRHM, launched for the duration of 11th Plan period, is expected to address the gaps in the provision of effective health care to rural population with special focus on 18 states having weak infrastructure. The Mission is for inclusive health development in which societies under different programmes will be merged and resources pooled at district level. The Mission provides for appointment of Accredited Social Health Activist (ASHA) in each village. Mobile clinics to reach the excluded ones are other features of this mission. Public-Private Partnership is another strategy aimed at improving equity and reducing expenses.

Employment

Employment is an area which shows up where our growth process is failing on inclusiveness. Daily status unemployment ratio increased to 8.3% in 2004-05. Employment in organized sector declined despite fairly healthy GDP growth. Employment generation should be made an integral part of the growth process. Hence strategies should be devised to accelerate growth of employment and also of the wages of the poorly paid. Targeting faster growth in GDP and doubling of agricultural growth will help in this process though it must be noted that this alone may not be sufficient. On the supply side, the labour force will increase by about 52 million during 11th Plan if it grows at the same rate as current projections of working age population. The increase would be much higher, around 65 million, if female participation rates rise at the pace observed during 1999-2005. Since this increase will be over and above the present backlog of about 35 million unemployed on a typical day, and since inclusiveness requires a shift of employment from agriculture to non-agriculture, we must plan for at least 65 million additional non-agricultural opportunities in the 11th Plan. Policy initiatives are needed to help achieve this growth in employment. Labour intensive manufacturing sectors such as food processing, leather products, footwear, textiles and service sectors such as tourism and construction need to be boosted. Other ongoing employment programmes aimed to manage vulnerability and structural changes like NREGP, self-employment programmes, National Social Assistance Programme, etc. need to be strengthened with proper monitoring so that benefits of these programmes reach scheduled castes and tribes.

Ensuring Gender Equity

Gender bias is deeply ingrained in our social psyche and this is reflected in indicators such as skewed sex ratio, literacy and health gaps of boys and girls. To bring gender equity, Ministries and Departments must ensure adequate provisions in the policies and schemes. Strict adherence to gender budgeting is another prerequisite for gender equity. The 11th Plan must have a special focus on four aspects—violence against women, economic empowerment, political participation and women's health.

CONCLUSION

The strategy for inclusive growth can succeed only if both the private and the public sectors join hands and play the role expected of them. Agriculture, small and medium enterprises and the large corporate sector accounts for 76% of the total investment and will be crucial for achieving the growth and employment objectives. The centre and the states must create the environment that will encourage efficient expansion and investment in the private sector, especially in key labour-intensive areas which would help to generate new high quality employment and also improve the quality of existing employment. The public sector has major responsibilities in developing infrastructure either directly or through PPPs, and in supporting agriculture irrigation, rural development health and education that are crucial for ensuring inclusive growth.

References

Papola, T.S., Reducing Imbalance in Regional Development : An Essential Ingredient of Strategy for "Inclusive Growth". Inaugural address at the National Seminar on "Making Growth Inclusive with Special Regional Development".

Planning Commission (October 2006), Approach paper to the Eleventh Five Year Plan (2007-12), Government of India.

Ruddar Dutt and K.P.M. Sundaram (2004), Indian Economy, S. Chand and Company, New Delhi.

Publication Division, Government of India, *Yojana* (different volumes).

Economic Growth, Employment and Inclusion

Rashmi Akhoury

OECD survey pegs the organized sector's share in employment to be just 6 percent on the eve of economic reforms. The external sector is booming. Inclusive Growth calls for human face of growth. Income and asset distribution have worsened during the last decade. Post-liberalization, job creation which will lead to economic prosperity, had been slowing down. Trend is that unorganized sector employment was not "necessarily of better quality" than that in stressed agriculture. The trickle down thesis to measure the impact on inclusion or exclusion of population is not worthy. The report aims to contribute to the national agenda of inclusive growth by focusing on those population groups who face variety of socio-economic and institutional barriers.

INTRODUCTION

At the time of India's independence, the socio-economic

scenario was characterized by a predominantly rural economy with feudal structure. There was wide spread poverty, dismal literacy rate, geographically and culturally isolated population, a rigid social structure and extremely poor transport and communication system. The state leaders and policy-makers during the initial years of development planning were also not adequately acclimatized to development activities. In view of the impediments to social and economic development, the fulcrum of the planning process had been pivoted on the strategic goal of economic development with social justice. Thus, the planning process in India, over the years, underscored the development of backward areas and disadvantaged population groups.

On the face of it, the results have been most gratifying. The rate of GDP growth in India has spurted in the last four years to 9 percent, making it the second-fastest growing economy in the world, after China. But at the same time the outcome of this growth has not necessarily been pro-poor. If anything, income and asset distribution have worsened during the last decade. The result is a heightened degree of social unrest, mostly in the country side. In nutshell, even the basic subsistence needs of millions of people are not being met. At the beginning of new millennium, 260 million people in the country did not have income to access a consumption basket which defines poverty line. Of these 75% were in the rural areas. India is the home to 22% of the world's poor. Such a high incidence of poverty is a matter of concern in view of the fact that poverty eradication has been one of the major objective of the development planning process. Indeed, poverty is a global issue. Its eradication is considered integral to humanity's quest for sustainable development.

A comprehensive definition of "inclusive growth" and the structure of strategy compatibility between newer instruments and the "human face" of growth remains hard to come by. Doubts about the sustainability of the current growth trajectory is an issue often debated, remains credible on this count. India celebrates significant GDP growth numbers more recently. This brings the boast of the Central policy-makers that more growth means "more inclusive" growth. This runs contrary to the experience of acceleration revitalizing "divisive growth". It is divisive between urban and rural dimensions. It is divisive between coastal and inland State of the Union. It is divisive in terms of location and commitment of Central investments directly by government and indirectly by the public sector enterprises. .

The Deputy Chairman of the Planning Commission acknowledged recently the distinction between "good" employment and not-so-good jobs based on regularity, scaling up prospects and availability of social security. This is what can distinguish the new era employment from that in agriculture that is seasonal, fluctuating from weather conditions, and relations of production in farm and factory. The more recent OECD survey pegs the organized sector's share in employment to be just six percent from 10 percent or so on the eve of economic reforms. Three elements in policy consequences from the current growth appear. Firstly, a tenuous link of growth number itself as "inclusion" is assumed. Secondly, the reality of grossly unequal rewards from the current strategy of growth is suppressed. Does inclusion confine itself to the sphere of population ? The result of a survey by Merill Lynch and Capgemini is reported in the media as estimating that India had one lakh persons each with personal net worth of more than four crore rupees which makes for a share of 10 percent of the national GDP. Thus 0.001 percent of the more than one billion population own 10 percent of the country's wealth! Finally, aggressive social disaffection is spreading. The spread of the radical Left influence is witnessing phenomenal growth since the economic reforms started. There is growing resistance to "land grab" for industry under policy protection. People are losing livelihood from forced land acquisition and from informalising regular jobs in organized industry. A comprehensive definition of "inclusive growth" and the structure of strategy compatibility between newer instruments and the "human face" of growth remains hard to come by.

GROWTH QUALITY

TWO positive shifts require to be watched closely. Statistical growth rate of the GDP has moved to an average level of roughly eight per cent in the course of the Tenth Plan.

It is a significant acceleration from the level of about six percent in the earlier two decades. Another significant recent shift is in relative stability of growth from quarter to quarter. There are, however, three negative or at the best indifferent trends. Growth rates vary widely from State to State. The swing in per capita income between 1991 and 2006 is from the low of less than two-fold in the State of Bihar to a high of nearly four-fold in Maharashtra. A breakthrough in bridging the difference relative to past trends is not in sight. Secondly, fluctuations still bedevil sector-growth rates. Agriculture figures negatively but even core infrastructure sectors display such a trend. A correlation between the electricity growth rate and the growth of energy intensive industry such as manufacturing is not always easy to establish. Finally, a validated analysis of contributors to the productivity growth rates in manufacturing and services is not available. Even in the highly rated IT sector, a media report indicated productivity in the USA being more than double that in India. So, if the current spurt in the growth rate is produced by the new fiscal capitalism and accounting processes in which the global fund figures significantly, then serious long-term imbalances in the total factor productivity cannot be ruled out. As Martin Wolf points out, the new global financial capital remains untested, Doubts about sustainability of the current growth trajectory, an issue often debated, remains credible on this count.

The external sector is booming as the last five years have seen strong global growth, India's exports have accelerated as never before. However, imports have grown more robustly. So, the current account deficit gap is increasing. Apart from crude and gas imports, we are increasing our dependence on import of coal, machinery, luxury goods and other commodities, foreign trade is not adding to our foreign exchange surplus as in China and the South East Asian countries. NRI deposits and remittances from Indians working aboard provide the real cushion. According to the World Bank, India received during 2005-06 foreign remittance worth $ 26.6 billion or Rs. 1.09 lakh crore. It is no longer the Middle East but North America that leads and contributes almost 40 percent of the total. And Bihar and UP are the States that receive substantial part of it. What happens when the cyclical downturn sets in remains uncertain.

But why has foreign debt shown a sharp increase to about $ 155 billion? It is racing to catch up with the foreign exchange reserves, It is no longer contributed by government borrowing. India's corporate sectors enjoy the luxury of raising loans as external commercial borrowing (EBC). It is not for infrastructure projects of fixed asset creation, the excuse is relatively cheap money for importing raw materials and other goods. Private companies are competing with one another rather than taking the consortium mode for intermediation. Is this completion adding to the cost of money so raised as also heavier burden in case of default or currency fluctuations? Finally, the government is facilitating acquisition of companies abroad by Indian enterprises, Last year, the outflow on this account was almost equal to the inflow of FDI. This is not like investment abroad in the energy sector but for pure trading. The global experience with M&A in terms of return and success is mixed. Expansion of global exposure might be contributing to the Indian footprint in foreign lands but it has potential adverse consequences during the apprehended downturn.

Finally, a clear picture of the relative contribution from the small and medium enterprises and the large corporate house is not easily available. The government is propping up the so called global scale of production and offering increasing sops for the same. This is revealed from a reply in the Lok Sabha that the SME sector is making larger contribution to productions as also exports. If that is so, then the scale of incentive at present is perverse. Budget paper relating to tax exemptions admit this reality. It is indicated that is one reason for the phenomenon of " jobless" growths. It amounts to the job creating industry being discriminated for the largesse of public finance and other incentive to be cornered by the larger private corporate sector. Public policy seems to favour the two-tier economy to sustain the growth momentum that deepens multiple disparities.

However, the picture on inequality is different, the Gini Index (a measure of inequality in distribution of Income of consumption) was 32.5 in India in 1999-2000 while it was 44.7 in China in 2001. So, India had far lower income/consumption inequality than in China.

One area of major concern is that in post-liberalization era job creation which is a major mechanism of inclusion of more people in economic prosperity, had been slowing down. Employment growth fell sharply in the post-reform year, from 2.6 per cent per annum over 1983-93 to 1.2 percent over 1993-2000.

The fall in employment growth rate was specially concentrated in organized sectors (particularly in the public sector). This trend had been reversed to some extent as the latest available National Sample Survey (NSS) data show employment growth during the period 2000-05 was 2.7 percent per annum. But, then again, the growth in jobs has been mostly concentrated (about 87 percent) in the unorganized sector .

The broad consensus seems to be that the rate of decline in poverty in the post-reform period (1994-2005) is not higher compared to the pre-reform period, despite a higher growth rate of GDP in the post-reform era.

Interestingly, however, a recent National Council of Applied Economic Research study using 2004-05 data for the BPL (Below Poverty Line) families finds that 30.3 percent of urban poor' own colour TVs, 24.9 percent own two wheelers, 10.5 refrigerators and 55.6 percent pressure cookers.

Further, the study shows that around 60 percent of all 4009 million odd BPL population resides in a few relatively low income states (used to be called BIMARU before some states were further sub-divided into more states) like Bihar, Orissa, UP, MP, Rajasthan, Chhattisgarh and Jharkhand

Such studies underline that poverty and its manifestations in various forms is much more concentrated in the rural areas of some specific states and regions within the states. At the same time, all the official poor in India are not necessarily the destitute that we usually associate with the term poverty. There was no question of poor family owing a colour TV set or a refrigerator some 15 years back.

Overall, though the picture is still pretty bad (specially on malnutrition and child mortality,) real poverty (in the sense of utter destitution) is now concentrated in a few pockets (like the remote tribal belts) where the benefits of growth and development have not yet percolated. Government's limited resources should best be focused on the development of infrastructure and connectivity in a time bound manner for such areas.

DIMENSION OF EMPLOYMENT

OECD economic outlook 2007 was widely flashed recently to sustain a thesis that Indian growth was creating job. This was only in terms of absolute numbers and in comparative terms with the other BRIC countries. Brazil, Russia and China added much less numbers than India since 2000. Why should it not provide any consolation? There are four reasons. First, the growth in employment has been faster since 2000 in the informal sector, an area suffering from data deficiency. ILO noted earlier in its 2006 Global Employment Trend that unorganized sector employment was not "necessarily of better quality" than that in stressed agriculture. Secondly, the employment elasticity of growth, that is, potential to create jobs with every one percent growth of GDP, has remained static at 0.3 percent during this period. This results from highly capital intensive growth. Thirdly, the organized sector growth is shrinking in relation to the pre-reform period. It has come down to six percent in 2005 from more that 10 percent earlier. Fourthly, the employment to population ratio at 50.5 percent in India is the lowest in relation to every other BRIC country. A more volatile problem persists, namely, finding suitable jobs for youth and women. The accelerated growth rate has not reduced the unemployment overburden of the past. It has added to it.

What have the country's surveys revealed? Both the NSSO and the Economic Census have, more recently, confirmed growth in number in relation to the situation during 1990s. What are the caveats here? First, employment growth has resulted from reversion of agricultural growth to a positive 1.3 per cent compared to being negative during the 1990s. Secondly, the work participation rate between 1983 and 2004 by the usual status indicates positive decline for the rural female and stagnation for the urban female. Thirdly, the census of small industry in different periods shows reduction in small enterprises and reduction of employment in relatively larger enterprises. This indicates a policy bias; against reservation for small industry for one larger enterprises hiring employees on contract to be retrenched at pleasure. Fourthly, in relative sectoral comparison, service sector shows the highest growth followed by manufacturing, with the lowest by agriculture. This is one element of the currently debated agricultural crisis. Finally, small States and Union Territories show exceptionally high growth of employment relative to the principal high growing states. Quality is casualty since these small States have no organized industrial base. This is the phenomenon of jobless growth.

High growth of SDP in States led by manufacturing indicates stagnant or declining growth of stable employment. That is what reflects the share of organized employment in the economy declining to only six per cent. One explanation is that public sector that led to the growth of organized sector employment had now a low priority in policy. It has followed the policy incentive for downsizing to scale up profit . It does not engage in labour intensive activities. Public policy preference for private enterprise has created moral hazards for public enterprises. A reversal can result only when governments provide concrete indication that they are serious about increasing "good" employment. Good employment is one that is regular, offers compensation commensurate with productivity and sets the example of innovating social security.

One measure of such employment is located in the level of wage and ratios between the highest and the lower levels. The OECD report indicates that while in China, the real wage in manufacturing trebled between 1990 and 2005, in India the increase was a mere 2.7 per cent. The march of growing wage inequality in India relative to other is demonstrated in just one lakh persons having a net worth of a little over four crore rupees. The 1999-2000 employment-unemployment survey had come to the damning conclusion that compensation to labour from increased productivity is very meagre indeed. This has not changed much since then. The NSSO 2004-05 indicates employment rate exceeding growth in persons coming on the labour market. Based on this, the Prime Minister's Economic Advisory Council has projected that everybody seeking jobs will get it by 2011. This is too good to be realistic unless confirmed in census 2011. There is growing evidence that grossly inflated compensation for capital has no relation to its contribution to employment. This phenomenon cannot but fuel vastly expanding economic inequality. And inequality in wages when the impression goes round of over-exploitation of labour, including technical manpower, is a recipe for depressed manpower productivity.

Post-liberalization job creation—a major mechanism of inclusion of more—people in economic prosperity has been slowing down. The theme of the Eleventh Five Year Plan (2007-12) and beyond is faster and more inclusive growth meaning that the benefits of faster economic growth should reach a much higher number of poor and disadvantaged people

But how inclusive has been the Indian growth story?

There is no single measure by which one can judge inclusiveness. However, human development indicators collectively give some broad idea about the performance on inclusiveness.

For example, in terms of country ranking by Human Development Index (HDI)—a composite measure of achievement in health, education and standard of living India stood at 128 out of 177 countries in 2005 (124 in 2000). China's position was 81 in 2005 (96 in 2000) and Bangladesh ranked at 140 in 2005 (145 in 2000) The disturbing fact is that India's relative ranking is worsening whereas that of China and even Bangladesh has been improving over the same period,

According to the latest available World Bank indicators, in 2007 the adult literacy rate for India is 66 per cent as against 93 per cent for China and 92 per cent for Indonesia. So, India is far behind China or Indonesia (two other populous countries) in terms of mass educational attainments Moreover, by restricting the excretion of industrial employment (which requires workers with basic literacy and numeracy at the minimum, though that may not be enough, this would stand in the way of a faster and more inclusive growth in future.

Life expectancy at birth for India is (2007 data): 63 (Male) and 62 (Female). For China, the corresponding figures are 71 and 75. The infant mortality rate per 1000 for India was 52, while it was 18 for China Regarding births attended by skilled health staff, India's attainment is 46.6 per cent as against 98.4

per cent for China. Again, India lags behind China in providing basic health and medical services.

In terms of malnutrition (underweight) of children under five years of age, India's figure (2006) is 43.5 per cent as against 32.8 per cent for Somalia and 31.7 per cent for Sudan. India's performance on malnutrition is worse than all countries (including sub-Saharan Africa) for which data were available for comparable periods.

On the basis of international poverty line of \$ 1.25 a day, the poverty ratio (percentage of people below the poverty line) was 49.4 for India in 1993-94. After a decade in 2004-05 it became 41.6 signifying a 7.8 percentage point improvement over a decade. By contrast, China went down by 12.5 percentage point in just over three years.

MODEL FOR GROWTH AND EMPLOYMENT

It is assumed that production structure is following, which satisfies constant returns to scale; $\alpha + \beta = 1$.

$$Y = AF(K,N) = AK^{\alpha}N^{\beta} \tag{1}$$

Here, Y, K, N, A are output, capital stock, employment and technology shock respectively, The labour demand (=N^D) condition is following, equalizing marginal productivity to real Wage,

$$AF_N(K,N^D) = (1-\alpha)A\left(\frac{K}{N^D}\right)^{\alpha} = W \tag{2}$$

To focus on the effect of economic growth on labor demand, we use the concept of labour per capital, L/k = n, which simplifies the labour demand function as following,

$$(1-\alpha)An^{-\alpha} = W \tag{3}$$

Capital accumulation through economic growth affects labour demand as following.

$$\frac{\partial n}{\partial \alpha} = \frac{1+(\alpha-1)\ln\alpha}{\alpha(\alpha-1)n^{-1}} < 0 \tag{4}$$

It means that labour demand per capital decreases as the value of alpha is larger, As mentioned above, this parameter is the elasticity of output with respect to capital and affects the convergence speed in transitional dynamics of neoclassical growth model. In other words, the parameter affects both the growth rate and job creation in the growing economy.

Since the employment is determined in the labour market equilibrium of labour demand and supply, we need to specify labour supply and demand functions as following.

$$N^S = N^S(W, \Psi) \qquad (10)$$

$$AF_N(K, N^D) = W \qquad (11)$$

In (10), $N^S\Psi$, are labour supply and other structural determinants of labour supply respectively. First, the equilibrium employment is determined by substituting (11) into (10)

$$N = N^S(AF_N(K, N), \Psi) \qquad (12)$$

Using this employment equation, one can derive elasticity of employment with respect to capital.

$$\eta_{NK} = \frac{\varepsilon^S{}_{NW}\zeta_{NK}}{(1-\varepsilon^S{}_{NW}\zeta_{NN})} \qquad (14)$$

Here $\varepsilon^S{}_{NW}$ = labor supply elasticity with respect to real wages, ζ_{NK} and ζ_{NN} are elasticity of marginal product of labour with respect to capital and labour respectively. Employment elasticity with respect to growth of output may be defined as following.

$$\eta_{NY} = \frac{\varepsilon^S{}_{NW}\zeta_{NK}\varepsilon_{KY}}{(1-\varepsilon^S{}_{NW}\zeta_{NN})} \qquad (15)$$

One can see that the employment elasticity is affected by preference and technology structure. There are four factors determining the elasticity: the elasticity of labour supply with respect to real wages, elasticity of marginal product with respect to labour, elasticity of marginal product with respect to capital, elasticity of output with respect to capital. The first one is from preference structure and the other three from technology structure, important point is that employment elasticity with respect to output growth is determined both by preference and technology structure.

Next one can also derive wage elasticity of output growth as following :

$$\eta_{WY} = \frac{\zeta^{S}_{NW}\varepsilon_{KY}}{(1-\varepsilon^{S}_{NW}\zeta_{NN})} \tag{16}$$

The same four factors determining employment elasticity determine wage elasticity. Other factors except ε^{S}_{NW} are affecting both elasticities in the same direction as the value of ε^{S}_{NW} gets bigger, however, employment elasticity increases while wage elasticity decreases. The larger the value of ζ_{NK}, ζ_{NN} and ε^{S}_{KY} is, the bigger the employment elasticity is, which is a quite intuitive result.

To be more specific, if we assume that production function is Cobb-Douglass, employment and wage elasticity is simplified as following :

$$\eta_{WY} = \frac{\varepsilon^{S}_{NW}}{(1+\alpha\varepsilon^{S}_{NW})} \tag{17}$$

$$\eta_{WY} = \frac{1}{(1+\alpha\varepsilon^{S}_{NW})} \tag{18}$$

These derivations are more readable than (15) and (16). Output elasticity has a negative relationship with capital coefficient and a positive relationship with wage elasticity of labour supply. Wage elasticity has a negative relationship with capital coefficient and the elasticity of labour supply with respect to wage. This result is intuitively right. As the elasticity of labour supply with respect to wage becomes more elastic, the resulting increase of labour demand from economic growth may be transformed into more employment rather than higher wage.

The Directorate General of Employment and Training, Ministry of Labour and Employment released its first Annual Report to the people on Employment in New Delhi. One of the central idea of the Report is that high economic growth and growth of quality employment reinforces each other. Recognizing low level of earnings and poor working conditions of casual labourers and a part of self-employed worker, the report argues for increasing the share of organized sector employment in total employment of the country particularly in the manufacturing and service sectors.

The report strongly puts the idea of re-defining 'economic activity' for public debate so that women's contribution to economic growth could be recognized properly in economic terms and a number of social and family-related barriers could be addressed through policy interventions. The Report firmly puts on the agenda to best utilize the demographic dividends by focusing on generating gainful employment for youth, in general, and young women, in particular.

The report particularly aims to focus on generating employment and enhancing employability of workers among less advantaged. It is widely believed that poverty in India, though significantly declined over the years, is continuing mainly because of non-inclusion of different less advantaged population groups in development process. The report attempts to identify some of the important sources of such exclusion in the labour market and focus on required policy measures for inclusive growth.

The Report notes that given very low proportion of skilled workers at present, a suitable and workable framework to enhance the employability of workers is essential, The same can be achieved by providing training to workers at various levels with emphasis on recognizing local skills and certifying informally acquired skills along with the expansion of skill development institutions The Report also argues for rationalization of labour laws and broadening the ambit of labour reforms for achieving equitable employment growth. It sets out short-term and medium-term strategies to ensure gainful employment opportunities for all the working people with particular emphasis on the disadvantaged groups.

The President of India in her address on 4 June, 2009 to the Joint Session of both Houses of Parliament, had announced that the Government will bring out five reports to the people on education, health, employment, environment and infrastructure. Ministry of Labour and Employment (MOL & E) has been entrusted with the responsibility of bringing out the report on employment being the nodal Ministry on employment-related matters. The present Annual Report is first in the series.

The inclusion of employment as one of the themes of these reports underline the Government's commitment and priority attached to this subject and its potential for advancing the objective of inclusive economic growth and development. The present report aims to contribute to the national agenda of inclusive growth by focusing on those population groups who face variety of socio economic and institutional entry barriers and fail to earn a respectable living status despite being engaged in economic activities. This Report to the people on Employment provides a framework to understand the contemporary employment scenario.

Major short-term strategies include, employment growth to be targeted at least 2.5 per cent annum compatible with the 9 percent growth in the economy, promote labour intensive and high employment elasticity sectors to achieve the quantitative employment growth targets. Focus should be on inclusion of women and vulnerable groups with their specific needs of training and skill development. Mahatma Gandhi National Rural Employment Guarantee Act (MGNREGA) must reach all poor households with 100 days of assured employment An urban employment guarantee scheme on the lines of MGNREGA may be considered National Floor Minimum Wage should be given statutory sanction. Statutory provisions to provide social security and improved conditions of work and remuneration of contract workers at par with the regular employees. Expand the outreach of Rashtriya Swasthya Bima Yojana (RSBY) scheme to all poor households, well calibrated withdrawal of stimulus package for labour intensive exporting enterprises e.g. textiles handicrafts, gems and jewellery. Developing Information base and E-monitoring on real time basis and compilation of employment/unemployment data on annual basis regularly are required.

Key medium-term strategies and targets are—focus on self- employed and casual workers for improving livelihood, enhance the scope of employment in the organized sector, enhance regular employment for less advantaged groups and in poorer states, comprehensive coverage of unorganized sector workers under social security schemes, rationalization and simplification of labour regulations and broadening the ambit of labour reforms, promote diversification of rural workforce to off-farm and non-farm activities, promote the technology, green jobs and encourage greening the workplace. Detailed skill mapping mechanism to be evolved. Credible and independent accreditation and certification process to be created. Upgradation on all training providing institutions and strengthening delivery through public-private partnership (PPP) Mode, creating large number of skill development institutions and pool of trainers to expand the outreach of skill development initiatives. Target regions with concentration of vulnerable social groups such as Scheduled Tribes, Scheduled Castes, minorities, women, illiterate less skilled for active labour market policies and ISO Certification of skill development institutions and assessing bodies.

EVIDENCE ON ECONOMIC INCLUSIVENESS

Employment, to be inclusive, has to be sensitive to certain norms. First, irregular and casual jobs need to be excluded from any enumeration. Since food and survival are daily necessity, there must be a daily income norm indexed to the price of essential survival commodities. Secondly, the government should lay down a national minimum wages as suggested by the Rural Labour Commission decades ago. Sharp differences over the level of wage in the National Rural Employment Guarantee Act lending to bound-rate of rupees sixty per day when the overall per capita income is rising is irrational. Third, the current political practice of token insurance and/or other schemes as social security in almost every budget must be replaced by a binding social security system for workers below a certain threshold. Sixteen years of economic reforms has not brought to any conclusion a legislation on social security for the unorganized sector. A legislation that is in the making is seen only as a bundle of pious intentions. Its firm commitment remains. "By this Act the Central Government may formulate and notify from time to time suitable welfare schemes for different sections of unorganized sector workers on the recommendation of the National Advisory Board." Fourth, social security must become a change on every enterprise, old and new. Finally, with emphasis having shifted to business efficiency and profitability, a national business fund that sustain access to quality manpower should appear. Such a trust fund with a suitable structure of government participation can add to a labour-intensive enterprise, if needed, on sub-minimum wage initially for them to migrate in reasonable period to more remunerative enterprise. If the liberalized system is really as efficient as is touted, then it should show the potential to be inclusive in such real term in employment delivery.

Does poverty reduction connect with the employment-led inclusive growth? When started, it was considered as merely a "holding on" policy framework till the poor are integrated in the growth policy itself. The outcome was a selective action approach that sought to aid enterprise in small and tiny sector supported by a policy of reservation and protection. Directed bank credit and state policy of procurement was focused on to this end. Private enterprise was given income tax exemption for undertaking activities for poverty alleviation. Low level of housing was added in the PAP. The PDS also gave it the needed income redistribution prop. In effect, India's anti-poverty strategy was a two-tier undertaking that could converge at some stage. It created minimalist redistribution condition on the one hand and a low grade welfare component of self and wage employment on the other. It aimed at fostering public-private partnership to strengthen a bottom-up effort for growth. Economic liberalization seemingly adopted it but without a plan to serve the inherent long-term objective. It has failed to innovate on the old platform for it to become part of the growth strategy. Therefore, its output is declining. In a way, the current state of poverty alleviation reflects failure of the policy of "growth with social justice". The new slogan of more inclusive growth confirms the dilution of the constitutionally mandated doctrine of economic justice.

Growing inequality of income stratifies "dualisation of income". Exclusion of the marginalized in modernizing sectors of the economy; "informalisation" trend in large and medium sectors; and the doctrine of merit in the skill-based economy are adding to social polarization and alienation among the workers—educated as well as unskilled. From one account, in the 21st century, almost 35 percent of the working population in the informal economy are under the poverty line. Spreading social protest and sporadic violence are symptoms of a deeper malaise that defies containment policies. This is demonstrated best in the spread of the "Naxalite movement" despite putting an internal security tag to commit more funds for coercive action. The PAP started as merely the entry point for empowering the poor to wrest their share in the national economy within a reasonable period. This is now a distant dream.

The trickle-down thesis has no firm yardstick to measure its impact on inclusion or exclusion of population. The outcome is an outlandish position that "nine percent growth is widely inclusive". The effort in such a view is to protect the politics of polarization and shield the lifestyles of the affluent contrasting the growing deterioration of lifestyle of the "outclass". But the current trickle down mechanism has no takers in the "outclass". It has to test positive in terms of a minimum basket of needs delivered in a manner that it helps the struggle against exclusion. It is tested in the form of food and nutrition security but public policy is in disarray in this respect at present. The latest NSSO output confirms that a mere 27 percent of the population in rural India consume fruit and vegetable, source for micro-nutrient that is needed for immunity. India's failure in managing child malnutrition is so dismal that the world has stopped looking at it. The government is busy depressing the cost of money and scaling up the security of profit for large corporate enterprises but has no policy for security of livelihood of the poor. A RBI study of the utilization of remittances from aboard in 2006 revealed that "a predominant portion of remittances (54 percent) is spent on food, education and healthcare". This confirms the distress migration. An NCAER study concludes that 81 per cent of Indian households save but many out of them remain financially fragile when income and expenditure are taken into account. Rural non-farm employment has expanded but largely from public sector infrastructure investment. If that investment declines, rural income will also decline. Businessman Atul Churiwal of Merchant Chamber of Commerce stated on July 11 that "farmer's income eroded by 50 percent in the last few years, in real terms". The landless labourers' condition suffers more. All this evidence shows how hollow vending of economic inclusion remains.

The government claims implicitly that the higher growth is from private sector investment. This will look credible when employment expansion and workers' income growth enters the private corporate sector discourse. Two negative articulations for industry are already being presented. First, a complaint is heard that public sector rural infrastructure investment and minimum wage are forcing decline in urban migration and eroding the competitiveness in certain industries. Second, the growing shortage of skilled manpower for knowledge and modernizing industries shows a modest interest in taking over just 300 industrial training institutes by the private sector out of about 5000 set-up over decades by exclusively government investments. The Finance Minister states that there is no paucity of financial resources. But the reality seems otherwise, in-so-far as projects targeting inclusion are involved. The Rural Development Ministry demanded extension of employment guarantee to 200 additional districts this year. The Budget committed funds for just 131 instead. The Supreme Court ruled that the ICDS be extended to all the remaining blocks by December this year. The Budget does not see merit in it, The government displays distinct reluctance to legislate affirmative action in private industry. The USA boasts of such legislation and industry lobbied President Reagan during the 1980s not to scrap it. It would seem that all the sound and fury about more inclusive growth only tends to conceal the poverty of public commitment. Decent employment-led inclusive growth remains elusive. Credible action remains far short of the stated objective, This reality cannot but generate increasing social turmoil in the years to come.

REFERENCES

Choi, C.K., 1995, "The Theory and Evidence of Intertemporal Substitution in Labour Supply Function", *Journal of Korean Labour Economic Associations*, 18, 1.

Choi, C.K., 2006, "Building an identified Equilibrium Model of Aggregate Labour Market", *Journal of Korean Econometric Association*, 17, 4.

Kapos, Stepen, 2005, "The 'Employment Intensity' of Growth: Trends and Macroeconomic Determinants", ILO.

Dopke, J., 2001, "The 'Employment Intensity of Growth in Europe". Kiel Working Paper No. 1021, Kiel Institute of World Economics.

Islam, I. and Nazara, S., 2000. "Estimating Employment Elasticity for the Indonesian Economy". ILO Technical Note, Jakarta.

Mazumdar, D., 2003. "Trends in Employment and the Employment Elasticity in Manufacturing, 1971-92: An International Comparison". *Cambridge Journal of Economics,* 27:563-582.

Padalino, S. and Vivarelli, M., 1997. "The Employment Intensity of Economic Growth in the G-7 Countries". *International Labour Review,* Summer 1997; 136, 2.

Piacentini, P. and Pini, P., 2000. Growth and Employment, in Vivarelli, M. and Pianta, M. 2000 (eds). The Employment Impact of Innovation: Evidence and Policy, London, Routledge, 44-76.

William Seyfried, "Examining the Relationship between Employment and Economic Growth in the Ten Largest States", *Southern Economic Journal.*

Martin Wolf, "The New Capitalism", *Financial Times,* London, June 19, 2007.

The Times of India (Daily), New Delhi, June 20, 2007.

Barbara Harriss, White and Anushree Sinha (ed.), Trade Liberalization and India's Informal Economy, Oxford, 2007.

Swaminathan, S. Anklesaria Aiyar, *The Times of India,* June 24, 2007.

The Pioneer (Daily), Delhi, July 2007.

Sanjiv Shankaran, Mint (daily), February 21, 2007.

The Statesman (Daily), New Delhi, July 12, 2007.

Challenges of Inclusive Growth in India

Reeta Kumari

The divide between 'two India' is now increasingly sharp. Growing India is co-existing with India caught in low level development trap. Growth should be shared and equity realized. Agricultural incomes are six times lower than non-agricultural sector. Fiscal and financial policies need to be fine-tuned. Next, climate change and reckless mismanagement of environment are causing heavy damage to our economy. Public and Private sectors should become equal and willing partners to achieve higher and inclusive growth. This partnership should be encouraged. Better governance, higher agricultural productivity, more and more number of educational institutions and improvement in infrastructure will ensure inclusive growth.

"India is a country with many poor people but it is not a poor country." With a population of just over 1 billion, in which about 300 millions live below the poverty line, India is the largest democracy in the world and one of the most important countries in terms of meeting global development goals. In the past decade, India has accelerated economic growth, and maintained a vibrant democracy. It has also emerged as a global power—the fourth largest economy in purchasing power parity terms, and a leading player in information technology, telecommunications and business outsourcing.

India's annual GDP growth has been strong and steady at more than 7 percent over the past decade, accelerating to over 9 percent in the three years before the 2008 global financial crisis. Growth followed wide-ranging structural reforms that began in 1991. Between 1997 and 2005, poverty rates fell down from 36 percent to 28 percent. Life expectancy rose significantly to 65 years, reducing the gap with China to about 8 years (composed of gap of 14 years in the early 1980s).

Since 1995, the International Development Association (IDA), the arm of the World Bank that serves the world's poorest countries, provided interest-free credits and grants totaling US $ 14.9 billion to India. During this time, the International Bank for Reconstruction and Development (IBRD), which serves credit-worthy countries, extended loans of US $ 15.8 billion to the country.

The Reform process that began in 1991 was gradual; there was no "big bang". As a result, reforms have become accountable for results. Also note-worthy is the growing role played by states, with greater competition to reform, increased accountability. In India's deregulated and open economy, those states in which government have delivered better governance, public services have attracted greater and more private investment. Conversely, those States where political leaders have not done so, have been punished by a flight of both capital and people. Going forwards, the challenge will be to improve the prospects of the poorest and low income states.

Investment rates, backed by growing savings and led by private investment, have now risen close to 40 percent of GDP, compared to about 24 percent a decade ago. Foreign direct investment grew rapidly until the global financial crisis in 2008.

In the last five years, export growth has accelerated to an average of 27 percent per year. Fiscal deficits have remained high, but prior to the Indian Fiscal Year 2008, there was a declining trend under the fiscal responsibility acts at the centre and the States.

Poverty has fallen to about 28 percent, although the momentum of decline may have slowed for reasons examined below. Growth has helped considerably in progressing towards the Millennium Development Goals (MDGs) but delivery of public services to India's 300 million poor, poses major challenge.

Investment as a growth engine for India was running out of steam in 2008 when bottlenecks in the economy became increasingly apparent. In addition, high International Commodity prices and rising interest rates in response to inflationary pressure lowered corporate profitability. In the last quarter of 2008, large capital outflows put pressure on reserves and rupee. A credit crunch and falling export demand led to a sharp slowdown in growth to less than 6 percent of GDP in the fourth quarter of 2008 and the first-quarter of 2009. The government reacted to the slowdown with swift easing of monetary policy and a sizeable fiscal stimulus. Because of the high commodity prices that were only partially passed on to consumers in the first half of the years, and the fiscal stimulus measures in the last quarter of the fiscal year, the Central Government deficit including off-budget borrowing for oil and other subsidies reached 12 percent of GDP, the highest in two decades.

The picture of "two India's" is now increasingly sharp. While one India is on a rapid development trajectory, the other is progressing much slowly and is caught in a low level development trap. Significant differences persist in poverty levels and human development indicators along gender, ethnic and regional lines.

CHALLENGES AHEAD

Despite India's progress over the past decade, poverty, low agriculture growth, low quality employment, rural-urban divides, poor health and education, regional disparities and environmental pollution in India remain daunting.

1. Poverty

India is still very much a low-income country with per capita income of about US $ 720; over 300 million people live in absolute poverty on less than a dollar a day—the largest geographic concentration of poverty in the World. Another sizeable 350 million people are just above the poverty line with incomes below US $ 2 per day and with few assets, savings or human capital to distinguish them from those below the poverty line.

Few Facts about Poverty in India

- Large number of people suffer from income poverty in India.
- The official poverty lines are anchored to a fixed commodity basket corresponding to the poverty line. (Rs. 49.09 per person per month at 1973-74 prices for rural areas and Rs. 56.64 for urban areas).
- The suggested rural commodity basket by the Expert Group contained 2400 Kcal per capital per day in rural areas and the urban food basket had 2100 Kcal per capita per day in 1973-74.
- Numbers of poor (in million)

Year	*Numbers (in million)*
1973-74	321
1983	323
1993-94	320
2004-05	302

- Income poverty declined from 55% in the early 1970's to 28% in 2004-05.
- Although there has been progress in decline, still more than 300 million are below poverty line.
- 80% of the poor are from rural areas.
- Poverty concentrated in few States (Bihar, Uttar Pradesh and Madhya Pradesh and Orissa, Chhattisgarh and Jharkhand).

- Concentrated among agricultural labourers, casual workers, Scheduled Castes and Scheduled Tribes.

Determinants of Rural Poverty

- Poor agricultural growth
- Relative food prices
- Development of non-farm sector.
- Rural wages.
- Government's development expenditure
- Infrastructure
- Human development.

Policies for Poverty Alleviation

India Adopted Two Relevant Approach

- *Growth approach*: All three sectors contribute (agriculture, industry and services).
- *Direct approach*: Safety nets or anti-poverty programme.
- *Self-employment programme*. (Women's groups), wage employment programme, food subsidies, nutrition programmes for children, old age and maternity benefits.
- *Public distribution system* : Subsidized food.
- *National Rural Employment Guarantee Scheme (NREGS)*—Giving 100 days of wage employment to the poor.

2. Low Agricultural Growth

Since agriculture holds the key to food self-sufficiency, rural incomes and relative stability in prices, the budget package for farmers is expected to provide for waiver of debt for smaller farmers, a moratorium on interest payments, lowering of farm credit rates and a range of measures to improve farm productivity.

Facts about Agriculture Sector

- 65% of people depend upon agriculture for their livelihood.
- Declaration in growth from 3.5% during 1981-97 to 2% during 1997-2005. Also decline in yield growth.
- Land and water problem, vulnerability to world commodity prices, farmers', suicides, 45% of farmers want to leave agriculture but do not know where to go.
- Disparities in growth across regions and crops: Agricultural growth rate declined more in rain-fed areas.

Problems in Indian Agricultural Sector

- *Long-term factors* : Steeper decline in per capita land availability. Shrinking of farm size.
- Slow reduction in Share of employment (Still 55%).
- Main problem is low labour productivity in agriculture. Gap between agricultural and non-agricultural sector is widening.

Three Goals for Inclusive Agricultural Development

1. Achieve 4% growth in agriculture and raise incomes. Increasing productivity (Land, Labour) diversification to high value agriculture and rural non-farm by maintaining food security.
2. *Second goal is sharing growth (equity)* : Focus on small and marginal farmers, lagging regions, women, etc. On lagging regions, focus on eastern India and other rain-fed areas.
3. Third is to maintain sustainability of agriculture by focusing on environmental concerns.

After the above analysis, it is clear that the pace of growth in agriculture sector is just below the 4% target. Agricultural incomes are six times lower than non-agricultural sector. To achieve the goals of inclusive agricultural development, there are major issues still to sort out in agricultural policy. There has to be a clear policy towards accelerating agricultural growth. The problem is particularly severe in the three poorest states of Bihar, U.P. and Orissa. In these states, management of water resources has become a major problem and in fact, significant investments are required to prevent flooding and to improve agricultural practices.

3. Low Quality Employment

In India, employment opportunities largely depend on the private sector. Jobs are increasingly informal and casual and India has a massive unskilled labour with low wages.

Facts a bout Employment Status in India

Share in Output and Employment of Different Sectors

- Agriculture : 20% in GDP, 57% in employment.
- Industry : 23% in GDP, 18% in Employment.
- Services: 57% in GDP, 25% in Employment.
- Employment growth increased in recent years but quality is low.
- Problem of working poor is grim.
- Poverty is much higher than unemployment.
- There were 458 million workers in India in 2004-05.
- Out of this, 423 million workers are informal/ unorganized workers (92%).
- Growth in employment is more in unorganized sector.
- Thus, quality of employment is the biggest problem.
- Workers in this sector do not have social security.
- Government is trying to provide minimum social security to unorganized workers.

After the analysis of the facts about employment status in India, it is obvious that exploitation of labour is widely prevalent. Despite the promulgation of minimum wages, the feudal system in the rural areas and industry in the urban conglomerates continue to fleece labour, paying them wages far below those prescribed. In certain areas, politicians and political parties have their own vested interests in keeping people poor and deprived. They have a readymade electoral constituency which they fear to lose with education and prosperity.

4. Poor Health and Education

Major population especially poor class suffers from malnutrition and illiteracy. Malnutrition stunts physical, mental and cognitive growth and makes children more susceptible to respiratory and diarrheal illness. Malnourished children are more likely to die as a result of common and easily preventable childhood diseases than those who are adequately nourished. According to a UNICEF report, 1.95 million children below the age of five die annually in India mainly from preventable causes that are directly or indirectly attributable to malnutrition. The children who survive the ravages of malnutrition are more vulnerable to infection, do not reach their full height potential and experience impaired cognitive development. This means they do less well in school, earn less as adults and contribute less to the economy.

On the other side, majority of the Indian population is still illiterate or semi-literate. India has the third largest pool of scientists, engineers and doctors in the World, but it has yet to reach anywhere near its full potential. Analysis shows that the literacy rate of the population continues to be low at 64.8 percent according to 2001 census. Furthermore, less than 9 percent of those passing grade 12, actually go in for higher education. This implies that a large proportion of the population is totally outside the school curriculum and even among those who go to the school, overwhelming proportion do not secure the skill levels necessary for secure employment, higher productivity and wages.

5. Environmental Change

The most important challenge faced by the policy-makers today is dealing with climate change. Reckless mismanagement of environment has created unsustainable ecological debt, which, the future generation will have to suffer.

Even in the present generation, the poor will suffer the most due to adverse impact on agricultural productivity, leading submergence of low level coastal areas and increased frequency of extreme events. Overwhelming proportion of greenhouse gas emissions are from developed countries and the share of the United States alone is 23 percent. However, it is the poor in the developing countries who will have to bear the brunt of the adverse impact of climate change.

India is highly vulnerable to climate change as it reduces agricultural productivity and endangers food security, displaces a large number of people when the sea level rises and exposes the poor to the incidence of extreme events. It is estimated that one metre rise in the sea level will displace 7 million persons in India (ADB, 1995). It is therefore, imperative that the country adopts measures aimed at both adaptation to and mitigation of climate change. The most important measure of adaptation is development itself and acceleration of inclusive growth is the key to combat adversities.

It is adopting appropriate mitigation strategy that India faces a dilemma. Although India is seen to be the fifth largest emitter of greenhouse gases (Sathye, Shukla and Rabindranath, 2006), India's share in CO_2 emissions is mere 4% with this low level of emissions. Measures at mitigation by India are unlikely to have any impact on climate change (India, 2008a). At the same time, accelerating growth in the economy would require substantial augmentation of the infrastructure, particularly electricity. Over 79 percent of the prevailing electricity generating capacity is thermal which is predominantly coal-based. The biggest challenge of accelerating growth in an environmental sustainable manner is a real challenge.

The challenges of inclusive, sustainable growth and service delivery are at the center of the government's priorities. Responsibility for action, especially on implementation and enforcement, lies as much with the central as with the State Governments.

Achieving Rapid, Inclusive Growth

India has made less progress than other countries in reducing poverty, and resentment about the unequal distribution of the benefits of growth contributes to social conflicts. Moreover, structural factors and the current slowdown and volatility of the global economy constrain future growth. The Eleventh Plan states that "The target is not just faster growth but also inclusive growth, i.e. a growth process which yields broad based benefits and ensures equality of opportunity for all."

Macroeconomic, fiscal, and financial policies need to be conducive to inclusive growth and stability at the Central and State levels. There is a need to remove infrastructure and skills constraints to growth in both urban and rural areas by forming private sector participation, for example, improving agricultural productivity, rural connectivity and rural livelihoods.

The Politics of Growth and Inclusivity

Despite all the issues holding back the republic and the problems plaguing its development as a nation, the economy has been galloping quite steadily.

India is growing at nearly 9%. We would like to sustain growth at this level for the next ten to twenty years, even taking it up to 10% or higher. Only then would we be closer to realizing our dream of being a developed country. And I would like to see this growth being all pervasive and all encompassing in every sense of the word. It ought to be truly inclusive. All sections of society must get the benefits of this growth in full measure and only then, will be able to take this growth forward by participating fully and wholeheartedly.

This can only happen if the government and the private sector become equal and willing partners. All impediments in the path of public-private partnership should be removed. China has taken a leap ahead of India in this respect with single window clearances and special economic zones. India is slowly trying to cut its red-tape procedures. It has set-up Special Economic Zones (SEZs), giving a host of incentives to industry, at certain selected locations. However, SEZs have also led to a host of unsavory allegations at times. The government needs to come out with transparent procedures for such schemes and also make people, especially farmers whose lands are acquired, willing partners and share holders in the process. Only then we will be able to achieve our economic growth goals.

While on the subject of economic growth and its impediments, we must also refer to the impact and consequences of increasing world fuel prices and the associated threat that looms large over India's future economic growth. Within the last one year, the fuel prices have more than doubled from 65 dollars to nearly 140 dollars a barrel of crude oil, upsetting the entire economic applecart. We can scarcely dream of ten percent growth without sufficient sources of energy. Nuclear power is urgently needed to fill the fuel gap for large scale power generation in India. To ward-off the impending energy crisis, there is an urgent need for all political parties to support efforts at getting India to gain access to relevant technology and fuel resources.

With Inflation figures shooting to a 13 year high at 11.05 percent, the government is mulling some urgent measures to control the situation. However, there are limits to managing the supply side, there has been a record production of wheat and rice and the country has adequate stock of these foodgrains. The government would now take steps to quell inflationary expectation. These may include a rise in interest rates by the Central Bank.

The high inflation rate would probably force the Reserve Bank Of India to increase the interest rates to curtail demand. This will affect the profitability of Companies and Economic growth as a whole. While, in the current fiscal year, GDP growth might be managed at 8%, but if inflationary pressure continues, it is bound to go down in the coming year. The good thing in this scenario is that the savings rate in India is at a high of 35%. With rising interest rates, investors would be tempted to save money. This should help the government to sustain the growth rate.

Prescriptions : Collective Efforts for Inclusive Growth

India has the potential of becoming a leading economy and has the unique opportunity to make that growth inclusive, provided there is willingness on the part of all sections of society to put in hard and disciplined work together with serious, sustained and purposeful planning.

First, there is much that needs to be done to build up India's potential. Better governance, more and better educational institutions, higher agricultural productivity, controlled inflation and improvement in infrastructure are some of the major and more important steps required in this direction. I mention these specifically because each of these steps has a bearing on the inclusiveness of growth as well.

Agriculture is extremely important for inclusive growth, since a large majority of the Indian population is dependent on farming. Improved agricultural productivity would bring in its wake increased family incomes for this vast majority. This together with better infrastructure in the countryside—greater rural connectivity, rural electrification and investment in irrigation, would aid tremendously in tackling rural poverty, as well as add to the overall prosperity of the nation. The "India Shining" campaign of the previous government failed to impress the people precisely for this reason because a majority of the rural populace had remained outside the purview of the increase in national GDP.

Better governance is the need of the hour, more so because the government in India still has a majority stake in almost all essential sectors, e.g. in the crucial sectors of health, sanitation and water. It is in social sectors that we find the political parties least interested especially once they come to power after elections. Yet these are the fields which need to be paid more attention. If we are to improve human development alongside economic growth; with the current situation, it is no wonder that India figures extremely low on world human development index reports. There is a need for more public-private partnerships. The private sector should take more social responsibility and contribute towards making growth more inclusive.

The outstanding success that the country achieved in the telecommunication field—high density across the country and world's cheapest call rates affordable by all needs to be reproduced in other areas. The problem of a massive parallel black economy, which has evaded a solution so far, needs to be tackled urgently and these funds brought into the much needed social sectors.

Education is extremely important for improving the skill levels of the population so that everyone can be an equal partner in the country's growth. More and better universities, schools, and technical institutes should be created. Inflation, which is running today, affects the poor man the most, severely limiting inclusiveness of growth. We need to fix acceptable inflation targets and constantly monitor them so that they do not go beyond the outer agreed limits. Similarly, India's fiscal deficit remains one of the highest in the World, almost 7% of GDP in real terms.

Political parties, across the spectrum, need to look beyond petty politics, sit down and agree on parameters for inflation and fiscal deficit beyond which certain tough economic measures must come into play automatically. Finally, rights of women, children, minority communities and the other marginalized sections of society must be constantly watched and protected if we wish to reach our goal of a truly developed society.

India has been endowed with some of the World's most essential minerals, beautiful places, diverse cultures and capable and talented people. It is time we stop squandering this advantage and make the most of what most countries can never even dream to have. There is much to be done, but if done and done correctly, then nothing can stop us from reaching the pinnacle of the world.

References

India (2008), Economic Outlook for 2008-09, Economic Advisory Council to the Prime Minister. Government of India.

India (2008a), Eleventh Five Year Plan : Inclusive Growth (Vol. I), Planning Commission, Government of India.

Sathye, Jaynath, P.R. Shukla and N.H. Ravindranath (2006), "Climate Change, Sustainable Development of India; Global and National Concerns". *Current Science*, Vol. 90, No. 3.

UNDP (2008), Human Development Report, 2007-08, United Nations Development Programme, 2007.

Inclusive Growth of India and States : An Approach of Rural Non-Farm Sector

AVIRAL PANDEY, PRAVIN KUMAR
AND REENA KUMARI

The process of economic growth has not been inclusive, it has bypassed the poor states, the poor people and the rural India. Punjab and Haryana are getting lion's share of public expenditure on agriculture. Villages of India are backward in health, education and other social infrastructure services as compared to urban areas. Rural Non Farm Sector is a source of improvement and income generation in rural areas and thus RNFS can play its role in bringing greater integration between rural and urban economies and also contributing to rural and overall development. It can be a tool to poverty alleviation as well.

INTRODUCTION

India's recent growth performance has been spectacular, the economy is booming. Over the last two decades due to the adoption of new-liberal policies, the Indian economy has made rapid strides. Following the initiation of structural reforms the Indian economy has grown at an average annual rate of 7.97% between 1992-93 and 2008-09. With sharp declaration in population growth per capita GDP at 1999-2000 prices have registered a growth of 7.2% per annum during 2003-04 to 2007-08. The growth figures have put India in commendable position today. It is now world's second fastest growing economy after China, 4th largest economy of the world in terms of GDP, PPP, and its share in world GDP has increased from 4.3% in 1991 to almost 4.6% in 2008 (IMF, 2008).

The list of achievement is very lengthy and progress indeed praiseworthy. India has truly emerged at the international scene and is stated to finally develop into a major economic power in the next five decade. A number of projections for the Indian economy are being made and it is projected that by 2050 India along with Brazil, Russia and China will form BRIC and will challenge the G-7 and US economies because of their size and economic dynamism.

The magnificent achievement and encouraging projections have given Indians a lot to cheer and feel happy about. However, all have not gone well with the Indian economy. It is a widely accepted fact that the fruits of development have not been evenly distributed. The process of economic growth has not been inclusive. It has tended to benefit the rich and prosperous states at the cost of the poor and backward states, the urban India at the cost of rural India and rich at the cost of poor. The growth process has bypassed or excluded the poor states, poor people and rural India. The exclusive growth by splitting the society into groups of the favoured and deprived ones is threatening to play spoil sport to India's oft quoted outstanding success story.

The exclusiveness of the growth process has forced to think in terms of inclusive growth, a process that includes all sections of the society. A number of alternative paths are being suggested to make inclusive growth a reality. The present paper attempts a solution in form of development of non-farm sector. It attempts to prove that if impetus is given on the development of non-farm sector, it by creating gainful employment in the non-agricultural sector, encouraging population to shift to productive employment and generating demand, will raise the level of income of the poor thereby reducing interpersonal inequality, by promoting development of rural sector, reduce urban-rural divide and by giving the economies of backward states a new lease of life and reduce regional inequality. The present paper aims at exploring the ways in which non-farm sector can make the growth process inclusive.

In this paper an attempt is made to analyze how Rural Non Farm Sector can be used as a tool of inclusive growth. *The paper* is divided in following four sections. *Part I* briefly narrates India's growth experience and shows how the process has remained exclusive. *Part II* talks about the theoretical aspects of "inclusive growth". *Part III* is the heart of paper and deals with how RNFS can be used as a tool to promote Inclusive Growth. *Part IV* gives final conclusion. *Part V*. Offers some suggestions.

PART I

INDIA'S GROWTH EXPERIENCE

India's growth story has been a mixed one. On the one hand we have the positives high growth across manufacturing and services sector, booming equity and commodity markets and on the other hand *we have negative exclusive growth, poor growth in agriculture.* After Independence government of India started "Five Years Plan" to achieve the economic goal of development. To increase productivity and irrigation facilities planners paid attention and increased funding agriculture sector. The Nehru-Mahalanobis growth strategy paid special emphasis on building "Industrial Atmosphere" for stable growth. Government started many social welfare and employment schemes to reduce poverty and gaps between rich and poor. But when we re-look the growth process of India, we find that work done by the planners is exclusive in nature. In

India, all segments of economy do not posses good positions. Agriculture which is an important sector of economy is growing at a dismal rate of 2 or 3% whereas industry is growing at 9% and service sector at 13-14%. The growth process definitely has not done appropriate task. Agriculture where 59% (about 60 crore people) are involved today contribute only 17% of GDP of India while it contributed 50% in 1947-48. We can feel happy about the growth of the service sector and industry, but this growth has not increased jobs. The growth has been "jobless growth". Regional disparity has increased over the years in India. The unskilled labour in India is mainly engaged in the manufacturing and agriculture sector. The daily wages offered to the labours in eastern India is substantially low as compared to that of the northern part of India. For example, the daily wage earned by a labour in the manufacture sector in Bihar is approximately Rs. 40 per day compared to other parts of India, where it is Rs. 100 per day. Punjab and Haryana are getting lion's share of Public expenditure of Agriculture.

According to Bhattacharya and Sekthiwl[1] at constant prices (1993-94) percentage growth of SDP per annum was 5.12% in Andhra Pradesh, 3.46 in Bihar, 8.23% in Goa, 8.28% in Gujarat, 4.6% in Rajasthan, 7.24% in Uttar Pradesh during 1999-2000. Coefficient of Variation was 0.14 in 1980-90, 0.29% in 1999-2000. This is clear from the Table 1. The variation indicates the increasing disparities between these states. Some good states like Karnataka, Gujarat, Maharashtra got the lion's share in FDI since 1990. This was due to infrastructure development in these states. So the gap between the states is become widening.

Rural urban disparity is clear from Table 2 that big rural population is lower and lower-middle class. There is also rural-urban gap in measuring of HDI Index in which the value for rural sector is just 0.340 in the case of urban it is 0.511.

A recent World Bank Report on India (Sustaining Reform, Reducing Poverty, 2003) as also the UNDP's Human Development Report, 2003 have expressed grave concern over the widening interstate disparities and the growing rural-urban gap in India. 93% population in rural India earns less than 915 rupees. This shows the joy of urban person enjoying.

TABLE 1
Growth Rate of SDP at Constant Prices

(Per cent per annum)

State	*1980-90*	*1990-2000*	*1980-2000*
Andhra Pradesh	4.81	5.12	5.05
Assam	3.91	2.47	3.49
Bihar	5.20	3.46	3.85
Gujarat	5.71	8.28	6.80
Haryana	6.68	6.71	7.80
Kerala	4.50	6.00	5.97
Madhya Pradesh	5.18	5.45	5.89
Orissa	5.85	3.60	3.90
Uttar Pradesh	5.88	4.24	5.15
Coefficient of variation	0.14	0.29	0.22

Sources : Research paper—Regional growth and disparity in India: A comparison of pre and post-Reform decades, Bhattacharya and Sekthiwl.

TABLE 2
Income Groups in India

Income groups	*Household income*	
	Rural	*Urban*
Low (2000)	65.4	36.7
Lower-Middle (2001-40000)	23.2	33.1
Middle (40001-62000)	7.5	17.1
Upper-Middle (62001-86000)	2.5	7.8
High (>86000)	1.4	5.3

Source : Human Development Report of India, 1999.

The disparities among income earners are clear from the fact that 10% top income earners have 33% of the GDP. One-fourth of people earn less than $ 0.40/day which is Government poverty threshold limits. Gini coefficient in India was 32.5% in 1999-2000 which expresses the inequality in India.

If anybody thinks about this exclusive growth, then they can find about a mysterious point that states which have been excluded and left out are basically states in which urbanization is low. Planners have not done sufficient exercise to minimize rural-urban gap in between these states. The gap is growing with fast speeds. If one sees opportunities in India, villagers have not enough opportunities. They are backward in education, health and other social infrastructural services as compared to urban areas. To decrease rural-urban gap former President of India A.P.J. Abdul Kalam proposed the view of "PURA" (Provision of Urban Amenities in Rural Area) vision. The main concern is to think that "what are the factors which divide rural-urban economies?" "PURA" vision can come in success by creating various activities and infrastructure services which are developed in urban areas. If there exists sufficient opportunity for jobs for villagers, then villages can be developed and the gap between "rural-urban" can decrease. From various studies and looking facts in villages "Non-Farm Activities" in villages have attracted all of economists. "Non-Farm Sector Employment" is creating various opportunities and facilitating various facilities in villages. After globalization in the war of competition, every one wants to minimize the "cost of production". Some activities like "processing" are profitable in rural areas. So all activities as "Rural Non-Farm Sector" is a great concern to achieve inclusive growth in India. Rural Non-Farm Sector will also facilitate market to urban producer. So if once a process of "RNFS" starts then it will include not only rural area but also urban area. In villages agriculture is important but recent experiences and studies had made clear that Agriculture cannot create much job in future. But Non-Farm Sector is playing increasing role in job creation. So there is need of a growth plan for "RNFS".

PART II

THEORETICAL ASPECTS OF INCLUSIVE GROWTH

The word "inclusive" has become not only fashionable but also quite relevant in our country. The Oxford Dictionary gives many meanings to the word and the most inclusive meaning is "not excluding any section of society". In this sense, the title of the approach paper on the eleventh five year plan "Towards faster and more inclusive growth" reflects the need to make growth more inclusive in terms of benefits flowing through more employment and income to those sections of society which have been bypassed high rates of economic growth witnessed in recent year.

"Inclusive growth" expresses target in terms of social object. It is growth which comes from all sections of economy and covers all sections of economy. There is a gap between poor and rich, villages and towns, men and women, if the growth decreases this gap, then the growth will be inclusive in nature.

Inclusive growth gives importance to all sections of the society. If agriculture grows at 4%, industry at 9%, service at 11% then average growth $\text{GDP} = \frac{4+9+11}{3} = \frac{24}{3} = 8\%$. In recent growth phenomena, we say that we are enjoying 8% growth then one can find that section agriculture grows just a 4% which gives employment to 59% of total population. Agricultural has been bypassed in the past and it is being bypassed in the present also. On the other hand, industry and service sector growth do not create sufficient job. In fact, employment growth declined from 2.7% per year in 1987 to 1% in 1994-2000.

Inclusive growth strategy as propagated by Planning Commission of India basically targets to eliminate poverty specially "Rural poverty" and distribute the fruits of development more equitably. Rural poverty is associated with limited access to land and livestock, poor education and health care as also low paid occupations and social status. All problems are associated with need of employment. If there is sufficient employment and income to all people then this will generate new demand. Thus demands for several things like Non-food materials introduce a new market. These markets will attract new investment. Investment will increase productive activities. Thus employment will generate an era of growth.

PART III

HOW RNFS CAN BE USED AS A TOOL TO PROMOTE "INCLUSIVE GROWTH"

The non-farm sector, particularly in rural areas is being accorded wider cognition in recent years as a potent instrument for alleviating rural poverty and providing employment opportunities. Arguments for paying attention to the non-farm sector generally centre on the sector's perceived potential in absorbing a growing rural labour force, in slowing rural-urban migration, in contributing to national income growth and in promoting a more equitable distribution of income.

The concept of RNFS is defined as employment in many diversified activities such as manufacture, processing, repair, construction, mining, trade and commerce, transport and other several activities in rural area.

The traditional image of farm household countries has been that they focus almost exclusively on farming and undertake little rural non-farm activity. Policy debate still tends to equate with rural income and rural/urban relations with farm and non-farm relations. Policy-makers have neglected importance of RNFS. Nevertheless there is mounting evidence that RNFS income is an important source for farm and other rural households including the landless poor as well as rural town residents. In this section focus is on RNFS so as to enable closer examination of what can be done with rural areas themselves to create overall economic activity and employment. India has 7.50 lakh villages and majority of population (72%) of the country lives in these villages which contributes 18.55 of GDP.[2] Yet this sector continues to support more than half billion people providing employment to 52% 0f workforce. The rural economy is the main base of Indian economy. If rural economy of country is staggering, it will affect country's economy adversely. Villagers are mostly depending on Agriculture sector. But they are not satisfied in Agriculture sector because growth has not included them to share the fruits.

Agriculture has some negatives because of its nature. Some definite incidents happen by nature as drought, flood, etc. tends farmers to differentiate their work in various other activities which is generally called "RNFS". In recent decade role of RNFS is increasing in rural economy to absorb surplus labour. According to NCAR survey a large share of employment and incomes are provided by RNFS in recent years.

There are several reasons why the promotion of RNFS activity can be of great interest to developing country like India. First evidence shows that RNFS incomes are an important factor in household economics and therefore also in food security since it allow greater access to food. This source of income may also prevent rapid or excessive urbanization as well as natural resources degradation through over exploitation. RNFS activity affects the performance of agriculture by providing farmers with cash to invest in productivity enhancing inputs development. Of RNFS activity in the food system (including agro-processing, distribution and the provision of farm inputs) may increase the profitability of farming by increasing the availability of inputs and improving access to market outlets. RNFS can play greater role in agriculture-based states like Bihar, U.P., Orissa, and M.P.

Linkage of Agriculture	*Secondary Sector (Construction and Manufacturing)*	*Tertiary sector trading and services*
Production Forward	Processing and Packaging industries. Construction of storage and marketing facilities	Transport and trade
Production Backward	Agriculture tools and equipment	Agricultural and Veterinary services inputs supply
Consumption	Household items. Home improvement	Domestic services Transportation sales of consumer goods

We can see the conceptual linkage of Non Farm Sector to other Sector of economy in following chart. There are some database results which are based on N.S.S. data (Not considering NSS data for 1987-78 that was a drought year). The percentage of RNFE in total rural employment increased from 16.6% in 1977-88 to 23.8 in 1999-2000. Yearly increase in the percentage of RNFE is 0.35% per annum during the reform period of 1993-94 to 2000. Total number of workers have increased 71.52 million in 1999-2000 from 36.1 million in 1977-78. From 1993-94 to 1999-2000 RNFE was divided into 36% in Construction, 27% in Manufacturing, 25.5% in Transport and Storage and 13% in Retail trade. Importance of RNFS is clear from the fact due to lower growth rate of employment in "RNFS", it has to be seen the low overall growth in employment (overall 1%) during the reform period. But 90% of additional employment during the reform period was due to RNFS as compared to 39% in the earlier period.

Average growth rate of non agriculture sector was 4.9% during 1951-52 to 1967-68, 6.4% during 1981 to 1990-91, 6.6% during 1991-92, 10.7 in 2005-06 to 2006-07 at 1999-2000 prices (Chapter 7, Economic Survey, 2007-08). Beside agriculture there are so many non-farm activities which are growing much faster than agriculture. For India, the estimates regarding growth in output or income of the rural non-farm sector are not available. However, one can get an indication of the performance of this sector from the changes in its share in employment. Table 3 gives the share of workers in secondary and tertiary sector in rural India from 1977-78 to 1999-2000. However, since there was drought in 1987-88, which drove a sizeable workforce to rural non-farm activities, especially for construction under public workers. The data for this year needs to be excluded for the purpose of comparison (Devanand Sharma, 1999).

The Rural Non-Farm Sector (RNFS) plays a significant role in providing employment and income for the poor in rural areas. As population pressure grows in land-scarce states, growth in agricultural production cannot absorb increasing rural labour force in agricultural employment. The urban industrial sector cannot grow fast enough to absorb the surplus labours released from agriculture. This leaves the RNFS to absorb the population released from agriculture and unable to absorb in urban industries. The Non-farm economy accounts for 40 to 60% of total national employment and rural Non-farm economy accounts for 20 to 50% of total rural employment (ADB, 2000).[3]

Table 3
Broad Sectoral Distribution of Workers in Rural India (Usual Status PS + SS); 1977-78 to 1999-2000

Year	*Primary*	*Secondary*	*Tertiary*	*Rural non-agricultural (3+4)*
1977-78	83.4	8.0	8.6	16.6
1983	81.5	9.0	9.4	18.4
1987-88	78.3	11.3	10.3	21.6
1993-94	78.2	10.2	11.5	21.7
1999-2000	76.1	11.3	12.5	23.8

PS and SS refer to principal status and subsidiary status respectively.
Source : Study of Dev (2002).

Many studies indicate that the RNFS growth based on growth linkage to successful farmers and their employees, to demand booming services has a better chance to cut poverty. Most traditional RNFS participation reflecting family skills, land shortage or the need to diversify against seasonal employment or annual drought risk is linked to poverty so it should not be neglected; but modern linkage-based RNFS is more promising way out of poverty (e.g. Mellor, 1976, Hazell, 1984, 1989, 1990).[4] Studies of rural area of Asia (India) reveal strong linkage between agricultural growth and rural Non-farm economy, which tends to follow agricultural growth and depends mostly on local and regional demand.

The theoretical proposition on processes and patterns of development and the empirical observation of the country suggest that the rural non-farm sector can be made to play role in bringing greater integration between rural and urban economies and generally contributing to rural and overall development. The diversification of the demand basket in India from cereals to other food items and non-crop-based agriculture products like animal husbandry and forest-based products, provides the demand base for the growth of the RNFS.

The RNFS can be an important for poverty alleviation if disadvantaged groups increase their participation in its activities. So it is necessary to recognize the importance of non-farm activities in faster and balanced growth not only in rural areas but in the economy as a whole and therefore it is important to treat the RNFS as a strategic element in the development strategy rather than a transient and survival induced appendage to agriculture.

CONCLUSION

Inclusive growth is a hard task. But a well practical growth plan can achieve this goal. In this growth model we have to induce policies for "ignored people". It is well defined that growth covered urban areas but rural areas are still underdeveloped. So rural development is need for inclusive growth in India. Linkages to farm sector, industrial sector, service sector, through forward and backward linkages with RNFS have a bright future in India, when all economies are trying to achieve sustainable development. The approach of growth through RNFS was also proposed by Gandhi in his "sarvoday gram yojna". So in India where majority of people are poor, uneducated and having not any technological knowledge RNFS can make a joyful growth path for them and thus in inclusive growth.

SUGGESTIONS

It is true that RNFS have created a job full growth for rural India. But inclusive growth has a "Complete Economic Target". So government has to focus on those areas which were bypassed. A five pronged strategy is needed for enhancement in the livelihoods, for the rural poor for inclusive growth in India. First, the government should have policies to improve education and skills of the workers. Second, they should have several policies to increase employment for the unskilled workers. Third, the incomes of the women have to be improved by creating opportunities in the higher productivity sectors. Fourth, the government should provide infrastructural support to rural India also. Fifth, a good governance and health facilities should be provided by government which will enhance the productivity of factors of production.

Notes and References

1. Research Paper, "Regional Growth and Disparity in India"—A Comparison of Pre and Post-Reform Decades. Bhattacharya, B.D. and Sekthiwl.
2. For India Inc. Rural Market is a Shot in Dark, *The Economic Times,* New Delhi, 29 January 2002, p. 1.
3. Asian Development Bank (2000): Rural Asia—Beyond the Green Revolution, Manila.
4. Fan, S. and P. Hazell (2000), Should Developing Countries Invest More in Less Favored Areas? *Economic and Political Weekly,* April.

References

Ahluwalia, Montek S. (2000), "Economic Performance of States in Post-Reforms Period", *Economic and Political Weekly,* May 6, pp. 1637-48.

Bhattacharya, B.B. and Sekthiwl S. Research Paper—"Regional Growth and Disparity in India"—A Comparison of Pre and Post-Reform Decades, www.iegindia.org/workpap/wp244.pdf

Chadha, G.K. (2003), Rural Nonfarm Sector in the Indian Economy: Growth, Challenges and Future Direction. Mimeo. *International Food Policy Research Institute,* Washington D.C.

Deaton, Angus and Dreze, Jean (2002), "Poverty and Inequality in India—A Re-Examination", *Economic and Political Weekly,* September 7, pp. 3729-48.

Dev, S. Mahendra (2002), Pro-Poor Growth In India : What do we know about the Employment Effects of Growth, 1980-2000?, Working Paper 161, presented at ODI.

Economic Growth in the States of India, IMF Staff Papers, Vol. 43, No. 1, March, pp. 123-71.

Hazell, P.B.R. (1984), Rural Growth Linkages and Rural Development Strategy. Paper Presented at the Fourth European Congress of Agricultural Economics, September 3–7, Kiel, Germany.

Hazell, P.B.R., and S. Haggblade (1989), Farm-nonfarm growth linkages and the welfare of the poor. Paper presented at the World Bank/IFPRI Poverty Research Conference, October 2, Airlie House, Va., U.S.A.

———, 1990, Rural-urban Growth Linkages in India. Working Paper No. 430. Washington D.C.: World Bank.

Mellor, J.W., 1976. The New Economics of Growth: A Strategy for India and the Developing World. Ithaca, N.Y., U.S.A.: Cornell University Press.

India's Present Rural Scenario and Challenges of Inclusive Growth

REETA KUMARI BHAGAT

Social and Physical infrastructure lack in rural areas. Development has not percolated in our villages in perceptible manner. Dr. Abdul Kalam's advocacy of providing urban facilities in rural areas can change the position for the better. Second Green Revolution can make a turn around. Boost to agriculture, rural infrastructure and rural non-farm activities will revive employment opportunities in rural India. MGNREGS can add to social and physical infrastructure. Self-help groups can help the rural poor. The rural orientation of the 11th plan reflects the will of the Government to change our rural scenario.

Development of rural areas is the major challenge of inclusive growth. Development schemes, programmes must reach the rural India, otherwise the overall development process at macro-level, leaving behind those in villages is meaningless.

'The soul of India lives in its villages', said the father of the nation, M.K. Gandhi. Almost after a century, it still holds true for India. More than seventy percent of the country's population lives in villages. The major challenges before our policy-makers are to draft policies to eliminate poverty, generate employment and develop infrastructure in the rural areas for inclusive development of our country.

Development implies overall possible change in the physical quality of life of the people. This positive change includes both economic, as well as social aspects and involves as improvement in the general standard of living. Therefore, development not only calls for economic growth, but also implies equitable distribution of the gains of economic growth all over country.

If we examine the Indian situation which is very much indicative of the state of development in the Third World, despite the sustained economic growth maintained during the last few years and the great hype about the benefits of globalization and liberalization of the economy, there has been very little change in the conditions in the rural countryside, specially of the poorer sections of the population. In fact, recent surveys make startling revelations about their livelihood, education and health conditions. Moreover, apart from the severe lack of social infrastructure, the physical infrastructure development has also been quite slow though one has to agree that some progress has been made in the last years.

The *National Sample Survey report on* 'Level and Pattern of Consumer expenditure 2004-05 on revealed that one-third of the rural population or over 200 million still live on less than Rs. 12 a day. States like Bihar, Jharkhand, Orissa, Chhattisgarh, Madhya Pradesh, and UP remained the poorest states in the country in terms of 'monthly per capita consumer expenditure' (MPCI) of rural population. Compared with 30 percent at the all India level, in Orissa and Chhattisgarh as many as 55-57 percent of the village population was living below the level of Rs. 365, which is 12 a day, the report said adding that 10 percent of the all India rural population was living at just

Rs. 12 a day. It is significant to mention here that apart from Orissa even Bihar and Jharkhand, which are considered mineral-rich states, 46 percent of population are at Rs. 12 a day. In Karnataka and Maharashtra, the well-developed states of the country, 32 and 30 percent of the population were living on this paltry income respectively. It is thus quite clear that the development process has not percolated to a major section of the rural population.

Another report of the '*World Food Programme, 2006*', has pointed out that 50 percent of the world's hungry are in India. Moreover, 35 percent of the country population, around 360 million is food insecure, consuming less than 80 percent of the minimum energy requirement. Nearly-nine out of 10 pregnant women between 15 and 49 years are malnourished and anemic. It may be pertinent to mention here that anemia in women is indeed a big problem especially in rural areas, and anemia causes 20 percent infant mortality.

The conditions of children are no less precarious. Three in four children are anemic and one in three stunted and this has been revealed by the recent *National Family Health Survey*, carried out simultaneously in 29 states during 2005 and 2006. With 21 percent stunted children, the worst affected state is Uttar Pradesh where 46 percent children are malnourished, both physically and mentally, because they do not get nutritious food to eat. It is a matter of concern that all the National Family Survey, between 1992-2006, has indicated the same abysmal trend. "The nutritional status of children has gone up marginally but in some states like Gujarat and Madhya Pradesh, it has actually worsened. India cannot hope to compete in the global market in the future if the physical and mental development of children is stunted, observed *UNICEF*. India's hunger indices—measured by child nutrition, child mortality and calorie-deficient people are however marginally high, its ranks at the lowest of 93 in a group of 199 developing countries on the Global Hunger Index, 2006. India has been citied as one of the countries that has been unable to use its economic resources effectively in reducing hunger and undernutrition.

Even with the revised *Human Development Index,* which used the yardstick of GDP per capita together with the supplements of life expectancy and a composite measure of education, including literacy and school enrolment, India climbed slightly from the rank of 132 out of 174 countries in 1999 to 127 out of 177 in 2005. However, it fared poorly by the old measurement of GDP per capita by being ranked 131 out of 177 in the *'United Nation Human Development Report, 2005'*.

All these pictures speak very poorly of a country, which boasts of high economic growth and is considered to be one of the emerging economies. The picture that is evident from the above scenario reflects that the benefits of development has not percolated to the lower echelons of society but cornered by the richer sections of society. One can thus safely say that uneven development between the urban and the rural sectors and between the rich and the poor have had very little effect on the major sections of the Indian population, which is indeed tragic for country of India's size and dimension.

The question that obviously arises at this juncture is whether the right strategy of development has been followed in the country and, if not, what alternative strategy should be pursued. At the very outset, it may be pointed out that the neglect of the rural countryside over the years has had a disastrous effect on the social and economic conditions of the rural population. The increase in various types of activities like militancy, terrorism and inter-religious conflicts may be attributed to widening gulf between the rich and the poor and also between the uneven and imbalanced nature of development.

The most significant aspect that comes to our mind is the advocacy of Dr. A.P.J. Abdul Kalam, on regeneration of the rural sector and his *'theory of providing urban facilities in rural areas'*. Even at the 1st Asia-Pacific Ministerial Conference on 'Human Settlements', Dr. Kalam suggested the creation of four types of connectivity namely, *physical, electronic, knowledge and economic,* linking cities and rural growth centers so as to minimize the need for rural-urban migration. He also stressed the need to preserve rural heritage and culture, and the rural environment through optimum utilization of local resources, drawing much from Mahatma Gandhi's thinking and philosophy.

This, however, is not being followed in the country, as there has not been proper decentralization of political and economic power at the *grass root levels* though this was envisaged in the 73rd and the 74th amendment to the constitution. Reversing the neglect of the rural sector has been a major task before the government and one cannot deny that some action has been taken in this regard by the government since the new millennium. One may mention here programmes like Bharat-Nirman, National Rural Health Mission, National Rural Employment Guarantee Scheme (NREGS), etc. that have been trying to develop the rural infrastructure so as to ensure better livelihood conditions for the masses.

The emphasis in the coming years has thus geared towards regenerating the rural sector, especially in the 11th Plan period. Obviously the core area is modernization of agriculture, which the Prime Minister has also been talking about in terms of ushering in a *Second Green Revolution*. According to him, a double digit growth rate cannot be accomplished without a turnaround of the rural economy. Even the approach paper of the 11th Plan concedes that deceleration in agriculture growth from 3.2 percent between 1980 and 1996-97 to 1.5 percent subsequently has adversely affected the landless, the marginalized and the middle farmers. It has thus called for 4 percent growth rate in the agriculture sector, enhance the scope of employment and spread the scope of basic education and health to every nook and corner across the country.

In this backdrop, expectations are that 11th Plan will give a boost to the agriculture, rural infrastructure and rural non-farm activities, thereby reviving job opportunities in the rural areas in addition to laying a road map towards effective management of food economy. The new budget has attempted to lay stress on the *'common man'* and *'rural India'*, taking steps for consolidating efforts on rural development, employment, food security, education, health and housing.

Some of the important steps and programmes concerning social and physical infrastructure in the Rural India have been analyzed below.

1. Rural Employment

The low work participation rates in the rural areas are due to the non-availability of employment opportunities and the necessary investment needed for job avenues in rural sectors. 'Mahatma Gandhi National Rural Employment Guarantee Scheme' (MNREGS), in this context, is expected to have the potential to create job opportunities at the grass root level and remove such demand side rigidities from the rural scenario. The scheme has completed four years of its implementation and has provided 100 days employment to around 40 million rural households. Considering the importance of spread and outreach of the wage employment, an amount of Rs. 40,100 crore has been provided to this scheme which is Rs. 1,000 crore more than the allocation made for the scheme during 2009-10.

The Government has proposed to restructure the ongoing rural self-employment programme, i.e., 'Swarnjayanti Gram Swarozgar Yojana' as the 'National Rural Livelihood Mission' with a view to eradicate poverty in a time-bound manner. It has allocated Rs. 2,683 crore to this programme which, in addition to its self-employment initiatives would focus at meeting the specific needs of women farmers. Efforts are proposed for linking the poor and the asset-less to the formal banking network through constitution of self-help groups or activity groups in rural areas. It is felt that the Self Help Groups constituted and assisted by various agencies like Ministry of Rural Development, National Bank for Agriculture and Rural Development, Rashtriya Mahila Kosh, etc. would be an effective medium for socio-economic transformation in rural areas as this group-based participatory development approach is most likely to ensure social, economic and political empowerment to the poor.

2. Rural Health

The enhanced allocation to Ministry of Health and Family Welfare from Rs. 19,534 crore in 2009-10 to Rs. 22,300 crore in 2010-11 indicated the government's concern over the quality of life of the masses. The country's health sector has continued to witness a wide inter-state, male-female and rural-urban disparities in its outcomes and impacts. The National Rural Health Mission which was implemented from April 2005 envisaged accessible, affordable and accountable quality health services to the poorest households in the remote rural regions of the country. The allocation of fund for National Rural Health Mission was Rs. 13,910 crore *vis-à-vis* Rs. 12,096 crore during 2009-10. This increment in the allocation is to establish a fully functional, community-owned, decentralized health delivery system and would fulfil the vision of *'Health for All'*. Implementing and supporting a regular annual health survey for compilation of district and sub-district health data base would help in better health administration in the districts.

3. Rural Housing

Under Phase I of the Rural Housing component of Bharat Nirman, 60 lakh houses were envisaged through the 'Indira Awas Yojana' all over the country during the four years from 2005-06 to 2008-09. Against this target, 71.76 lakh houses were constructed. During the Current financial year 2009-10, as against the target of construction of 40.52 lakh houses, 18.57 lakh houses have been constructed. The Government has proposed to construct 120 lakh houses during the next five-year period starting the year 2009-10. Considering the double digit inflationary situation in the economy, the centre has proposed the enhancement of the unit cost of construction of houses.

4. Agriculture

The 11th Plan tried to give a big push to agriculture, as this sector provides livelihood to two-thirds of our population. Besides directing the policy initiatives towards improving productivity and production, emphasis is on bringing in the eastern India under green revolution. Provisions are made to pump in Rs. 400 crore to prepare eastern India to bring in a green revolution as this region was largely unaffected by the first round of 'Green Revolution of late 1960s'. Budget 2010-11 has also emphasized on the opening up of retail trade to reduce large price differentials prevalent between the producers and consumes of the agro-produce. A four pronged policy strategy has been planned in the budget to ensure sustainable growth in this sector. *This includes enhancing agricultural production, reducing agro-wastages, strengthening credit supply channels at rural areas and promoting food processing sector for processing, value addition of the agro-produce*. To ensure adequate and timely credit to the needy, small and marginal farmers, the budget 2010-11 has announced the extension of the geographic coverage of banks by providing additional banking licenses to the private sector player and non-banking financial companies. Further, regional rural banks would be provided financial support with a view to strengthen these banks for onward lending to the prospective rural farmers.

5. Food Security

The centre has reaffirmed the early introduction of a Bill on 'Food Security laws' under which a BPL family would be legally entitled to 25 kg of rice and/or wheat per month at Rs. 3 a kg. Currently, a BPL family is entitled to 35 kg of rice at Rs. 4.15 per kilo or wheat at Rs. 5.65 a kilo per month. While four crore BPL families are benefiting from the current provision, after the enactment of the food security laws, an additional 2 crore families would be added to the existing list of beneficiaries. While this is a laudable step taken by the Government in ensuring food security to the poor, it is expected that to fulfil the intended objective of access to food at affordable prices, the government would look into the issues of pilferage in the supply of foodgrain, inefficient food management, high transport cost, quality of the foodgrains supplied to the beneficiaries, etc. in the proposed law.

The large allocation for various flagship programmes is expected to build on the foundations already laid by the *'Bharat Nirman Programme and other social sector programmes'*. The benefits of the programmes providing opportunities for improved living conditions and ensuring adequate livelihood to the rural people is expected to work through a multiplier effect. To achieve the targets set for each of the programmes, a facilitating physical and social infrastructure is an important pre-requisite. Therefore, the Eleventh Five Year Plan (2007-12) has laid the thrust on the creation of an enabling rural infrastructure. The priority given to social sector and *rural development schemes and projects* indicates that the Government is on a mission to revive the recessionary phase of the economy by boosting demand and removing both demand and supply side constraints in the economy. The government has reposed its focus on social sector and rural development initiatives and to spend 37 percent of the plan outlay in 2010-11 on social sector programmes and another 25 percent allocations are earmarked for rural infrastructure.

The rural orientation of the 11th Plan highlights the fact that the policy-makers of the country have understood urgent policy initiatives required for agricultural and rural development to make a turnaround in the growth of the agriculture and allied sector and strengthen and widen existing rural infrastructure sectors. The sudden deceleration of economic growth due to the global financial meltdown would generate domestic demand for goods and services and would ensure an all inclusive growth. In this context, the government attempting to address technological issues in agriculture entails the doubling of agricultural credit flow, providing employment to the needy, empowering the poor, bringing more children under the purview of formal education, enhancing skill sets of the population, improving rural health care and pushing developmental initiatives.

The emphasis of the Government on social sectors is aimed at ensuring Rural development and Inclusive growth. While outlays are provided by the central government, outcomes are decided by the performance of State-governments and Local-self-governments. Thus, to achieve the objective of rural development and inclusive growth with economic stability, a common effort is needed:

1. Converge all resources directed towards development intervention.
2. Successfully implement welfare plans and programmes.
3. Bring in effective monitoring mechanism to match the outlays with the intended outcome.

To achieve these objectives revamping of the Panchayats and greater power to them are given high priority during the 11th Plan period, their operation and achievement *vis-à-vis* targets for their better administration at grass-root level. The Economic Survey, 2009-10, in spite of deceleration in the growth scale of the country's GDP during 2008-09 and 2009-10, expressed its optimism towards achieving the country's growth target of 8.75 percent, during the financial year 2010-11. Besides, the greatest challenge has been to ensure the plan objective of an all inclusive growth.

The Gandhian concept of development visualizes self-supporting rural economies for which each village would be perceived as a complete republic, independent of its neighbours for its basic wants like food, clothing, education, water, etc. Similarly, the Buddhist model of development places, the individual human being, rather than maximization of economic growth or capital accumulation as the central focus. These theories have great relevance today.

The future of modern India unequivocally depends upon the face of rural India. The benefits of schemes launched by the centre are trickling down at the implementation level. In many of the schemes, the states are major stakeholders. Their full cooperation and people's participation in making any scheme a success is necessary. If the Government follows up its various action plans with avowed commitment, most of scourges currently plaguing the rural economy would be wiped out and rural progress ushered in the rural India to make a marked difference in the quality of life to millions of people.

References

Anil, K. Rajvanshi, India Shining needs Sustainable Rural Development, in Project Monitor, May 15-31, 2004 issue on India Vision, 2020.

Yojana, March 2009, p. 12.

APJ Kalam, Speech 26th January 2006.

Kurukshetra, May 2006, p. 27.

Yojana, March 2010, p. 33.

The Economic Challenger, No. 8, Issue 30, January-March 2006.

The Hindu Survey of Indian Agriculture, 2006.

23

Inclusive Growth and Education in India

SHASHI PRABHA

Education is key to making of human capital. Educational system needs not to be discriminatory; rather it should impart quality education to all. Gaping chasm in quality of education between private and public schools is a matter of concern. Disparity and exclusion should give way to "quality education for all". Works of Lucas (1988), Barro (1999) and Duraisami (2002) all suggest the importance of education in ensuring economic growth. Inequality based on income, gender, religion, caste, region, etc. needs to be addressed. Primary education and female education are more important for ensuring proper economic development as well as proper development of personality.

Education is considered to have a strong correlation with social and economic development. In contemporary times the focus is on knowledge economy. The role of education becomes all the more important in the development of human capital. A society of literate and skilled citizens has more chance of development of economic and social levels. Education can reduce poverty and social injustice by providing underprivileged persons an opportunity for upward social mobility and social inclusion.

However, this engine of growth encounters pitfalls. A lack of political commitment of the state has resulted in multiple education systems which are inherently discriminating and biased in nature. A large number of students who make it to schools, however drop out by class V. According to NEP, about 72% make it to grade V which means a drop-out rate of 28% (2007).

Such a large number of students outside schools means that they are deprived of opportunities to learn and acquire skills for playing a meaningful role in the society. Social exclusion is a great loss at individual and social levels. Most of those out of school children experience poverty and unemployment and some get involved in some criminal activity.

Constitutionally, the provision of basic education to citizens is the state responsibility. Is the state carrying out this responsibility? The state needs to analyze the reasons behind the number of out of school children. They come from poor families and cannot afford the luxury of education despite their desire.

Besides enrolment in school, it should also ensure the provision of quality education that is the quality of building, faculty, management, text books, curriculum, examinations, medium of instruction as well as socio-economic conditions of the children.

The widening difference between private and public schools is responsible for the gaping chasm between resources and opportunities given to the poor and the rich. Children from elite schools have enhanced chances of employment and social integration whereas children from public schools, no matter how bright they are, are disadvantaged in terms of getting exposure to quality education.

The famous slogan "Education for all" needs to be revisited. Is it sufficient to enroll every child in school? The continuance of disparity and exclusion goes on depending on the quality of school. Thus, the slogan needs to focus on "Quality education for all". It is quality aspect which is missing in disadvantaged schools. Instead of some constructive measures to improve the conditions, the state is taking the easy route of offering private schools as an alternative. But these schools can be complementary to the system and should not be presented as an alternative to public education. Education has failed miserably to reduce the poverty gaps, social justice and oppression.

The analysis of education as an economic commodity has a long history. Within development and growth economics, the importance of education as an economic variable also has a distinguished history. Lewis (1962) questioned appropriate mix of skills, type education to be emphasized, the relationship between the education and the capacity of the economy to absorb educated workers in productive employment.

ECONOMIC GROWTH OF EDUCATION

Lucas (1988) was pioneer in understanding not only the relationship between education and growth but also why there might be a strong case for policy intervention to promote educational set-up. Within the context of a 'new growth' model Lucas suggested that productivity of any worker is higher when working in an environment peopled by high productivity workers through a kind of learning by watching mechanism.

Barro (1999) found that once other factors were controlled, human capital did indeed have a positive influence on growth. Barro's analysis was focused on the positive impact of growth of basic educational variables—namely, primary and secondary schooling. Using Indian date from Crabowsky, he used time series techniques to study the causal impact of primary, secondary and tertiary education on Indian growth performance. The result confirmed the importance of primary education with weaker evidence of secondary education and no evidence of tertiary education. The most important finding is the importance of female education (of all levels) in the growth process. This supports the results of Duraisamy (2002) that rates of return to education were higher for women. Nagaraj *et. al.* (2000) do find strong evidence of the role of primary education in generating growth and in reducing educational disparities across the state and inter-state inequality.

EDUCATION AND DEVELOPMENT

Economic growth can not be seen as synonymous with economic development. For all but the most ardent believers in 'trickle down' economic growth will be seen at best as a necessity for economic development. It is certainly not sufficient. In broader perspective of economic development, it becomes apparent that the role of education and educational policy becomes even greater.

In India the set of issues which might reasonably be encompassed within the umbrella of economic development might include inequality and exclusion of all types—whether based on income, caste, religion, region, health, fertility, infant mortality and child labour.

In the broadest term, the empirical research by economists suggests that in India, a very important factor impinging on these issues is woman education. For example, Dreze and Murthy (2001) show that a major factor determining low fertility is high female education whilst general indicators of modernization like urbanization, poverty reduction and male literacy have no 'such impact'.

The picture with respect to caste issue is less promising. Despite considerable government investment into the education of the backward castes, there is little evidence of economic benefit to these castes, partly because of the inability of the education to deliver superior jobs. This leads naturally to a "disgusted worker" effect and withdrawal of funds for educational purposes.

The consensus of the empirical literature appears to be that rates of return are indeed (inverted) U-shaped. Rates of return to education are higher in those areas where development is low. But it is the primary educational variable that has the largest positive impact. Similarly, the policy of investing in educating backward castes without compensatory changes in labour market policy have shown to be potentially counter-productive.

Thus, education is every sense is one of the fundamental factors of development. No county can achieve sustainable economic development without substantial investment in human capital. The major part of human capital is formed by education and training and rest by medical care. The attitude of planners has changed, instead of considering education as a consumption, they regard it as investment.

People invest in education with a view to increase their productive capacity and increase their consumption bundle. It is recognized fact that education also increases consumption efficiency. Education capital (knowledge, skills and work capacity) can be formed in many ways. The most obvious is through formal education starting from primary school, continuing through secondary school and going on to higher education like college, university or a technical institute. Another equally important method is on-the-job training sometimes systematically provided within the work environment. In addition to these, individuals develop themselves though reading, independent study, observing and learning from others and personal experience. Thus, human education capital formation is a life long process for most people. It covers work-oriented activities in schools, factories, farms, government, armies, political organizations and trade unions. At the early age, family is the most important source of education for children.

Education can improve the capacity of individual to live a decent life and to escape from hunger trap. It can also enable rural people's capacity to diversify assets and activities to access information on health and sanitation to enhance human agency in addition to increasing productivity in agricultural sector, these are all essential elements to ensure food security in the long run. The way to reach food security is to strengthen the capacity of rural people. The concept of capacity is associated closely with notion such as empowerment. The role of education is not only to impart knowledge and skills but also to contribute to the empowerment of people by improving their self-confidence, widen their frame of reference and give them the tools to participate in wider process of social and economic change.

So, policy should be made with specific emphasis on rural areas and keeping in mind the multiple advantages provided by an educated and skilled society. Only then egalitarian society will emerge and inclusive growth achieved.

References

Ozturk Ilhan (2001) The Role of Education in Economic Development, Theoretical Perspective, published in *Journal of Rural Development and Administration*, Winter XXXIII (2001).

NCERT Report, 2006.

Annual Status of Education, Report, Government of Bihar 2007.

Importance of Education in Economic Development, *Education News Achieve*, 2007-10 to 2007-10, Pakistan Education News.

Inclusive Growth in India : From Utopian Dream to Achievable Goal

KUMKUM JHA

Many regions in India failed to take due advantage of economic reforms resulting in wide inter-state and intra-state variations in economic growth. Another aspect is big urban-rural divide. The employment opportunities are limited in rural areas. Agriculture sector is not doing well. Women constitute the largest under privileged group. Inclusive growth is the need of the hour.

It is heartening to note that India has been able to achieve remarkable economic development in the last ten years. The credit largely goes to the economic reforms, liberalization and globalization of economy. Its growth rate has been around 8 to 10% during the last eight to ten years. Considering the odds that India faces in the form of gigantic population burden, huge deficit in infrastructure like roads, electricity, irrigation, scarcity of capital and allied resources caste and creed ridden sick social structure, widespread corruption and inefficient, biased and apathetic administrative apparatus, India's tremendous success looks an incredible story. Our vast and committed manpower in the farms and factories have toiled relentlessly to achieve this unbelievable feat. The miracle has happened and it proves that India possesses immense capabilities and potentials and can be a rightful claimant of the prime position in global economy. Despite the great economic slowdown which has come as a cyclone and devastated the great economies of the economic giants like U.S.A, U.K. and other European countries has only a moderate effect on Indian economic growth. India has been able to retain growth rate of 6.7% in 2008-09 after growing at close to 9% for four straight years before the melt down hit India. It is expected to grown at the rate of 7.5% in 2010 year, although the recovery in the world economy remains fragile and is expected to slow in the second half of 2010 as reported by the World Bank. Indian industry has led the acceleration in the growth of broader economy. Factory out put has been growing from 10 to 20% in different sectors. Similarly, IT Sector and services sector have registered wonderful performance.

COUNTRY OF CONTRASTS

India is a vast country. It is a cauldron of mixed cultures, multiple languages, numerous religions, countless castes and sub-castes, varied climates and different soils but still there is an underlying oneness, this unity amongst diversity is a unique feature of great Indian story. There are a number of affluent industrialists and businessmen who have made their mark in the global economy but at the same time crores of Indians are living a life of extreme poverty and destitution. In our mega cities a large number of our fellow country men are enjoying the cozy comforts of life while their rural counterparts are forced to live in thatched and muddy houses where even safe drinking water, bare minimum clothing and food stuffs are scarce. This paradox of many Indians residing in one India is tale of our modern India. India is growing economically and so is its poverty. Though National Sample Organization data

(2004-05) suggests that about 45 percent Indian population is living below standard conditions. Arjun Sen Gupta report estimates that India's 77% population is living miserably. Suresh Tendulkar's report also confirms that many states like Bihar, Orissa, Jharkhand, M.P, Chhattisgarh, and U.P have vast population of poors.

REGIONAL DISPARITY IN ECONOMIC DEVELOPMENT

Many regions of India failed to take due advantage of economic reforms resulting in wide inter-state and intra-state variations in economic growth. Ahluwalia (2000) while commenting on "State Level performance under economic reforms in India" observed that the rising regional inequality, as measured by an increase in the Gini-Coefficient from 1986-87 to 1997-98, has important implications for poverty

TABLE 1
Rate of Growth of Gross State Domestic Product (Percent per Year)

Sl. No.	*State*	*1980-81 to 1990-91*	*1991-92 to 1998-99*
1.	Bihar	4.66	2.88
2.	Rajasthan	6.60	5.85
3.	Uttar Pradesh	4.95	3.58
4.	Orissa	4.29	3.56
5.	Madhya Pradesh	4.56	5.89
6.	Andhra Pradesh	5.65	5.20
7.	Tamil Nadu	5.38	6.02
8.	Kerala	3.57	5.61
9.	Karnataka	5.29	5.87
10.	West Bengal	4.71	6.97
11.	Gujarat	5.08	8.15
12.	Haryana	6.43	5.13
13.	Maharashtra	6.02	8.01
14.	Punjab	5.32	4.77
	Combined GSDP of 14 States	5.24	5.90

reduction. The growth performance of 14 major states in the pre and post-reform period was studied on the basis of GSDP (Gross State Domestic Product).

This table shows only four States viz. Gujarat (8.2%), Maharashtra (8.0%), West Bengal (7%), and Tamil Nadu (6%), registered strong growth rate. However, the BIMARU States of poor performers did show divergent directions in economic development. Bihar and UP performed very poorly but the other two members (MP and Rajasthan) did reasonably well. The deceleration of growth in the poorer states has important implications. It is a matter of great concern. It can be seen as a defeat of one of the main objectives of Indian Plans, i.e, balanced regional development by reducing regional inequality. There is a common perception that developed states go on developing while backward states lag far behind.

TABLE 2
Annual Rates of Growth of Per Capita Gross State Domestic Product (Percent Per Year)

Sl. No.	*State*	*1980-81 to 1990-91*	*1991-92 to 1998-99*
1.	Bihar	2.45	1.27
2.	Rajasthan	3.96	3.48
3.	UP	2.60	1.28
4.	Orissa	2.38	2.08
5.	MP	2.08	3.67
6.	AP	3.34	3.67
7.	Tamil Nadu	3.87	4.78
8.	Kerala	2.19	4.35
9.	Karnataka	3.28	4.08
10.	West Bengal	2.39	5.14
11.	Gujarat	3.08	6.73
12.	Haryana	3.86	2.85
13.	Maharashtra	3.58	6.19
14.	Punjab	3.33	2.93
	Combijed GSDP 14 States	3.03	4.02

This raises a question, "Have economic reforms caused regional in equality?" It is commonly agreed that even though the reforms themselves are non-discriminatory, they will affect states differently because of differences in state specific characteristics and this could lead to a deceleration in some states. For example, opening the economy to foreign trade can be viewed as improving efficiency of resources use in the economy as a whole and thus potentially benefit all states, but if some states have a greater comparative advantage in exports, while others have developed a production structure excessively dependent on uncompetitive import substituting industries, the process of opening up could well lead to an acceleration in growth in the former in the short-run while slowing it down in the latter, as investment is likely to move from the latter to the former, at least in the short-run. This implies of course that some of the factors that make for greater competitive advantage are impossible in the short-run. However over a period of time production structures, including factors that account for competitive advantage in the particular states, can change and states initially excluded from acceleration can catch up.

Nair (2003) studied economic reforms and regional disparities in economic and social development of India. Economic liberalization was brought about in a big way in India on the plea that growth could not trickle down under the earlier command and control regime. There was serious concern that some Indian states with large populations and vast natural resources were pockets of poverty. This concern has even greater relevance today because the changes over time in the boundaries and in the number of states in India have been such as to make each of them more and more linguistically, culturally and even ethnically homogenous. On the top of it, we also have the phenomenon of regional parties coming up in a big way in the last few years, having a say not only at the concerned state; but also as members of coalition governments at the centre. In such a scenario, widespread inter-state disparities in levels of economic and social development can have serious economic, social and even political consequences this being particularly so if these have persisted over long periods of time. He further concluded,

"There is a evidence in the study to suggest that infrastructural development is of great help in promoting regional development. This is particularly true if we consider an indicator of level of living like HDI and seems true to some extent also in the case of per capita NSDP. A detailed analysis of the development of industry at the state level in India indicates that infrastructural development is particularly helpful for the development of both registered and unregistered manufacturing. There are also two other indications with interesting policy implications. One is the already accepted finding that agricultural development is

TABLE 3

Per capita Net State Domestic Product at Current Prices for Major Indian States

(in Rupees)

State	*1999-2000*	*2001-02*	*2003-04*	*2005-06*
AP	15507	18630	22041	26211
Assam	12269	13153	15653	18598
Bihar	5766	6197	6993	7875
Gujarat	18864	19823	26922	34157
Haryana	21966	26077	31509	38832
Jharkhand	12747	10972	12941	19066
Karnataka	16758	17776	20515	27291
Kerala	19294	21047	25645	30668
MP	12384	12697	14306	15647
Maharashtra	23340	24450	29770	37081
Orissa	10567	11075	14252	17299
Punjab	25615	28949	31192	34929
Rajasthan	13477	14165	16704	17863
Tamil Nadu	19378	20924	24106	29958
UP	9405	9781	11250	13262
West Bengal	15826	17826	20806	25223
India	15839	17800	20936	25716

Source : *Economic Survey*, 2007-08, GoI.

beneficial for the development of unregistered manufacturing at the regional level. The other is the interesting hint here that measures to reduce poverty in a region don't always go against the objective of improving the relative position of a region in terms of its per capita net domestic products. Much more work possibly with the help of casualty tests and along the lines also of Datt and Ravilion (2002) needs to be done before more definite policy inferences can be drawn in this regard.

It is obvious that states like Bihar and UP have been greatly affected by poverty. Per capita income is even below one-third of the national average. It is but natural that there has been massive migration of poor skilled and unskilled labourers from these states to the relatively affluent states like—Gujarat, Maharashtra, Punjab, Haryana and Delhi. By dint of their hard labour they have earned good fortunes and have contributed a lot towards economic development of these developed states. Never-the-less some of the local residents of these states like Maharashtra, Assam and Delhi are reacting violently against poor migrants out of political agenda and sectarian considerations. These are dangerous developments and pose serious threat to national integration. This divisive and sectarian tendency has to be curbed with iron hand because our constitution guarantees every citizen to earn his or her livelihood at any place in the country. We cannot allow anyone to snatch this fundamental right of equal opportunity of employment and business.

Another aspect is big urban-rural divide in India. The basic facilities like hospitals, schools, electricity and communication, etc. are in a very bad shape in villages. The employment opportunities are limited in rural areas. Therefore, poor people, mainly unskilled labourers migrate on large-scale to cities in search of livelihood and better life. This is causing major problem in towns and cities which are overcrowded. This one-way traffic cannot go on endlessly. Villages have to improve. Basic amenities are to be developed so that they can attract and accommodate its residents.

We are celebrating 60th year of Indian republic. We must take stock of our national health, which along with education and nutrition is the moulding factor of human resources. A

Planning Commission study completed in 2009 on the basis of surveys conducted in several villages showed that health care expenses were responsible for more than half of all people pushing into poverty. NSSO (National sample survey organization) data for the year 2004-05 estimated that an additional 39 million people were pushed into poverty due to health care expenses in that year alone. Public spending on health care has been around just 1% of GDP while private spending has grown alarmingly to 4.2% of the GDP. It is estimated that more than 70% of the entire health expenditure in India is borne out by the people from their own resources. Sitaram Yechury, (2010) a noted communist leader exhorts, "what is required is a political will and a social commitment to vastly enhance public expenditure in health care." In context of public health Govt. of India has introduced the National Health Bill, 2009. It holds huge promise. The National Rural Health Mission is doing wonderful job in improving health care infrastructure particularly, in the remote rural areas but most of the states are struggling hard to cope up with the growing needs of health care. Demographic and lifestyle changes due to socio-economic development led to health transition where non-communicable diseases like diabetes, hypertension, stroke, cancer and coronary heart diseases have emerged as leading causes of death and disability resulting in heavy economic burden for the affected individuals, families and society as a whole. Many of these diseases are preventable. Mass public education is needed to motivate people to quit smoking and tobacco as well as fatty diets and alcohol and take plenty of vegetables as well as fruits and salads. Many diseases can be avoided by regular physical exercise. Tobacco is great killer; its use must be discouraged.

The present day health services are focused on diagnosis and treatment of various diseases. But as the old saying goes "Prevention is always better than cure". Our health services should promote preventive measures through massive national programmes.

SECTORAL DISPARITY

During the last few years there has been considerable

growth in industrial output, Tele sector, and IT sectors but agricultural growth has been stunted.

TABLE 4

Contribution of Various Sectors in GDP in India

	2007-08	*2008-09*
Agriculture, forestry and fisheries	4.9	1.6
Mining	3.3	3.6
Manufacturing	8.2	2.4
Electricity, Gas and Water resources	5.3	3.4
Infrastructure	10.1	7.2
Trade, Hotel and Restaurant	10.1	7.2
Transport, Storage and Communication	15.5	7.2
Finance and Insurance	11.7	7.8
Community Services and Private Services	6.8	13.1

CSO, Government of India.

It is obvious that agriculture sector is not doing well. Plight of farmers is well-known. In many parts of the country farmers are taking the extreme step of suicide under the unbearable burden of debt. On the other hand, spiraling prices of foodgrains, pulses, edible oil, sugar and tea has spoiled the budget of common people. Poor people are at the verge of starvation. Government of India has adopted National Agriculture Policy, 2007 under which targets for increasing production and productivity of agriculture, improving the economic situation of farmers, using new and innovative technology in agriculture as well as extension in irrigation facilities and export of agriculture produces, have been fixed at high levels. Our President Her Excellency Mrs. Pratibha Patil has drawn the attention of the nation towards the need of Second Green Revolution in her speech on the eve of Republic Day, 2010. She has emphasized the need of good quality seeds, better farming technique and effective water management besides disbursing credit to farmers on easy terms and extending better marketing facilities.

THE GENDER-GAP

Women constitute the largest underprivileged group in India. Despite tall claims, constitutional safeguards and judicial activities, our women are still away from equal opportunities. Their literacy, nutritional state, health statistics, employment quality and property profile are all below par. Girl children are not safe in homes and outdoor. It is heartening to note that the things are changing quickly in their favour. With reservation for women in Panchayati Raj Institutions, the process of political empowerment has taken rapid strides. Girls are getting better opportunities for education now. The central and state Governments are taking special steps to encourage women education and their economic empowerment. Recent reports published by WCD Ministry, Govt. of India, indicate that GDI score in India was 0.514 in 1996 and it rose to 0.596 in 2006. GDI is the Human Development Index (HDI) adjusted for disparities between men and women based on infant mortality, life expectancy, Literacy rate and decent living based on earned income. Similarly, Gender Empowerment Measures scores for India increased from 0.416 in 1996 to 0.497 in 2006. The parameters for GEM scores were political participation, decision-making power, participation power over economic resources.

DISPARITY AMONG SOCIAL AND RELIGIOUS GROUPS

It is a matter of great concern that despite several programmes and promises, some social and religious groups in India are relatively more poor and backward. Sachhar Commission and Rangnath Mishra Commission Reports depict the pathetic state of Indian muslims. The Govt. of India has started many new schemes for their development. They must be brought into the national mainstream of development and be empowered to participate in the process of economic growth at equal footing.

People from scheduled castes and tribes are largely unaware of their right and opportunities. Special drives are necessary to bring them to the path of progress. The fruits of reservation are being devoured by a few powerful sections. The real disadvantaged people need our special attention. Government's policies and programmes would be only effectively implemented if people at large are cooperative and actively supporting Governments endeavors.

CORRUPTION—THE GREAT SPOILSPORT

Corruption is the universal phenomenon in public life today. In the recent years names of senior ministers, chief ministers and even honorable justices have come under cloud. Lot of controversy has been generated. The Government machinery, business people and NGOs are all suspects. With tarnished image the bureaucracy is failing to deliver required results. Strict vigil on the whole system and exemplary punishment to the culprits is the call of the time. But popular perception is that only small fishes are caught and booked while the big players purchase immunity and freedom. Our policy-makers must ponder about this serious issue which is killing our instinct like powerful venom. In the recent past, the Govt. of Bihar has brought out a special law in which the movable and immovable properties of the corrupt officials and politicians would be confiscated and used by the Government for public welfare. The President of India has approved this law a few weeks back. Transparency at all levels of financial transaction is a must. Right to information has emerged as a strong weapon against corruption. This has brought all offices under public scrutiny and this would certainly prove as a strong deterrent against corruption.

INCLUSIVE GROTH : WHY AND HOW?

Inclusive growth is our long cherished dream which finds its root "Sarve bhawantu sukhinah". Sarvoday has been our avowed objective since freedom struggle.

Inclusive growth is the need of the hour. We cannot afford to neglect it anymore. The nation is craving for wholesome growth of all sections of people, all parts of the country and all sectors of economy. Of course, our resources are limited and we have may constrains but our greatest strength are the vast population of energetic and skilled young people who are ready to strive for change. Inclusive growth is the greatest challenge. We can achieve this target with hard labour and focused strategy. We can ensure inclusive growth by appropriate use of newer technology in the field of education, health, agriculture and industry. Infrastructure like road, power, communication and credit is to be strengthened in neglected areas on a priority basis. Sam Pitroda (2010), a noted telecom scientist finds the overall situation quite fertile for rapid growth through proper and judicious use of technology. There is no dearth of foreign exchange, telecom, IT, BPO. KPO sectors are getting plenty of outsourcing. Through expansions of internet facilities common people have got better access to basic services like information, health and education. Thus, these collective developments can be termed as "Knowledge economy" which will have decisive role in the 21st century as a catalyst of economic growth.

Our more than 40 crores of young Indians are the agents and architects of change and we are standing at doorstep of economic revolution. If they use the opportunity appropriately they can shape the destiny of the country and the whole world.

DANGER OF GLOBAL WARMING

Global warming is a burning issue. Our existence is at stake. Many parts of the country face the risk of sumberging in the sea. The great glaciers of the Himalayas are melting rapidly. These are due to pollution created by industries, Carbon emission is creating lot of troubles. Recently world leaders from developed as well as developing countries met together to ponder over this gigantic problem at Copenhagen. They decided to reduce pollution by developing carbon-friendly industries. This is costly affair and is proving as a deterrent for industrial growth. China and India have decided to protest and resist the pressure of carbon quota advocated by the European countries and USA. But we must strike a balance between environment and growth. We need both and can't afford to ignore any one of the two.

GOVERNMENT INITIATIVES

Government of India is very serious about inclusive growth. In fact this is the main theme of Eleventh Plan through which following objectives have been placed:

1. Accelerate growth rate of GDP from 8 to 10% and then maintain at 10% in the 12th Plan in order to double per capita income by 2016-17.
2. Increase agricultural GDP growth rate to 4% per year for broader spread of benefits.
3. Create 70 million new work opportunities.
4. Reduce educated unemployment to below 5%.
5. Raise real wage rate of unskilled workers to 20%.
6. Reduce the head-count ratio of consumption poverty by 10% points.

An important document "Vision 2020" released by Planning Commission on 23rd Jan. 2003 has aimed at achieving 9% growth rate along with eradication of illiteracy, poverty and unemployment and increasing per capita income by four-fold.

Government has started many national programmes in various sectors covering both rural and urban areas but the implementation is quite slow and tardy. We cannot leave everything on the shoulder of Government machinery. People's direct involvement in monitoring and accelerating implementation of various developmental schemes is a must for effective inclusive growth. Mr. Chaturanan Mishra, veteran communist leader has very nicely brought out the need of people's responsibility in successful implementation of Government various programmes in his recent article in *Hindustan Times*. Good governance is indispensable for rapid and inclusive growth. Change of Bihar Government in 2005 has ensured very rapid economic growth and the recent data is around 11.3% which just below Gujarat. It is really a remarkable achievement.

SUMMARY

Though India has shown praiseworthy pace of economic growth despite heavy odds, the benefit of post-reforms spurt in growth has not trickled down to all sections of people, all regions of the country and all sectors of economy equally. The recent World Bank Report (2010) suggests that Indian Economic growth would be around 7.5% this year but still poverty will increase in India. This riddle, this paradox is due to economic disparity If India has to grow in the coming years it will have to ensure inclusive growth. This is the new age mantra and guarantee for uninterrupted and smooth growth. But inclusive growth is an uphill task taking into consideration, the limited resources and sick socio-political milieu of the country. Problems galore but there is a way ahead. Success is within our reach. Millions of our energetic young men are capable of changing the face of India. The innovative strategies drawn properly and implemented effectively can accelerate growth, weed out corruption, red-tapism and bureaucratic inefficiency and apathy and bring about social justice with rapid growth. Adopting newer technologies in the field of agriculture for promotion of agriculture production and productivity is urgently required if we have to sustain our growth. We are at the brink of food scarcity and danger signals of soaring prices of food items call for impetus on farming sectors. We need green and eco-friendly small and medium industries which provide employment to millions of our people both in urban and rural areas. Balanced industrial growth can prove to be catalyst of poverty alleviation programmes and bring about inclusive growth.

References

Ahluwalia, Montek S., "Economic Performance of States in the Post-Reform Period". *Economic and Political Weekly,* May 2000.

Lal, Deepak, Rakesh Mohan and Natarajan (2001) ; "Economic Reforms Poverty Alleviation: A Tale of Two Serveys", *National Council of Applied Economic Research,* New Delhi (mimed).

Cashin, P., and R. Sahay (1996) : "Regional Economic Growth and Convergence in India". *Finance and Development,* 33 (March), 49.52.

Datt, Gaurav (1999) : "Has Poverty Declined since Economic Reforms? *Economic and Political Weekly,* Vol. 34, No. 50.

Bhattacharya, B.B., and Sakthivel (2004) : "Regional Growth and Disparity in India: Comparison of Pre- and Post-Reforms Decades", *Economic and Political Weekly,* Vol. 39, No. 10.

Dholakia, Ravindra H. (2003) : "Regional Disparity in Economic and Human Development in India", *Economic and Political Weekly*, Vol. 38 No. 39.

Bhattacharya, B.B. and S. Sakthivel (2004) : Regional Growth and Disparity in India, *Economic and Political Weekly*, March, pp. 1071-77.

Kurian, N.J. (2000) : "Widening Regional Disparity in India: Some Indicators", *EPW*, Vol. 35, No. 7, pp. 38-55.

Planning Commission (2002) : National Human Development Report, 2001, Government of India, New Delhi.

Nair, K.R.G., Economic Reforms and Regional Disparities in Economic and Social Development in India, Centre for Policy Research, AVH, 2004.

Educational and Economic Development of Weaker Classes

KAWITA KUMARI

Man is a capital and education is linked directly with productivity. Investment in education is investment in the future of the country. Weaker sections of the society, divided into several groups are deprived, so far getting proper education and training are concerned. The position and percentage of education in minorities is still disappointing. Half of the women population is still illiterate. The literacy rate in SCs, STs and backward classes is low compared to other groups or castes. Physically handicapped and mentally retarded persons require special care. Socially handicapped persons should be brought into mainstream. Proper education and training should be provided to such groups. The author is optimistic by ending with the words of Tagore that "if you weep for the setting sun, you miss the stars".

The development of a nation depends on its citizens. Basically, human resource is a key to progress and development of a nation. In the eyes of economists, man is a capital and education is directly linked with productivity. Souz has tried to co-relate human capital with the highly educated people. Really speaking, the very foundation of development of human capital is education. The economists now firmly believe that the achievement of economic development lies in improving human resources and not in physical or material resources alone. In one sentence we may say that destiny of a nation is folded within its human resources as the flower within the close embrace of petals.

By imparting education to people, we ensure development of human resources in the country. Education not only gives knowledge, it also enhances efficiency and capabilities. A report issued by University Grants Commission clearly states *investment in education is investment in future of the Country"*. It makes us aware of new technology and it consequently leads to production and prosperity. The educated man is morally, socially mentally, emotionally, and economically developed. Once Vivekanand said :

> "Education is not the amount of information that is put into your brain and runs out undigested all along your life. We must have life building, man making, character making, assimilation of ideas. Real education is that which enables one to stand on one's own legs"

Now-a-days education is no longer a luxury; it is essential for survival. Money and human resources are equally important for economic development of the country. The scholars Marshall and Bacon have found in their research and survey that it is education that ensures socio-economic development of the country. The countries which fail to provide education to its people, continue to remain poor and undeveloped. The people can take full advantage of physical and material resources only if they are educated. Even the farmers and labourers, who are educated, work in skilled and more efficient way contributing a lot in production.

It needs to be taken note of that with rise in Gross domestic product (GDP) since 1999, the Human Development Index has recorded slowdown from 115 position to 128 in 2005 as per the Report for 2007-08. In age of repaid economic growth, the quality of human life in India has not improved as compared to rest of the world. Referring to weaker classes clearly means group of people who have not been able to develop so far because of socio, political, religious and some other circumstances and situations. This situation is more intense in villages as compared to urban life.

It is necessary to bring the weaker classes to mainstream of social life by emphasizing more and more on education. If we want to ensure economic development to these classes many programmes on education need to be formulated and chalked out for these classes. The constitution of India in its Article 15 (4 & 5) clearly states that there will be no discrimination on grounds of caste, creed, religion, sex or place of birth and the state will provide all assistance to socially and educationally classes including those coming under scheduled caste/scheduled tribes by launching even special drive.

KINDS OF WEAKER CLASSES

1. Economically weaker classes
2. Religion-based weaker classes
3. Gender-based weaker classes
4. Caste-based weaker classes
5. Physically handicapped classes
6. Mentally handicapped classes
7. Socially handicapped classes

1. Economically Weaker Classes

A large population of our country is under poverty line. The poor people find themselves helpless to provide basic needs and facilities to their children. The children help the guardian in domestic and field work too. These children, even if they go to schools, hardly concentrate and moreover they are too poor to purchase books and other items needed in day-to-day use. Since independence, many policies and programmes were adopted and implemented under different plan periods to eradicate poverty but not much has been achieved. The constitution of India in its Article 45 clearly advocates compulsory and pre-education to all children of 14 years and it was to be achieved within a decade but it remains unfulfilled even after six decades of our independence. The World Bank and different international organizations, too, are providing financial assistance to achieve the target of providing compulsory and free education. The government too provides mid-day meal, free books and dress in Primary Schools to encourage children to join the schools. It is estimated that by 2016, all children will be at least literate and poverty will not come in the way. The Government is committed to implement Right to Education Bill, 2009. It has also been proposed that in private schools, the participation of poor children be ensured at least up to 25%.

2. Religion-based Weaker Classes

India is a country of diversities. The Hindus who constitute the majority speak Hindi. The people belonging to different religions do also live here and speak their mother tongues. The religious minorities constitute 18% of the population and out of which 12% are Muslims, 2.5% are Christians, 2% Sikhs, 0.7% Buddhists and 0.5% Jains. In democratic form of Government, usually majority dominates the system and there does exist the possibility of undermining the voice of the minorities. The framers of the constitution of India took every care to guarantee religious freedom, linguistic identity and cultural heritage of the minorities. As such, minorities have been given right to get education of their choice by opening minority institutions in Article 29 and 30. For the reason that education is a successful and effective tool to achieve the target. In Article 350 there is a provision for primary education through their Mother Tongue and the State Governments and the local institutions have the responsibility in this regard. The Constitution in its Article 350-B also gives special provisions for linguistic minorities. It is not out of context to mention here that despite rights given to minorities and special policies and programmes being launched by the Centre and the State Governments for the minorities, the position and percentage of education in minorities is still disappointing. The High Power Panel under the chairmanship of Dr. Gopal Singh constituted by the Home Ministry had identified Muslims and Neo Buddhists at the national level as educationally backward. The new Education Policy adopted in 1986 too, lays emphasis on these groups. The former Prime Minister Mrs. Indira Gandhi in May 1983 announced 15 point guidelines for welfare of the minorities out of which 11 and 12 were concentrated on education to minorities. Referring to low percentage of minorities in government jobs in point 11, it has been stressed that special coaching classes be undertaken in educational institutions for minorities to enhance their participation in jobs while in point 12, there is commitment for providing special opportunity to minorities for their entry in technical training institutions.

The following programmes are being undertaken for minorities :

- Coaching Classes for Competitive Examinations.
- Community Polytechnic in Minorities populated areas.
- Training to Principals, Teachers and Managers of minorities schools.
- Review of Syllabus in national perspective.

In addition to all these programmes the State Governments are also launching special drive for welfare of the educationally minorities groups. There is need to focus special attention to education to girls and higher and vocational education to minorities. The literacy drive in women of minorities groups needs to be given top priority. In fact, we need to underline the factors responsible for educational backwardness of minorities taking into account socio- economic circumstances and monitor the programmes being launched for educational development of minorities to come to better results.

3. Gender-based Weaker Classes

There is immediate need to focus on female education to speed up rural economic development. It remains a harsh reality that girls are not given so much attention as compared to boys particularly in rural life. Since their birth, girl child is discriminated against. To confine the girls within the four walls of the house is the biggest hurdle to female education. It is generally said if you educate a boy, you educate and individual, if you educate a girl you educate a family. Two worst enemies of women, said a government report on international women year, have been the traditional female and conservative male. Since Mughal period, the female education has been neglected and paid no adequate attention. During British rule the situation improved a bit but as compared to male, it remained almost dismal. As per the 2001 census report, the literacy rate in India is 65.38% out of which male literacy is 75.83% and female 54.16%. Kerala is the only state where literacy rate is above 90% and achievement lies in the fact the percentage of male and female literacy is almost equal. During last decade, the States like Rajasthan registered 22.48% rise in literacy, Chhattisgarh 22.27, M.P. 19.44%, Andhra Pradesh 17.2% while Bihar showed deplorable figure which is merely 10.04%. Wood in his declaration (1954) had suggested special grants to encourage female education and since then all commissions constituted from time to time on this issue had made valuable suggestions and the following are some of the important ones :

- Female education be listed as important and urgent programme in coming years and existing difference between boys and girls be reduced.
- Necessary grants for female education be released on priority basis.
- Special mechanism be set-up at the centre and the states for better co-ordination on female education.
- Part time and full time employment guarantee to women be ensured.

In every plan period special attention should be given on education.

Women Literacy in India

1951	-	8.86%
2001	-	54.16%

The above figures show improvement but it still remains a fact that half of the women population is still illiterate. 50% reservation has been given to women in Panchayats and Primary Schools. However the initiatives like providing free books, cycles, dress and other incentives have been able to promote women education. It is a happy signal to brighter future.

4. Caste-based Weaker Classes

The caste system in India is very old and intense. Some caste normally called Sudras are supposed to be low castes and they are discriminated against particularly in rural areas. Untouchability is a social disgrace or stigma. These groups are socially deprived and weaker and as such they are economically backward. The Scheduled Castes and Scheduled Tribes constitute a large population. The Scheduled castes are generally regarded as untouchables. The society continues to get the services of these people subjecting them to exploitation, torture and social inequality. Mahatma Gandhi once wrote: *"I may not be born again, be it happens, I like to be born in a family of scavengers so that I may relieve them of the inhuman, unhealthy and hateful practice of carrying night soil."*

The Scheduled Tribes live in remote forests totally unaware of the fruits of developed society and civilization. Some other castes are categorized as backwards. These deprived castes have not been getting proper education because of many socio-economic factors. The census 2001 clearly underlines the fact that literacy rate in scheduled caste, schedule tribe and backward castes is low as compared to other groups or castes. The female literacy in these deprived castes is much low. The dropout rates in children of these classes is much below the normal. The Tables 1, 2 and 3 noted speak for themselves.

The tables present a comparative study of the position of education in SC/ST and Backward classes in relation to total population. It is crystal clear that education in these deprived classes is lower in comparison to other groups.

Dhebar Commission (1960-61), Kothari Commission (1964-66), New Education Policy 1986 and POA's 1992 have given valuable suggestions to promote and tone up education to

Table 1
Literacy Rate in Different Classes in India

	SC	*ST*	*Backward Classes*	*Total Population*
Male	39%	30%	65%	75.85%
Female	20%	14%	45%	54.16%
Total	30%	22%	55%	65.38%

Table 2
Admission of Children of Different Groups in Primary Schools

Academic Session		*SC*	*ST*	*Backward Classes*	*Total*
1980-81	Boys	72 Lacs	31 Lacs	2 Crore 20 Lacs	5 Crore 53 Lacs
	Girls	38 Lacs	15 Lacs	1 Crore 15 Lacs	2 Crore 85 Lacs
	Total	1 Crore 10 Lacs	46 Lacs	3 Crore 35 Lacs	8 Crore 38 Lacs
1990-91	Boys	97 Lacs	49 Lacs	2 Crore 45 Lacs	5 Crore 81 Lacs
	Girls	63 Lacs	30 Lacs	1 Crore 70 Lacs	4 Crore 10 Lacs
	Total	1 Crore 60 Lacs	79 Lacs	4 Crore 15 Lacs	9 Crore 91 Lacs
2000-01	Boys	1 Crore 24 Lacs	65 Lacs	2 Crore 90 Lacs	6 Crore 79 Lacs
	Girls	98 Lacs	40 Lacs	1 Crore 95 Lacs	4 Crore 95 Lacs
	Total	2 Crore 22 Lacs	1 Crore 5 Lacs	4 Crore 85 Lacs	11 Crore 84 Lacs

Table 3
Dropout Ratio in different Classes

Class	*SC*	*ST*	*Backward Classes*	*Total Population*
I-V	50%	62%	48%	45%
VI-VIII	30%	38%	27%	25%
IX-X	25%	32%	22%	20%

these classes. The government at the centre and the states, too, are implementing the policies and Programmes and much more needs to be done to achieve the target. Some of the important plans and programmes are as follows:

(a) To provide Scholarship.
(b) To provide hostel.
(c) To construct Schools in these areas.
(d) To start special coaching classes.
(e) To open Centre of Informal Education.
(f) To open Book Banks and provide Banks.
(g) Reservation in educational Institutions.
(h) Reservation in jobs.
(i) To provide grants to voluntary organization.
(j) To open Teaching centres.
(k) Special programmes on education for girls.

If these programmes are implemented honestly in their real spirit, it is sure that the boys and girls of the deprived classes namely SC, ST and Backward classes may be strengthened to compete with other groups of the society.

5. Physically Handicapped Classes

Under this group of physically handicapped, two types of people usually come, namely—those physically handicapped who are born handicapped, and secondly, those people who develop deformity after birth because of several factors. Before independence, there were 28 schools for blinds, 33 for deaf and dumb and 2 schools for leprosy patients. This arrangement was inadequate. After independence, the Education department and social welfare department, were given responsibility to ensure education as well as vocational education to physically handicapped. A central school for Blind was established in Dehradun, with printing press and library. On this model, a school for physically impaired has been established in Hyderabad. The teachers of these schools are given special training. With rise in population these schools are proving to be inadequate to meet the challenges. It is the duty of nation as a whole to provide education and training to physically handicapped of all kinds to help them to be self reliant to join the mainstream of our social life.

6. Mentally Handicapped Classes

Under this group, come those who are born mentally retarded. Before independence there were two schools in Bengal and one in Bombay for mentally retarded and handicapped. After independence, psychological lab has been established at Allahabad for these boys and girls. After 1952, special scholarship to this class was announced and since 1955-56, 50% of the expenditure incurred on it was shared by the Government at the centre and remaining 50% by the State Government but later total expenditure is being met by the centre.

This group needs Medical Hospitals and Psychological labs to identity their problems and ensure better conditions. Such facilities are lacking. The government at the centre has opened a centre for this group attached to a nursing college.

7. Socially Handicapped Classes

Under this group, come those who go abnormal because of bad and non-congenial social factors. This group of children do not get education for the factors such as poverty, customs and other reasons. Consequently they are socially unadjusted. Before independence, there were only 13 Reform Homes for this group. The rate of child crime is on sharp increase. The children resort to theft, cheating, anti-social activities after being discriminated and neglected in the society. A great thinker has rightly said :

> "The poverty of being unwanted, unloved and uncared for, is the greatest poverty".

The problem is complex and many-fold. The problem can not be solved by mere passing legislation and enforcing law but the need of the hour is to feel the pulse of the problem and open educational institutions and vocational training centers for this group to get them isolated from the life of crimes and neglect. Ram Krishna Mission is doing commendable job in this direction. Many religious groups and institutions are taking lead and it may be seen as a good beginning to achieve our goals. There is no denying the facts that education is an effective tool to achieve economic growth and development.

We, as a nation, need not weep and lament but strive tirelessly to help the deprived classes to enable the country to emerge stronger, brighter and more prosperous.

I conclude with the inspiring words of Tagore :

"If you weep for the setting sun, you miss the stars".

References

Bhartiya Siksha ka Itihas, Visay and Samasyayen, Prof. S.P. Gupta and Alka Gupta.

Bhartiya Siksha ka Itihas Aur Samasyayen, Dr. Sitaram Agrawal.

Teacher in Emerging Indian Society, Shiksha Chaturvedi and Mr. Swaroop Saxena.

Feasibility of Inclusive Education in Knowledge Economy of Bihar, Perspective and Initiative Act Higher level, people's dialogue on Education, volume, number, from 2007, Kumar Sanjeev.

P. Vijayalakshmi Pandit, Transforming India into a Knowledge Society with Inclusive Growth : Challenges and Strategies for Higher Education, *University News*, Vol . 47, Number 50, December, 14-20 2009.

Udayiman Bhartiya Samaj Mein Shiksha—Dr. Satya Narayan Dubey.

Shiksha ke Samasya Shidhant—Pathak and Tyagi.

Xth Plan profile of Higher Education in India—Issued by UGC.

Young India : Mahatma Gandhi.

Index